above

and

beyond

slickrock

forty mountain bike rides out of Moab, Utah

To the memory of Dave Minor,
whose effective but unassuming service has kept
public lands recreation accessible and desirable

Text, photos, and illustrations by Todd Campbell,

unless indicated otherwise
Comments, criticisms and suggestions
can be directed to the author c/o:

Moab Outabouts
P.O. Box 314
Moab, Utah
84532

Inquires concerning backcountry guide service,
on bike or on foot, and retail of photographic images
can also be directed to the above address.

Revised and Updated 1995

Published by Wasatch Publishers, Salt Lake City, Utah
Direct book orders to: Wasatch Book Distribution,
P.O. Box 11776, Salt Lake City, Utah 84147
801-575-6735

INTRODUCTION

I first met Todd when he came into the local bike shop in mid-1985. He was riding the most unlikely mountain bike I had ever seen (the first effort of a framebuilder friend of his, we soon dubbed it "the brass barbell"), and so filled the shop with his bold energy that he got himself thrown out.

He soon won his way back in, however, and I became better acquainted with him when he wrote to me later that winter requesting (make that insisting) that I hire him as a guide for my fledgling mountain bike touring company. This "Application for Employment" was scrawled on the back of a well used topo map, and that plus his general audacity convinced me to hire him on the spot. Thus began our working partnership, from which we have both moved on, and our friendship, which lasts (in spite of everything) to this day.

As you may know, this book is preceded by Todd's first effort, <u>Beyond Slickrock: Rides to Nowhere</u>. Written and published in 1987, it was an effective answer to the great need that existed at the time for a useful guide to the Moab area's most popular mountain bike rides. Modest in scope, it covered twelve rides in painstaking detail and included some small maps of those rides. Most of the routes were established jeep trails, though a couple were new trails or combinations of existing trails that Todd pioneered (often with the unsuspecting me along as fodder for the experiment), specifically for and do-able only by mountain bikes.

This new book is such an expansion on and refinement of the first book as to be something altogether different. The most obvious difference is the size and scope. Here you will find descriptions of 40 rides, covering 11 different areas in southeastern Utah, on open desert, canyon, and mountain terrain. To further assist route finding, there are over 80 maps, and for those of you who told your mothers that you kept the Playboy (or Playgirl) in your room so you could "read the articles," there are over 175 illustrative photos of the area covered by the book.

Also considerably expanded in this book are discussions of geology, history, lore and local environmental dynamics. Completely new are descriptions of multi-day rides, an assortment of rides in the mountains and high country of the region (which explains the word "Above" in the title), and most importantly, some information on rides not to do. The last item could be some of the book's most valuable guidance for your pleasure and safety.

At some point in an introduction like this the reader should be told of the author's qualifications. I could start by ticking off the obvious ones: Todd has pioneered or helped establish many of the routes described in this book, and he has ridden them all a zillion times. He has also put his muscle where his mouth is (always a relief to his riding partners) by working during the summers to clear obstacles, properly mark, and otherwise restore decrepit single tracks in the local mountains. He has worked (??!!) as a mountain bike guide in the area since such tours first started being offered, and has pursued the development of his photography skills with a vengeance.

This is all well and good, but I believe that all of Todd's qualifications are sprung from one salient characteristic of his. He has always instinctively embraced the mountain bike as a tool of transportation and personal independence rather than as a toy. Don't get me wrong, he has as much fun as anyone; but rather than being an end in itself, for Todd riding a mountain bike is a means to discover, explore, and hopefully appreciate the wondrous backcountry of southeastern Utah, or anywhere else for that matter. More than that, it is a means to discover the satisfaction of one's personal independence and self-reliance. He and I both hope that this book will assist you in that discovery.

John W. Groo
Castle Valley, Utah
1/20/91

CONTENTS

I. FOREWORD

The unlikelihood of Moab's prominence in the mountain bike culture is rivalled only by the unlikelihood of the geologic processes which combined to create it. The 10,000-year depositional "tides" of fluctuating seashores, the faulting, the uplifting, and of course, the erosion—all, in their turn, were the builders and sculptors of a giant, intricately detailed topography. Spectacles such as Delicate Arch, Balanced Rock, the Needles, the many slot canyons too narrow-seamed to emit sunshine—even the stairstepping layers of canyon to mesa to plateau and mountain—their chance patterns reflect an attention to detail in both the gross and minute. The scale of this topographic relief becomes understandable, almost conceivable, when you understand that at least a mile-thick overburden of rock and soil has been scoured through the canyonlands' rivers during only the last one-quarter of one percent of the earth's history. If the earth's creation were a feature length film, we'd have to stop-view its last few frames to even recognize the canyonlands as such.

And if we could preview its sequel, it would become abundantly clear that creation is just a sidelong view of destruction. The ground is eroding out from underneath us as if we live in clay-mation format.

A moment of geological time has coincided with a moment of mankind's incessant technology to create more fun, more efficient, more fun-efficient opportunities. Given a web of audacious mining roads, given a map fraught with misspelled names and mismarked places corrupted by fable and the lisps of sun-drunk sheepherders, and given—yes, granted—a mountain bike, there is no responsible act but to celebrate the moment.

May this book open your eyes to the opportunity.

II. DISCLAIMER

It is the author's hope that he's done all of the getting lost for you. The correlation of maps with route descriptions should preclude even topo-agnostics from becoming irretrievably lost. Getting un-lost, too, is usually just a function of time, perseverance, and not "burning bridges."

This book is bound to have flaws, including misprints and mismarked mileages, as any compilation of like scope will. Although it mentions several trails "suitable" to bicycle travel, the author does not suggest that anyone in particular ride any route in particular. It is impossible for the author to guess or judge someone's riding skills or attitudes or to note constantly changing trail conditions. Please use good judgement as to where, when, and under what circumstances you ride; not only to assure your safety and that of other trail users, but to assure the continued preservation of our public lands.

Be aware that mountain biking is a potentially strenuous activity with inherent risks and dangers. Hazards, whether natural or man made, whether mentioned within this text or not, can present themselves at any moment under a vast array of unusual situations and may occur where one did not previously exist. Ride at your own risk, exercising the "muscles" of prudence and responsibility.

Although most routes are on public lands, some trails cross parcels of private property inheld or adjacent to these public lands. Always respect the wishes and rights of a land owner and obey all signs restricting trail use. The author assumes no liability in the event of accident, injury or any action brought against anyone trespassing on or travelling any route mentioned in this book.

Finally, when on or off your bike, riding, hiking, or camping, abide by a code of ethics for backcountry travel. Remember, you are an ambassador for the privilege to bicycle off the paved strip.

Trail Etiquette

Trail etiquette means not only riding softly on the trail, but showing courtesy to other trail users. A modified version of the National Off Road Bicycling Association's Code of Ethics says it all:

1 • Yield the right of way to other non-motorized recreationists. People judge all cyclists by your actions. Move off the trail to allow horses to pass and stop to allow hikers adequate room to share the trail.

2 • Slow down and use caution when approaching others, and make your presence known well in advance. Simply yelling "bicycle" is not enough.

3 • Maintain control of your speed at all times and approach turns in anticipation of someone around the bend. Be able to stop SAFELY within the distance you can see down the trail.

4 • Stay on designated trails to avoid trampling native vegetation, and minimize potential erosion by not using wet or muddy trails or shortcutting switchbacks. Avoid wheel lockup. If a trail is steep enough to require locking wheels and skidding, dismount and walk your bike. Locking brakes contributes to needless trail damage. Do not ride cross-country. Water bars and dips are placed across trails to direct water off the trail and prevent erosion. Ride directly over the top or dismount and walk your bike.

5 • Do not disturb wildlife or livestock.

6 • Do not litter. Pack out what you pack in and carry out more than your share whenever possible.

7 • Respect public and private property, including trail use and no trespassing signs, and leave gates as you found them. If your route crosses private property, it is YOUR responsibility to obtain permission from the landowner. Bicycles are excluded from designated wilderness areas.

8 • Always be self-sufficient. Your destination and travel speed will be determined by your ability, your equipment, the terrain, and the present and potential weather conditions.

9 • Do not travel solo in remote areas. Leave word of your destination and when you plan to return.

10 • Observe the practice of minimum impact bicycling. "Take only pictures and leave only knobby prints."

11 • ALWAYS wear a helmet.

12 • If you abuse it—you lose it. Since mountain bikers are newcomers to the forests and deserts, we must prove ourselves to be responsible trail users.

"Lunchtime," a.k.a. "Soil Sampling"

In southeastern Utah, you're more likely to mountain bike on dirt roads than singletracks; therefore you are probably safest to assume that a car, truck, ATV, motorcycle, or bike is around the next bend, even though you may not have seen one for days. Ride with this eventuality in the back of your mind and a helmet on top of your head.

Riding "cleanly" means more out here than not dabbing a foot on technical sections of trail. It means deviating to take an all-slickrock line around a patch of microbiotic crust, the dark and coarse mat of organisms that function as "the building block of the desert" by stabilizing and actually establishing productive soil. It means having the sense to dismount for a declivity that might otherwise mean a broken collarbone to you and a wrecked day to your friends. It means leaving your dog at the trailhead so it doesn't drag in with bloody paws or a limp from having gotten "undertire" too many times. But ultimately, it means replacing infatuation with (pushing the limits of) your machine with infatuation for the beauty around you, beauty that is as large as the amount of time you spend admiring it.

III. HOW TO USE THIS GUIDEBOOK

You don't need an odometer to use this book. The map alone provides enough information to get through a ride. Just orient the map to the landform and note the intersections of critical routefinding importance (which have cumulative mileage depicted on both the map and its corresponding Route Description). For greater precision, note spur roads as you pass them, and compare the terrain you're riding through to the map occasionally to anticipate the way ahead and to check that you're still on the described route. If you have an odometer, you won't have to pay as much attention to turnoffs and spurs, for you can simply "dial in" to the Mileage Log at any time to pick up your approximate whereabouts.

To minimize the tedium of stopping constantly to consult the map and Route Description, I suggest you do your "homework" by reading and comparing them beforehand. Note that the Route Description and map mileages list ONLY what the author considers to be the points of critical routefinding importance, as well as background information and color commentary. This means that an abundance of spur roads will NOT be noted in the Route Description though they ARE dutifully recorded on the map of the route, so that **you should be able to dope out a route by using just the map.** (Be sure to check what the various map symbols stand for.)

The thing to keep in mind is that often a route will take a twist or turn that neither the map can portray nor your common sense anticipate. It may veer from an oft-used road onto a seldom-used track, and previous riders may have missed it too, their tracks left behind to lead you astray. (Also, many of the rides in this book are new to mountain bike use, with no telltale tracks to guide an uninformed rider.) This is why **you should, at the very least, preview the Mileage Log and Route Description before a first-time ride.**

Finally, when a note in the Mileage Log and Route Description is preceded by **(R)**ight or **(L)**eft, this assumes that the route BYPASSES the spur, sign, petroglyph or whatever.

Notes on How to Interpret the Maps

The front and rear inside covers have an overview map of the eleven riding areas covered by this book, and their aspect regarding paved roads and highways.

Each area has an index map that shows how individual rides' topographic maps relate to each other within the area. Some rides have as many as six pages of topo maps, A through F, and they appear throughout the book in an order that facilitates ease of use.

All the topographical map reproductions used in this book are oriented with the length of the page lined up to magnetic north for ease of use. "Topo" lines depict level contours marked with the elevation (above sea level) to which they correspond. The contour intervals are 80 feet (although sometimes supplemented by 40-foot intervals in relatively flat topographies), and the numbered boxes represent square miles. The red-inked overlay marks the featured route and only those aspects relevant to it. The cumulative mileages refer to entries in the Mileage Log and Route Description that are of routefinding or background significance.

Map Legend

Paved road	———————————
On-dirt road or doubletrack	— — — — — — —
Singletrack or hike-a-bike	— · — · — · — · — ·
Portage route or hiking access	· · · · · · · · · · · · · · ·
Road, track or trail continuing indefinitely	— — — ▶
Road, track or trail ending	— — — ǀ
Trailhead	T
"Trailtail"	t
Trailhead or trailtail off the edge of the map	(T) (t)
Seasonal water source (not necessarily potable!)	⚬̥
Petroglyphs or pictographs	✶
Natural bridge or arch	∩
Manmade structure or ruin	▫
Campsite	△

The Land of Standing Rocks

IV. ENVIRONMENTAL CONSIDERATIONS

Land Ownership

Southeastern Utah is typical of the west in that most of the land here is state or federally owned. In other words, you and I hold the "keys to the place." Ideally, it is managed to achieve the greatest good for the greatest number of people—the concept of multiple use. This means that many user groups share popular areas and usually, if one user-group's activity doesn't preclude others, a tenuous harmony prevails.

The Bureau of Land Management (BLM) administers most of the desert and lower elevation woodlands here. Three-fourths of the rides in this book, including most of the Slickrock Trail, cross BLM land. This government agency helped create the Kokopelli Trail, a multi-day mountain bike ride from near Grand Junction, Colorado, to Moab, as well as the San Rafael Trail, a 190 mile route connecting Moab to Skyline Drive.

The U.S. Forest Service (USFS) manages most of the alpine area here, including the La Sal and Abajo mountains. Like the BLM, it has traditionally managed the land largely as a commodity, but in a break with this tradition, the agency's director issued an internal Recreation Initiative several years ago. Its intent was to allocate more money to promote renewable uses of the forest. The mountain biking community has seen the fruits of this initiative in Idaho, Colorado and California, and we are now seeing it in Utah. In the summer of 1990, a group of Forest Service volunteers created a revised travel plan for the La Sal mountains (a district of the Manti La Sal National Forest) that effectively closed over 25 roads to motor vehicle travel while keeping all roads and trails open to mountain bike use.

The National Park Service (NPS) is perhaps the most visible of federal land agencies, if not because it imposes entry fees, then because of the minimum-impact restrictions issued to park visitors. These restrictions are compiled in sufficient quantity to make a body feel self-conscious about his or her presence there. You cannot ride off designated roads, camp without a permit, park anywhere you please, have open fires or let pets run around unleashed as you can on BLM and USFS lands (with discretion). However, you are insured of a more pristine environment because of these restrictions—a rare and refreshing tradeoff. Though Park Service lands may be desirable to visitors because of mere title appeal, they are some of the most revered scenic places in the world.

Land Use

An extractive, commodity-based land use has reigned for the better part of the one hundred twenty years since permanent caucasian settlement of the Moab Valley. But now, with the collapse of the domestic uranium market and the phasing out by economic attrition of public lands livestock ranching, has come the realization that not only is this stark bit of land often more esthetic in its undeveloped form, but it can create a measure of economic providence, too, in the form of recreation and tourism.

Recreation is a renewable resource. The softer and more sensitively we walk and ride upon the earth, the more it will inspire us. Specifically, leave gates as you find them to confine the effects of livestock. Keep your bike on the road and off the shortcuts. Don't modify the environment by cutting down trees or pushing in new campsites. Let the Indian ruins stand, as they have for a thousand years. And, perhaps even most importantly, please respect the rights and privacy of other people and their property.

In short, if we can be convinced that it takes infinitely more compassion to leave a wild place unsullied, untrammeled, and "undiscovered" than to treat it as the means to an end, the sum of our individual actions may yet engender a global consciousness.

"Slickrock Superheroes"

Town Etiquette

The late Dave Minor, a highly respected recreation coordinator for the BLM's Grand Resource Area, said that of all the places throughout the west in which he had worked, vandalism to public lands, trail signs, and other government installations was the worst near Moab. An attitude of contrariness to symbols of excessive regulation has always dogged the west, even while western states have received more than their fair share of government assistance. A few Moab residents seem to have transferred this attitude to the "invasion" of tourists. In light of the fact that this "invasion" has coincided with the industry-wide loss of high paying mining jobs (especially in this area's once-strong uranium business), it might be argued that any underlying resentment towards tourists seems to be a natural response to a feeling of being victimized by the economic necessity of having to cater to tourists to make a living in Moab. As perhaps the most "eccentric" type of tourist visiting Moab, mountain bikers provide an easy target on which to pin the blame for this community's struggle to accommodate tourism and growth.

Certain incidents of late have fueled animosity towards this ever-increasing tourism, not the least of which are the downright unsanitary conditions which have made the Colorado River corridor and Slickrock Trail area health hazards. (Arguably, state and federal land agencies failed to provide for necessities such as toilets.) People can show very little discrimination in selecting a campsite, especially if it is free and unrestricted. If they're not camping on top of one another, then they forge their way deep into the brush or across unmarred desert, too often leaving fire rings, blowing toilet paper, and other scars upon this slow-to-heal land. It's a poor statement. Moab's citizens need your help in stopping this abuse.

Motorcyclists and jeepers have been using the Slickrock Trail since at least 1971, well before mountain bikes were invented. Please show courtesy to motorists when on the paved or dirt roads here, as you would at home. With few exceptions, Moab's citizens live here because of the land's natural beauty, and have consciously forsaken the high salaries, refined culture and trendy consumptive habits of big city life. Moabites recognize and resent arrogant, gentry-like attitudes, and regard as hypocrites those "educated" vacationers who drive $20,000 cars yet won't even avoid sleeping in town parks, "showering" in public sinks, or leaving the free camp sites festered with litter.

The author hopes that this background will help mountain bikers understand that land abuse does not go unnoticed, and that routes are provided here as much to keep you from getting lost as to keep you on the trail, where environmental damage is minimized.

Camping Etiquette

As this book goes to press, many of the unrestricted camping areas near Moab face imminent restrictions—the necessary response to the growing health threats, fire hazards, habitat damage, and land access problems that accompanied the "discovery" of Moab. Although it's not exactly clear what changes will take place, it's hoped that some of the current impact can be dispersed by providing amenities at campsite clusters in critical areas, such as those near Highway 128 (the "River Road"), Kane Creek, and the Slickrock Trail. Toilets, tables, fire grills and information kiosks will be maintained by your donation.

The upshot of this is that we will all have cleaner, quieter camps, with day-use areas uncluttered by other people's belongings. It will be every bit as seemly as camping in a forest campground, plus provide you with a critical bit of education towards both maximizing your options and sustaining the quality of the environment, a "win/win" situation.

Until these services are available, however, most campers will still run off into the bushes to poop. It's imperative to dispose of human waste correctly, for feces can readily infect water sources. **YE SHALL NOT DEFECATE IN OR NEAR A WATER SOURCE OR POTENTIAL DRAINAGE.** It is the most inviolable unwritten law of this land. Canyons are natural conduits for flowing water, and in the shade and shelter of canyon walls, plants and animals find respite from the arid plateaus above. Those of us who visit the canyons must be mindful not to taint the precious water there. Please go as far away as you can from a drainage or potential drainage (at least one hundred feet) when selecting a place for your cat-hole, and find a place with FERTILE SOIL to dig a six inch-deep hole. Don't burn your toilet paper, as this has caused fires even in riparian areas and deserts. Consider packing it out in a baggy, as do menstruating women.

If you have established a base camp with several other people, consider renting a portable privy from town to be placed temporarily at your campsite. (Hauling and cleaning services are part of the rental cost.) Also, it is easy enough to create your own portable toilet with a snap-lid container and a bag to line it. Outfitters commonly use a "groover," made by lining a 20 mm-shell ammunition box with plastic garbage bags and flopping a toilet seat on top of it for a touch of class (thus minimizing its grooving effects to the bum). The Moab dump has a special pit, signed "Outfitters," where bagged human waste should be left. If your group is backcountry, consider making a community "cat-hole" or trench in a private place.

Note that mandatory carry-out of solid human waste (to centrally located disposal units) and the use of fire pans will be required for camping at undeveloped sites near Moab in the near future.

Trail Hazard

Archeological and Historic Sites

There are many ruins in the canyons and mesas here, both historic and prehistoric. With time spent here, you'll learn to recognize the remnants of once-sound structures. It's the rare canyon that doesn't show signs of ancient use, whether it be a faint petroglyph high on a south-facing wall, an arrowhead flake, or a few dust-covered stones at the base of an overhang. Modern signs are more obvious, like the tunnel and tailings of old uranium mines, washed out roadbeds, and conspicuous rock cairns which mark mining claims.

These ruins are well preserved because of the aridity (water being the great erosive force), and because a relatively small number of people ever discover them. Fitted and mortared stone walls that have stood for over a thousand years can be toppled in a single act of carelessness. In 1979, the 1906 Antiquities Act was amended to provide additional protection for historical and archeological resources. This law provides for the removal of artifacts or the disturbance of historical or archeological sites only with a permit to qualified archeologists to do so. Fines up to $250,000 and two years in prison can be levied on people who disturb these sites. Feel free to look at artifacts, but leave them where you find them, so that they will continue to hold their in-place significance. Touching rock "art" panels is clearly harmful to the resource, and "rubbing" glyphs for reproduction or taking latex casts is also illegal.

Please note that the removing of or "hiding" of artifacts is illegal and punishable by law. It is recognized that many people conceal their finds so that they are not immediately obvious to passers-by who might end up taking them. Some call this the "living museum" approach, a variation of "catch and release." Certainly, it is better than pocketing an irresistible arrowhead or potsherd, and it allows the satisfaction of showing the artifact to others during future visits to the area. However, it alters the exact context of the artifact, and context is THE crucial element in the study of archeology. Again, the moving or removing of artifacts is illegal. If you enjoy, then leave the artifact *in situ*, so much the better.

Canyonlands backcountry rangers monitor archeological sites in the Park, as digging and looting of comparable sites continues all across the Four Corners Region. Moab youths who found an Anasazi burden basket in the summer of 1990 reported it to a government archeologist. Not only did they receive the accolades of numerous professionals in the field, but the basket resides in a Moab museum for the public to view. Their behavior strikes a note for decency and honor.

Life on the Edge - the Anasazi

V. PERSONAL CONSIDERATIONS

Water in the High Desert

It's an old axiom, but it's true: Water is more precious than gold when you really need it.

By and large, you should carry all the water you will need on a ride with you. It is not uncommon to need four quarts of water DURING a three-to-four hour ride in the hot desert because, besides profuse sweating, an increased breath rate assists the evaporation of water from your lungs. **You can never carry too much**, as it is a hedge against the unforseen, a gift to your needy companions or an homage to the gods of the cactus blossom. Convective cooling, and therefore adequate saturation, is your body's only means of maintaining its internal "thermometer."

> Consider what happens to a man... He must keep his body temperature within just a few degrees of 98.6° F, or die. If the air temperature is much above this, he must cool himself principally by evaporating off sweat. The source of the perspiration is the water in his blood, which desert sunlight will tap at a rate of about a quart an hour. By the time two gallons are gone, about 10% of his body weight—the man becomes delirious, deaf and, rather more happily, insensitive to pain. When another 2% is gone, the blood thickens like boiled-down gravy so that the heart can no longer circulate it effectively. Thus the blood is unable to carry off heat from the inner organs to be dispersed through the skin, and the man very rapidly dies.
>
> Jerome Doolittle, <u>Canyons and Mesas</u>, 1974

The most common place to find water on most Moab area rides is in potholes. And on average, they provide the biologically "cleanest" source of backcountry water because they are temporary rainwater basins. However, many aquatic animals live in potholes, including shrimp, bivalves, snails, water striders, and the egg and larval forms of toads and flies. These species live whole life cycles, from dormant eggs to larvae to adults which lay eggs in as little as two weeks. They are beautifully but tenuously adapted to intermittent rainfall, and they are sensitive to pollutants such as salt, chain lubricant and sunscreen. If you take pothole water for any reason, take it well away from the pothole to drink or wash or whatever, for just one oily or sweaty drop will begin to change the pH of the pothole.

14

Like pothole water, all other waters taken from this area should be filtered, boiled or sterilized with iodine tablets. All flowing water hereabouts has probably been contaminated by either beavers or cows, both animals thought to be carriers of the *giardisis* cyst, or giardia, a parasite of the intestinal tract. Stock ponds are found often enough throughout the canyons, mesas, and mountains of the region, and they can quench a thirst in an emergency, as can the silty, filter-clogging waters of the Colorado and Green Rivers. The author would wish to say that he never had to rely on these sources, for not only is there the threat of biological hazard, these rivers are known to contain more than "background levels" of trace heavy metals, especially during spring runoff.

There are several gushing springs along riding routes, the best known of these being Kane Spring on the Kane Creek Road and Matrimony Spring near the junction of Highways 191 and 128. (Neither of these springs is monitored for contaminants.) Some springs are fed through pipes into giant metal stock tanks, troughs or hollow logs. You can easily intercept water before it dribbles into the container, and often this is potable without treatment. Seeps, or seeping springs occur in sheltered and north-facing alcoves and can provide your bottle with directly potable stone-filtered water if you are patient. The unsyncopated rhythm of their drips can be a soothing melody on a hot day.

A view from Canyonlands Overlook

Riding Seasons and Seasonal Hazards

The classic seasons for high desert riding are spring and fall, March through mid-May and mid-September through November. (One can tell because there are more wheels on top of visitors' cars than beneath them.) The La Sal and Abajo Mountains offer fine summer riding from June through October, subject, of course, to snow conditions. And even the dead of winter offers some rare opportunities to access frozen wash bottoms too sandy to ride another time.

Springtime around Moab brings shorter shadows, shirt sleeve temperatures, and blossoming plants. There is usually a dynamic storm or two, then come the bugs—the gnats on the plateaus, the deer flies in the verdant side canyons, and the mosquitoes on the river—to settle in by mid May. The mountains offer a retreat from insects until July, when the picnic flies accompany the cattle drives up out of the surrounding valleys. The high country insects are rarely as insufferable as the low country ones. With the first cold snaps of September, the bugs recede to a distant drone in sunlit places, and disappear altogether by mid-October.

Late spring and summer thundershowers can cause intense flash floods and create the opportunity to witness phenomenal electrical storms. People are struck by lightning every year in southern Utah, because storms move in so rapidly that they are taken unaware. If this happens to you, remember to avoid both high ridges and low drainages to shelter on mid-slopes, being mindful to crouch and stay clear of trees.

The vivid fall colors of aspen and cottonwood groves are preceded by three months of our heaviest rains, from August through October. In the last ten years, only October has averaged over an inch of rain. Rainy weather is excellent to ride in, as it firms up sandy soils and provides pothole water for drinking. Mountain soils, however, can become exceedingly gooey. Also, there are certain geologic formations in the desert with high clay content which are the wrong places to be when it is wet. (The individual ride descriptions note specifics on this matter.) Finally, bikers are reminded to wear bright colors when riding anytime from September through December, as one or another of the various hunting seasons is under way. Hunters deserve courteous treatment whether or not you agree with their motives and methods.

Mountain and dismountin' bikes

Techniques

The single most important piece of advice for mountain bikers new to this terrain is to use the front brake sparingly on descents. The notoriously shifty surfaces here, which can vary from deep sand to loose stone and back within a wheelbase's distance, increase the likelihood of front wheel washouts. Although the front brake is potentially 70% of your bike's total braking power, it is effective only as long as you stay on the bike. A tactile savvy is enhanced by keeping your weight back and low, off and behind your saddle when descending.

To avoid small obstacles, actually aim at them when approaching and you'll be better able to avoid them when the time comes to pass. Also, it is important to lift, or "pre-jump," the front wheel over dips and creases across the trail, especially when speedballing. In jarring terrain, it pays to relax your grip so as not to absorb all the punishment. "Posting" off of the saddle, while pedalling or not, can also reduce saddle shock. W. Nealy (in The Mountain Bike Way of Knowledge, 1989), introduces the idea of the "grin level," where even as you swallow the bumps, your legs act as compression devices in keeping your Cheshire Cat grin on a straight vector.

On hill climbs, there is a fine weight distribution between a churning, tractionless rear wheel and having the front wheel lift off the ground. It helps many people to envision themselves pulling back with their arms, a leveraging from the handlebars that applies force to the pedals. Balance, tenacity, and proper gear selection all play roles in dab-free climbing. Only experience can tell you how fast to approach and in which gear a climb should be taken, but you should assume a gear at the base of the hill which you can push to the top. The rule of thumb on thumbtip shifting?—**Conserve momentum and anticipate your shifts.**

Riding through sand is nearly as demanding technically as it is physically. Foremost in approaching sand is to maintain as much momentum as possible. If you begin to auger in, downshift before there is too much stress on the chain and try to churn steadily through. If it gets to the point where you're pulsing each pedal stroke, you're expending more energy than you would by getting off and pushing the beast, although the thrill of charging into and lurching, from a near trackstand, out of a deep sand bog is ecstatic, after a fashion. Not all sandy stretches need be "runaway bike ramps." Floating across deep sand also mandates that you let the bike steer itself. Keep your weight laterally centered and don't aim the bike. In fact, let it career off the humps and embankments to find its own path of least resistance. If and when you encounter deep sand, please don't establish multiple trails by detouring around it.

Carving the slickrock is one of the truly blissful experiences in life. One could spend a lifetime finding new and more outrageous routes to perfect. Riding the "rawk" is an expression of the mountain bike's most graceful act, and great riders make it look like ballet, not grunt work. Applied thrust, critical timing, and derring-do render these artists "sand-stoned," or tuned in to the greater possibilities that await. Ultimately, the slickrock is a controlled experiment, where the surface features will be nearly identical from one day to the next. There is no better gauge of a rider's progress.

Basically, the skills for riding slickrock are merely exaggerated trail skills. Arm strength is critical in keeping the bike where it needs to be. Get the weight **WAY** back and low in descending, **WAY** forward in climbing, and by all means, keep that inside pedal up when sidehilling. Pedal-gouging the rock can send you sailing, so it pays to perfect a side-vaulting dismount, where both feet hit the ground on the low side of the bike. The bike should be upright and brake-stabilized when you attempt this technique, of course, and its use should help you avoid what slickrock superhero Mark Doherty calls "the dreaded crotchsplit."

Briefly, here is a list of other techniques which might be useful:

• Always try to cross roots, sticks and branches perpendicularly to keep them from being sucked into your brakes, spokes or derailleurs.

• Jab the snow or mud out of your brakes even before it impairs your bike's braking, for that glob can wear your brake pads down to nothing in one good descent.

• Slow down the moment you see tire ruts running the length of the road. At speed, it's hard to cross or exit a rut at an angle perpendicular enough to keep from losing the rear wheel in a grinding slideout.

• Within reason, brake as little as possible. Speed absorbs trail shock and can dampen jarring impact to you and your bike, which is nicer to the trail surface, to boot.

• Pinch the saddle between your thighs when downhill "posting" for premium control. This is easier when the seat is lowered a few inches.

• "Ratchet," or alternate backward and forward pedalling, through roots and rocks to keep your pedals clear of obstruction. This technique is especially important on steep slickrock sidehills.

• Loosen your toe clips a bit in highly technical riding terrain for safer dismounts. Also, it's a good idea to always "get" your clip upon restarting, rather than letting it dangle to catch on things. Toe clips can keep your feet on the pedals when you might otherwise be doing a "flying 'W'."

• Brake and pedal at the same time to enhance your balance at slow speed on technical single tracks.

• Rocky outcrops can be a better line of travel than soil, even, as they provide better traction.

• Never tie garments or string or anything to a bike that can come off. A shirt lodged in the front brake has sent many a folk to the hospital.

• When you hike-a-bike, never be on the downhill side of your bike in case you lose your footing. If something is going to fall, it should be your bike, not you. Also, rearing the bike up on its back wheel can help you carry, kick, and cajole it along narrow trails and through rocky descents.

• If you begin to crash, ditch the bike. Holding on will complicate your fall and injure both you and the bike worse than a clean vaulting dismount.

The Moab Slickrock Bike Trail:
- experienced riders only
- do not travel alone
- please register
- and check your guns at the sign!

Equipment and Maintenance

Any well maintained fat tire bicycle can handle rugged terrain, but sooner or later it's going to rattle out of adjustment. In mountain biking, there is a premium on carrying and knowing how to use the necessary tools to fix a breakdown, for it's usually a long walk home. At the very least, you should have a tube patch kit (and/or spare tube), tire irons, a pump, and the axle nut wrench which removes your wheel if your bike doesn't have quick release skewers. If your tires aren't flat, you can at least scooter-kick the bike along. Most bolts can be hand tightened for temporary light duty, but it is more judicious to carry the wrenches that fit brakes, derailleurs, chain, mounting bolts, and even the bottom bracket, headset and spokes if you're hard on bikes. Carrying chain lube and a rag to wipe off any excess with is a good way to make friends.

Innovative tool use isn't necessarily high tech. A rock and a nail in a craftsman's hands is a lock ring tool in a mechanic's. Wadded underbrush can substitute for an innertube, and bailing wire and pliers can be used to fix anything from a broken chain to loose dentalwork. (Sometimes it seems that the bike industry does everything it can to make the simple and efficient unnecessarily high-tech, specialized, expensive and, dare I say—ugly—in what seems an attempt, if not a conspiracy, to strain the limits of our belief.)

Before departing on a ride, squeeze the front brake and rock the bike back and forth to see if the headset is loose. Feel whether the crank arms wobble laterally at any point in their rotation. Make sure the brake pads are flush with the rim when applied and not chafing a tire anywhere. Listen for a squeaky chain, a plea for lubrication. And finally, check your tires for sufficient air pressure and sidewall damage. **If any of these basic functions is awry, you'll want to deal with it before you ride.**

Tire pressure is best kept on the firm side to keep from "snakebiting" the tube against the rim, yet low enough to insure adequate traction on loose surface climbs. Depending on your weight and riding style, this ranges from probably 40 to 60 psi. Keeping tires aired up will also keep valve stems from twisting and sidewalls from creasing prematurely. In choosing tire brands, note that tire traction is primarily a function of a knobby's width, not its tread pattern. Innertube liners can help protect you from the ravages of cactus, goatheads, sand burrs, and sharp rocks.

A portage strap and 24-tooth small chainring, toe clips and extra water bottle cages are welcome additions to any mountain bike that sees backcountry use. Beyond the addition of these things, it all depends on how you define "superfluous." Often it is difficult to co-ordinate the use of too many essential add-ons.

"Cross Straining" with mountain bike   photo by Rachel Schmidt

Route finding on the White Rim, an exercise in imagination

Trail Finding

Most of the routes in this book use dirt roads created in the rush to mine uranium-bearing ores. Uranium has been recognized and mined in the area since 1872; before that, Ute and Navajo Indians used it for war paint. The Curies received a Nobel Prize in 1911 for isolating an ounce of radium from ores processed in this country's first plant, just over the border in Colorado. A second mining boom sought the ore for its vanadium content, a mineral used in paints and dyes of the time. By far the biggest frenzy for radioactive rock occurred in the wildcat boom of the early 50's. The commercial development of nuclear energy gave softrock miners their latest and greatest chance at personal fortunes. The legacy of this activity is a spiderweb of roads in and around the backcountry. Their destination is too often a scenic prominence, and the difficulty of building them was too extreme for it not to be believed that those miners loved the country they worked.

In following a road across slickrock hummocks, it can be easily lost, so continue straight from where you last saw it, taking the path wide enough for a motor vehicle to pass. Look not only for tire tracks in sandy depressions, oil, grease, transmission fluid and blackened rubber stains, but for the ribbed depressions on the rock made by the bulldozer that originally forged its way through. Some slickrock stretches are marked by small stone stacks called cairns. From a cairn, you can usually look ahead and see another cairn or obvious sign of the route. The Slickrock Trail, Poison Spider Mesa and Gold Bar Rim have routes painted on the rock. Try not to be offended by their presence. They manage to keep lots of the 50,000 or so people who ride here every year out of trouble.

Following single tracks through the woods can prove interesting at times, too. In the La Sals and Abajos, trees along the path are routinely "blazed," or hatcheted so that their bark scars with what is shaped like a two-foot tall, upside down exclamation mark at about eye level. Look for evidence of trail work—sawn trees, water bars, bank reinforcement, or even flagging tied to an occasional branch. When a track reaches an open meadow, it can become obscured by heavy grass. Go to the cow wallow that's sure to exist in the center of the clearing, then scan the 180° field-of-view before you for the most likely corridor back into the trees. Logs are sometimes laid along the trail to define it over barren ground, and cairns or conspicuously clumped groups of rocks seek to show you the way, even if cow traffic has disrupted the message. If you lose the trail, go back to the last place where you're sure you were on it and strike off in another likely direction. If you still don't find it, try spiralling out on foot from that point until you cross the trail or its most likely facsimile.

Preparedness

Be prepared to turn back, to cut your losses if you've over-extended your ability level somehow. Two mountain bikers died here in 1989, one from heat prostration and the other from a fall. Both were separated from their riding partners, and the resulting anxiety may have provoked them to use poor judgement. When riding with a group of people, be sure to communicate your intents and purposes as social protocol would dictate. Don't assume anything about a missing member of the group unless the possibility was specifically addressed beforehand. Try to familiarize everybody with the route, its elevation profile and length by sharing the map or guidebook.

In the author's five years of guiding, he's seen people make (and himself made) the goofiest assumptions about the whereabouts of the trail or the rest of the group, a syndrome dubbed "altitude confusion," or "fresh air and open space confusion," if you prefer. For safety reasons, party members should not be expected to read tracks, decide which way a flatwater river is flowing from afar, or determine what direction is due north. But if they are carrying their own tools, food, water, and extra clothing, they should be fine until you reconvene with them.

Finally, do wear a helmet. It's your best insurance against the unforseen mechanical mishap, error in judgement or lapse in reflex. There is no excuse anymore but vanity not to wear one, for they are so light. "If you've got a head worth saving, then you've got a helmet worth wearing."

Lu and Tatsy Warner in utter "tandemonium" — La Sal Mtns.

Navajo sandstone formation's slickrock

VI. A GEOLOGIC BRIEFING

Southeastern Utah is an "open book" of geology. The reason so much rock is exposed on the surface is that the entire Colorado Plateau, a provincial block of land that occupies almost half of Utah and lesser parts of Colorado, New Mexico, and Arizona, is in a period of drastic uplift. Under the vise-like pressures exerted from tectonic plate shifts, the Plateau began to rise about 10 million years ago, and rivers and streams which meandered across a relatively flat, low-lying plain were forced to cut indiscriminately into underlying formations simply to maintain their courses. With the increased vigor from a steepened gradient, flowing water scoured through over a vertical mile of sedimentary rock, causing layer after layer to recede in cliffs or slopes which now reveal the dramatic effects of 1.8 billion years of faulting, mountain building, intermittent flooding, and cyclical periods of erosion and deposition. This uplifting has hastened erosion such that soils, and thus plants, cannot be formed quickly enough to retard it, a condition which is exacerbated by arid "stress." Where rain is infrequent, plants are few and organic nutrients are scarce, little remains with which to create soil.

Visually distinctive rock formations are displayed in broad horizontal bands. They were originally transported here as rock, silt, shale, sand and calcium carbonate—the calcified remains of early sea life. At a glance, the various formations here show either the horizontal planes of waterborne strata or the obvious, tilted bedding planes of "cemented" sand dunes. The truly unique aspect of canyon country geology is that many of these now-visible formations were deposited near a then-fluctuating seashore. On-shore dunes, fresh water streams and salty sea water, in combination with a constantly fluctuating shoreline, deposited what has become interfingered limestone and sandstone. Sand turned to sandstone as more recently deposited sediments compressed, leached, and cemented underlying layers with calcite, silica, gypsum or iron oxide, the mineral which gives much of the rock its rusty hue.

The canyons of Canyonlands National Park were cut into the fallout of the Uncompahgre Uplift, a prominent range of the Ancestral Rocky Mountains. Thousands of cubic miles of debris that washed down from the Uncompahgre began filling a basin composed largely of the evaporite salt left from receding seas. (Due to dynamic glacial activity in the earth's polar regions, at least twenty-nine seas advanced into, then became trapped in the Paradox Basin to evaporate.) As this lopsided and increasingly heavy overburden compressed the salt, the salt flowed like wet putty to and through pressure-alleviating fault blocks. Where it squished upwards, overlying rocks were first arched, then pierced by these massive bodies of salt, some of which had concentrated up to 15,000 feet thick. As soon as this salt surfaced, water dissolved it, and in the void left by its dissolution, rock collapsed inward to form a valley.

Moab and Castle Valleys are but two of the many "salt valleys" that are the result of this impressive process. With the relatively recent (in geologic time) uplift of the Colorado Plateau, the Colorado River has penetrated the Paradox salt formation in places to further dissolve and undermine the relatively brittle rock on top of it, even as this rock is rapidly being eroded from above. The salt beds may still be rising, but mostly as a "rebound" from their compression caused by the lessened weight of eroding overburden above. So not only the inherent nature of the strata, but the rapid uplift of the land "through" the rivers, is the great determinant of what we see today.

The Paradox formation is one of over a dozen distinct formations that are identifiable from the trails in this book. (The "paradox" of it refers to the Paradox salt valley, which is cleaved perpendicularly by the Dolores River, just as the Colorado cleaves the Moab Valley.) The somewhat predictable way in which a formation erodes is a function of both its hardness and its proximity to softer underlying formations which can undercut it, or to harder overlying formations which can "caprock" or protect it from slabbing and spalling. Basically, this differential erosion creates cliffs, slopes, and benches. On a smaller scale, it creates arches and spires and balanced rocks which defy gravity … for a while.

Erosion can reduce a massively thick deposit to a thin surface remnant, or the deposit can be seen at the edge of its "boundary," where it tapered horizontally to nothing before erosion revealed it to the eye. Fault blocks frequently cut through and displace deposits, leaving a formation visible on one side and buried or elevated on the other. The classic local example of this is the Moab fault, which is most pronounced near the entrance to Arches National Park. On the west side of Highway 191, you see rock that usually lies 900 feet below the type of rock on the east side of the highway.

Each ride writeup includes a briefing about which rock formations it travels on, with occasional geologic elaboration in the Mileage Log and Route Description.

The Totem Pole, Monument Basin

VII. RIDES BY AREA

Canyonlands National Park's Island in the Sky Area

The only route in this district is probably the classic multi-day mountain bike ride in the desert southwest. The White Rim Trail wanders close to the edge of sheer dropoffs as it contours around the head of one deeply stamped drainage after another. Burnt orange cliffs tower over the Rim, even as the Rim towers over two great rivers below. The landscape is stark and exacting for it is waterless and treeless, and in its immensity, you can ride for hours and still be in sight of a landmark butte or mesa.

Logistics are everything on the White Rim, as a finite number of primitive campsites strictly managed by the Park Service make the competition for reservations fierce. It is usually impossible to acquire them on a walk-in basis, especially in the spring or fall. Commercial bike outfitters account for only 20% of the trail's use, and Moab's many outfitters offer an excellent range of supported overnight trips, from elegant to no-frills. At least one of the (average of) two sites per primitive camp is retained for non-commercial use (except in one-site camps). For reservations, write:

White Rim Reservations c/o Canyonlands National Park
125 West 200 South, Moab, Utah 84532
Phone: 801-259-4351

The Park Service has a stronger resource preservation mandate than the BLM or USFS, since it is charged with maintaining both the environmental resource and the visitor's experience. Too often this means rangers try to either "save visitors from themselves" or keep the Park from "being loved to death." And sometimes the Park's responsibilities come into conflict. For instance, firewood cannot be collected inside the Park. This is due to the scarcity of trees, whose absence would mean not only a loss of esthetic value or shade, but a denial of scarce nutrients to an already impoverished sandy soil.

There is no food, water, or gasoline available at the "Island." The Willow Flat campsite near the Green River Overlook is atop the Island mesa, accessible by paved road. The other campsites are backcountry on and around the White Rim, and require travel over rugged dirt roads to access. They accommodate no more than fifteen persons per permit. Vehicle camping can occur only at these established campsites. There are fire rings and "duck blind" pit toilets at the campsites, but firewood must be imported and toilet paper sometimes runs out before ranger patrols can restock it. Domestic pets must be leashed and remain in the vehicle corridor at all times. It's an unfair pressure on wildlife if pets are allowed to roam (in non-Park areas too), and it's probably unfair to the pet to suffer constant restraint, so consider leaving your animals at home. Besides, barking or whimpering can become annoying to visitors in adjacent sites.

Please remember that mountain bikes are managed as vehicles and are required to stay in vehicle corridors while in the Park, even when not in use. When making reservations, please take the time to learn the vehicle regulations as well as the environmental restrictions. Their intent is to insure a quality experience for you.

The White Rim Trail, (clockwise from top left)
Dave Lyle measuring the Holeman Slot
Colorado River gorge backdrop
Bego Gerhart admiring the airy view from Holeman Slot
Fort Bottom Lookout

THE WHITE RIM TRAIL

Type: Multi-day Loop (usually 3-5 days)
Length: 100.6 miles, including 9.9 miles on pavement
Difficulty: Physically moderate to difficult / Technically moderate
Best Season: The White Rim is most popular in spring, which may make it difficult to get campsite reservations. There are steep and sloppy places on the trail that are unsafe for even a chained four wheel drive rig when it's wet or icy. Fall is as nice as spring on the Rim, and subject to less tempestuous storming even though it sees more overall rain. By all means, avoid summer travel on the White Rim from June to mid-August, as it can reach 130° F on open ground.
Elevation: Trailhead/-tail—5,900 ft., High—6,280 ft., Low—3,950 ft.
Land Agencies: BLM and NPS
Route Summary: (Note that most references to the White Rim Trail include just the seventy or so miles from the base of the Horsethief Trail switchbacks to the base of the Shafer Trail switchbacks, the two 1,000-foot-plus descents used to access the White Rim. Since mountain biking this seventy miles with some type of support vehicle, whether it be merely a shuttle or a full blown four wheel drive sag wagon, means that, one way or another, you'll see all of the 100+ miles, this book takes the liberty of calling those 100+ miles the "White Rim Trail.")

The White Rim Trail route might best be thought of as three sides of a triangle: a 21 mile connector "side" across the Island's mesa top between the Shafer and Horsethief Trails; a bench "side" along the Green River from the Horsethief Trail 42 miles out to White Crack Overlook, the point of White Rim closest to the Confluence; and a final bench "side" along the Colorado River from White Crack Overlook 36 miles to the Shafer Trail. The "bench" sides are the more visually compelling and physically exalting sides of the triangle, so the mesa top side is often foregone by doing a vehicle shuttle before or after the ride. The White Rim sandstone is a "bench" in the sense that it is the middle tier of a "geologic wedding cake," the Island mesa top and the river corridor composing the tiers above and below it, respectively.

This trail is recommended as a counterclockwise loop because 1) the fast, 13 mile ride from Highway 313 to the Horsethief Trail is a nice warmup that contrasts well with the White Rim, and 2) there are more campsites on the Green River side, allowing you shorter mileage-days as you warm up to your task.

Options: There are many dead end spurs from the trail, none longer than five miles. Also, it connects to the Potash Trail, which parallels the Colorado River upstream to the Potash Plant, where paved Highway 279 continues in to Moab Valley. (Consult the Jughandle Loop ride.)
Attractions: The White Rim is particularly rewarding to those who like rim hiking, for a funhouse of caverns, slots, arches, and enticing downclimbs is

there to entertain you. Passions such as swimming, archeology, photography, botany and geology are easily indulged. The views can be dizzyingly sheer, intimate, or expansive—across a thousand square miles of incised rock. There is little natural shade or shelter, and the open space both bewilders and beguiles as it absorbs the noises even your presence makes, so to reinforce a kind of psychedelic sense of "personal puniness"—the hallmark of a classic place.

Riding Surface: Most of this occasionally-graded route is hardpacked sediments on a jeep trail, with the usual hazards such as loose surface rock, drift sand, ledges and gooey soil when wet.

Geology: The route starts on the "Island" amongst sediments between the Navajo sandstone's plainly visible outcrops of slickrock, and the Kayenta formation, the thin, ledgy-eroding deposit of off-white sandstone that caps the beetling orange Wingate sandstone cliffs, those that confine the entire Canyonlands Basin. At the head of the Horsethief Trail (mile 21.7), you'll gain the first closeup views of the Wingate with its harder Kayenta caprock. By the time you reach the intersection at the base of the switchbacks, you'll have entered the Chinle formation, a shale-, silt-, and sandstone that gets slippery as dog snot when wet. It almost always appears as a colorful slope abutting massive Wingate walls, which litter its surface with orange boulders. Where the Chinle appears ledgy, it is called the Mossback member, a sandstone element of the Chinle. The campsites on Murphy Hogback (mile 56) are located on a long finger of the Mossback member. By the time you reach the Canyonlands National Park boundary (mile 27.1) you'll have descended just enough to enter the Moenkopi formation mudstone, a study in texture which includes cemented clay crack castings, raindrop depressions, and tree roots.

As you leave Potato Bottom (mile 36), you'll see the trail's namesake—the White Rim sandstone—emerge from beneath the ground to border the Green River. You have just intersected the northern exposed edge of its lens-shaped deposit. The remainder of the White Rim Trail will stay on or above the White Rim, but the many reddish-brown basins below it are in the Organ Rock shale, which, despite its very different appearance is a component of the same Group as the White Rim—the Cutler Group. The Cutler dominates Canyonlands National Park, for it also includes Cedar Mesa sandstone—the red and white banded rock so prominent in the Maze and Needles Districts—and the Elephant Canyon limestone formation—the dominant layer along the river clear down from Potash to Lake Powell. Some poorly differentiated Cedar Mesa sandstone is visible in the round-edged benches beneath White Crack Overlook (mile 65), and the Elephant Canyon is glimpsed from the same overlook in the distant walls that define both rivers' inner gorges.

The origin of the Cutler Group deposits is the Ancestral Rocky Mountains, and the marked difference in the Group's various components is caused by the dynamic comings and goings of ancient seashores.

Anne Clare Erickson enjoying a birthday on the White Rim

Generally, the White Rim Trail's rock types were deposited in the following environments (in order of their appearance):

Navajo - windblown sand dunes
Kayenta - freshwater stream deposits
Wingate - windblown sand
Chinle - freshwater stream deposits
Moenkopi - marine tidal flat
White Rim - sand dunes and off-shore sand bars
Organ Rock - freshwater stream deposits
Cedar Mesa - windblown sand and marine sediments
Elephant Canyon - marine sediments

Notes: Licensed mountain bike outfitters in Moab provide a range of services on the White Rim, from simple shuttles to fully catered and provisioned trips with guides versed in first aid and any number of other skills. Theme trips such as tandem rides, combination whitewater trips, and instructional seminars are popular on the White Rim. Contact the **Grand County Travel Council, 805 N. Main St., Moab, Utah 84532, ph.(801) 259-8825** for a comprehensive list of companies. Since most overnight cyclists are vehicle supported, it's important to have at least one experienced four wheel driver per group in order to minimize the impacts to both vehicle and trail. Hazards like deep watercut furrows, protruding bedrock, loose boulders, ledges, deep sand, and clay soils that get slick when wet make driving this trail harder (and slower) than biking it.

Most of the plants abutting the trail are older than you and I, and sustaining life in a desert is a mark of their tenacity. However, they are as fragile as they are tenacious, and they "live on the edge" of more than the road. When pulling aside to let other vehicles pass, ALWAYS find some slickrock or a sandy drainage to pull onto. Back onto the road the same way you pulled off of it or straddle vegetation to avoid crushing it. The Park Service requires that you keep two wheels on the road when pulling aside. This may not always be the best way to observe a minimum impact ethic, so you be the judge.

The rangers on White Rim patrol spend an inordinate amount of time raking out mountain bike, motorcycle, and motor vehicle tracks that venture off the road. There are 66% more roads than hiking trails in the Park. Please don't drift off the roads even to nearby overlooks, because it is not only illegal, it is immoral. If you leave your bike lying on the edge of the road or camping area, traffic can pass without having to swerve off the road and inflict further environmental damage.

Logistics: Before making reservations, consult the map to spread your campsites appropriately over the number of days you'll be spending. With a support vehicle, the trail is as easily supported taken clockwise as it is counterclockwise.

White Rim Trail, (clockwise from top left)
    Musselman Arch
    Buttes of the Cross reflected in the Green River
    One of the thankless and unnecessary tasks of the Park Service Ranger
    The "Coke Bottles" near Musselman Arch

(The Route Description is narrated counterclockwise.) Arrange a shuttle between the parking lot at the top of the Horsethief Trail switchbacks and the Visitor Center near the Shafer Trail if you want to concentrate your time to the backcountry of the Canyonlands Basin. The thirteen mile pedal from Hwy. 313 to the Horsethief Trail (the Mineral Bottom access road/switchbacks) is a nice fast warmup at a trip's outset, but something of a monotonous grunt at the end of a trip. Shuttle vehicles can be left at the visitor center or other designated overnight parking areas in the Park, as well as along any road on BLM turf which surrounds the Park, but it is unnecessary (and considered bad form) to create new vehicle turnouts or campsites on ANY public land.

For self-supported riders, a counterclockwise route is suggested. The rivers supply the only reliable water near the trail, and the Green River side of the trail has several direct river accesses whereas the Colorado side has only one, via a sandy descent into Lathrop Canyon. All things being equal, the Green River side is the harder ride, thus the need to stock up on vital fluids before turning the corner to the east side. Once a self-supported rider leaves Queen Anne Bottom, it is at least forty-six waterless miles to Lathrop. (A body needs as much as two and a half gallons of water a day when exercising in dry heat.) The use of water caches or pothole water is an option that self-supported riders can usually avoid, as the numerous commercial outfitters and private groups on the Rim will often provide limited amounts of water.

More and more people are riding the entire 100 mile loop in one day, and again, a counterclockwise direction seems best for this marathon.

Trailhead Access: From downtown Moab (Main x Center St.'s), go north on Hwy. 191 12.5 miles to Hwy. 313, the road to Dead Horse Point and Canyonlands. From this turn, it is 21 miles to the Island Visitor Center (where you'll need to pick up your permit). Along the way, you'll pass the dirt Mineral Bottom spur just before highway mile marker 12 and the Shafer Trail spur at about mile marker 20, just before reaching the Visitor Center.

Mileage Log and Route Description:
0.0 Head north from the Island Visitor Center.
8.9 Turn left onto the Mineral Bottom access road.
21.7 The switchbacks mark the beginning of the Horsethief Trail. Notice the three crumpled autos if you stop to shake out your wrists halfway down. The switchbacks were bulldozed in the 1940's for minerals exploration access. Art Woods, the catskinner who cleared the trail across what was then a talus slope, endured a life threatening mishap in the process. Minutes after his three-day supply wagon left, Art sidehilled his machine too steeply and rolled it. His arm was pinched between the dozer's tread and some slickrock, and he immediately started losing blood. In a moment of astounding lucidity, he applied a tourniquet to his arm, withdrew his pocketknife and severed it completely off.

As rugged as the canyons he worked, Art lived well into his seventies, and continued to operate heavy machinery with skill and dexterity.

ISLAND IN THE SKY DISTRICT OF CANYONLANDS

To Moab

Hwy. 313

DEAD HORSE POINT STATE PARK

White Rim A

White Rim E

White Rim B

GLEN CANYON NATIONAL RECREATION AREA

White Rim C

White Rim D

Green River

Island in the Sky District

Colorado River

Maze District

Needles District

CANYONLANDS NATIONAL PARK

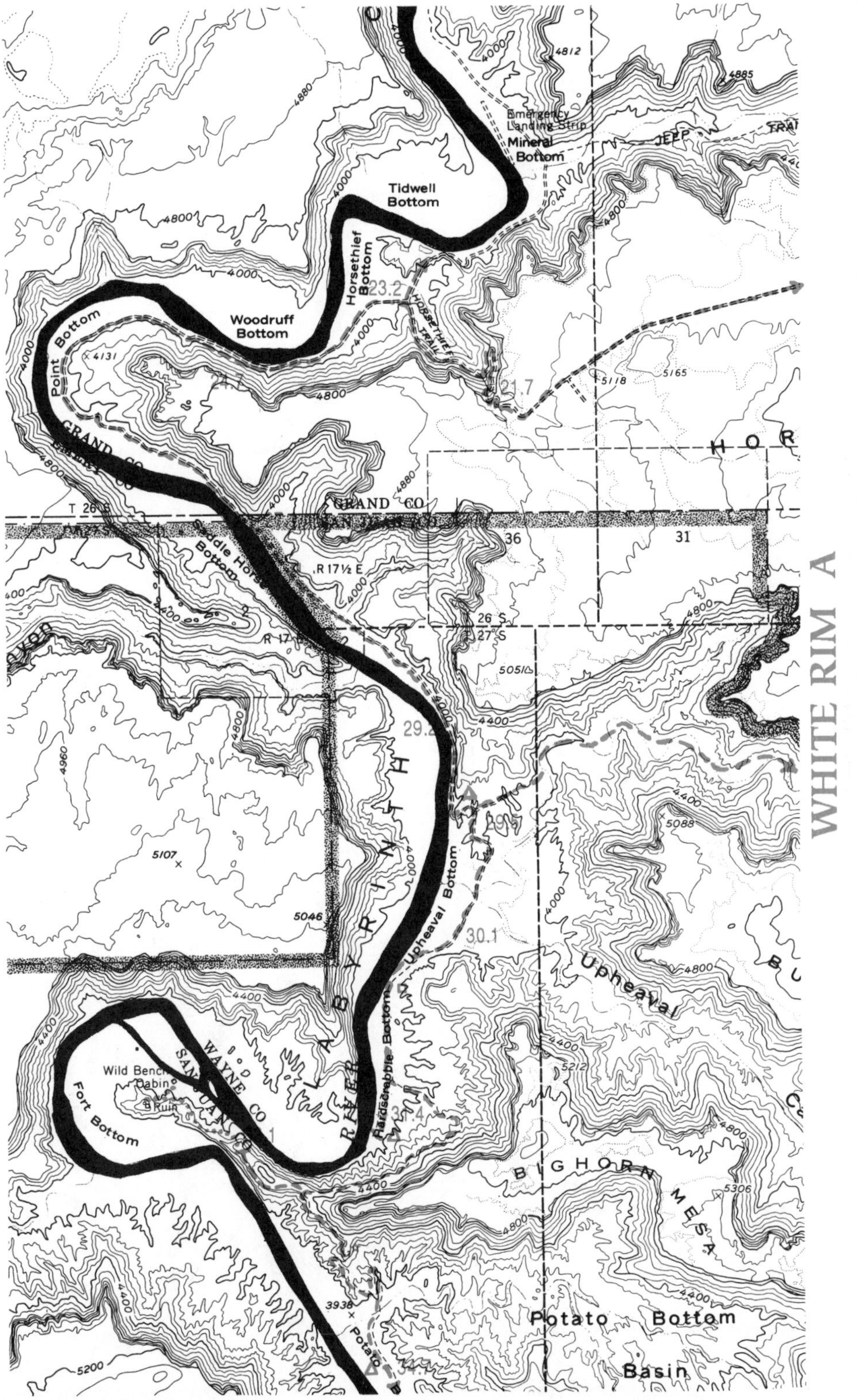

Emergency Landing Strip
Mineral Bottom
JEEP
TRAIL
Tidwell Bottom
Horsethief Bottom
Woodruff Bottom
Point Bottom
HORSETHIEF TRAIL
23.2
21.7
4131
4812
4885
5118
5165
4000
4800
4880
GRAND CO
EMERY CO
T 26 S
GRAND CO
SAN JUAN CO
Saddle Horse Bottom
R 17½ E
R 17 E
36
31
26 S
27 S
5051
4400
29.2
29.5
5088
5107
5046
4960
30.1
LABYRINTH
RIVER
Upheaval Bottom
Hardscrabble Bottom
Upheaval
Wild Bench Cabin
Ruin
Fort Bottom
WAYNE CO
SAN JUAN CO
31.4
5212
BIGHORN MESA
5306
3938
Potato Bottom
Basin
5200
HOR
WHITE RIM A

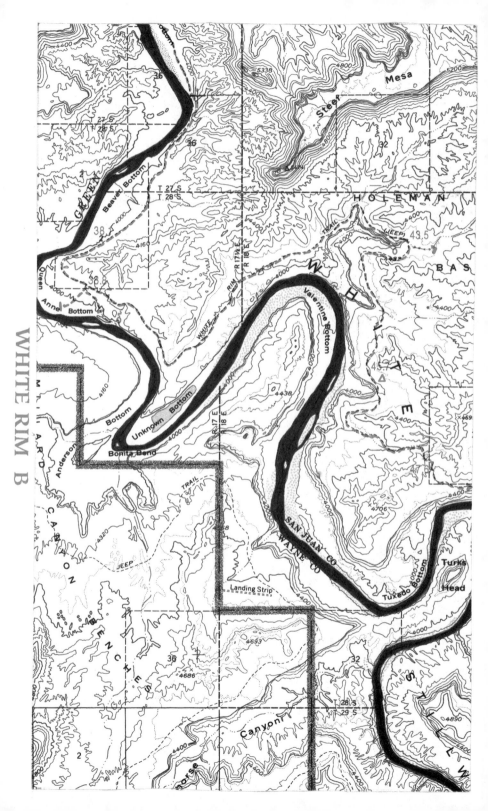

WHITE RIM B

WHITE RIM C

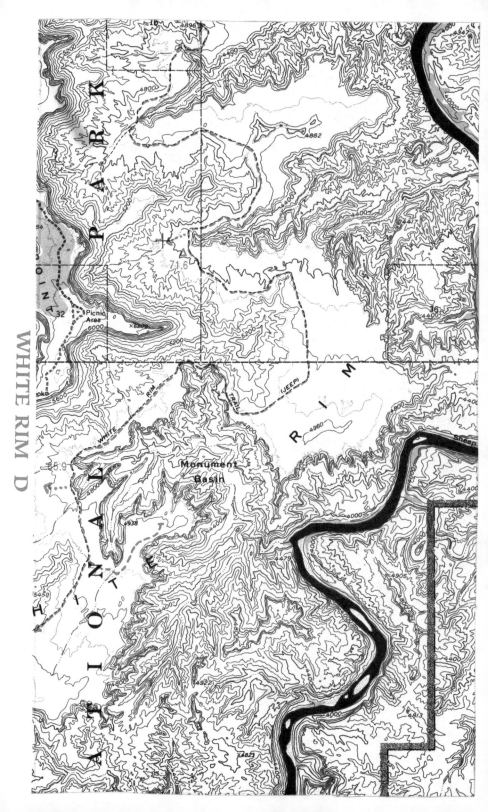

Red Sea

Red Sea Flat
×5895

Hwy 313

SHAFER TR South Fork

WHITE RIM

Shafer Canyon

99.8

13%

94

5600

16

5600

White Neck

×5950

Neck Spring

Rim Spring

612

6153

6247

5924

6000

5156

5059

Goose Neck

18

4808

Musselman Arch
4864
19

R
M

T
E
W
I

30

4400

×5398

Airport Tower
×5838

JEEP

WHITE RIM TRAIL

Buck

×4609

×4849

LATHROP

2

3983

36

33

Little Bridge Canyon

4973

6

5585

4604

4400

4800

4612

WHITE RIM E

23.2 Turn left at the base of the descent to avoid going to the boat put-in. (An inscription left by Denis Julien, the man who is thought to be the first Anglo to ply the river, occurs near the mouth of Hellroaring Canyon 3.5 miles past the put-in.)

24.7 (R) The feathery trees to trail's right are called tamarisk or salt cedar. Introduced from Asia early in the century in an attempt to control riverbank erosion, tamarisk worked beautifully, spreading a thousand miles up the Colorado River and its tributaries to boot. Its presence here is now a much lamented fact, however, as it chokes access to and from rivers while transpiring huge quantities of precious water into the atmosphere.

"It's not as bad as we used to think it was," states Dave May, a retired Chief Park Naturalist for Canyonlands. It seems that tamarisk literally creates riverbank, to the extent that the river channel becomes narrower with each succeeding year, in places just 25% of its former glory. The old growth tamarisk, now well removed from a river on whose bank it once seeded, provides habitat for the seedlings of indigenous species like cottonwood and willow. And since these species are better suited to on-shore conditions, they ultimately outcompete the tamarisk.

Tamarisk is most successful at river's side, since its seeds sprout in open air if lying on wet sand. Seasonal sand bars grow thick with its sprouts, and as the river rises with spring runoff, their density actually slows its current, precipitating out some of the water's silt content to settle around their slender trunks. On a collective scale, these sand bars can become permanent and bridge across a shallow channel to the near shore.

Here too, you can see how quickly the tamarisk has regenerated since Woodruff Bottom burned in 1987, crown sprouting from its parent source. In 1983 and 1984, and again in 1993, spring runoffs flooded many miles of the White Rim Trail. This area is muddy after rains, as clay-rich Chinle soil washes down onto the road to mingle with the river silts left from the flood. The river ran dry as recently as 1934, a fact that lends credibility to the notion that outlaws regularly crossed the river near here to escape pursuing posses, although the likelihood is that the posses were pursuing gold or cattle thieves, not horse thieves.

27.1 Park Boundary, replete with warnings, and imploring signs. You are responsible for knowing and abiding by all Park regulations, much as if the park were another country and its people's customs were to be honored. The park's "people" are bighorn sheep, lizards, blackbrush, fairy shrimp, etc.

29.2 Roof-mounted bikes have been smithereened on the overhanging rock at the skinny road cut above the river.

29.5 (L) The Taylor Canyon spur to Zeus and Moses, two Wingate towers which are popular rock climbs, ends in five miles, about a half mile from the towers.

30.1 (L) There is a view of distant Upheaval Dome from near the Upheaval drainage. The dome appears more as a giant crater from its rim. (Refer to Outtake #1 on page 48 concerning the dispute as to its origin.) A reddish-brown post marks the hiking trail up to the Dome and the rim beyond.

"I didn't see any sign, Mr. Ranger..."

Geologists Donald Baars and Peter Huntoon disagree about the origins of Upheaval Dome. Baars points out that it lies on the Colorado Lineament, a deep seated fault that runs beneath the course of the Colorado River. Like other salt plugs, it marks the spot where overburden deposits on the "squishy" salt squeezed it to the surface at a point of weakness. As the salt flow vented upwards, it pushed layers above it to the surface as well. Water then dissolved the near-surface salt, accounting for the sink effect of the dome.

Huntoon holds the maverick opinion that the dome is the remnant of a meteor strike. Although not the impact point of the so-called "Death Star" that darkened the atmosphere and caused mass extinctions, he believes it to be of the same swarm. Meteorites are composed of roughly 85% ice. The 15% solid matter has long since eroded and gone the way of the 6,000 feet of sediments that overlay the area when it was struck. The original crater, at eight miles wide, would have dwarfed the craters extant in Arizona.

Two interesting facts support Huntoon's posit: There is a "hydrocrack" or spontaneous fracture, such as those generally associated with meteorite impacts, emanating from Upheaval Dome. Material from 2,500 feet beneath the Dome's rim occupies this narrow crack. And a study of the White Rim sandstone dikes encircling the heart of the crater indicates that their particles were microfractured to 10% of their normal size, a fact best explainable by a sudden impact of immeasurable force.

One thing is apparent when you study a topo map of the region. There isn't anything shaped like Upheaval Dome for hundreds of miles around, which gives it that aspect of randomness that a meteor strike would inevitably have. To give perspective to the force of this impact, did you know that most shooting stars are no bigger than a grain of sand when they enter the earth's atmosphere?

31.4 (R) The furthest of the two campsites at Hardscrabble Bottom provides the easiest access to the river. Before you lies one of the difficult climbs on the trail. Keep your weight over the rear wheel, downshift BEFORE you need those winch gears, and most importantly, compose that "canyon-do" attitude.
33.1 (R) The hiking trail to Fort Bottom starts a half mile out this spur. There is an old cabin at the bottom said at times to have been a hospice, an outlaw's hideout, and a retreat. An old native American watchtower stands sentinel over a three mile length of river meander that in its narrowest place is separated from itself by just a few hundred yards. The fact that Hardscrabble Hill has long been a shortcut around this meander is evidenced by petroglyphs next to the road near where it begins the steep descent to Potato Bottom. From this point, try to spot the beginning of the White Rim sandstone in the distance, where the river turns to flow out of sight.

34.7 (R) Potato Bottom has three campsites, all of which provide muddy, bushbeating access to the river for a swim. The surefire easy access, however, is via the wash north of campsite "C."

38.1 (R) The surfacing of the White Rim sandstone marks the end of Labyrinth Canyon and the beginning of Stillwater Canyon. The White Rim is bereft of the various oxidized irons that color most other rock types. However, it does exhibit the dark, ciliated streaks of "desert varnish," or mineral stains which are leached from either the rock itself or the ground above it.

> ...the walls are symetrically curved and grandly arched, of a beautiful color, and reflected in the quiet waters in many places so as almost to deceive the eye and suggest to the beholder the thought that he is looking into profound depths.
>
> J. W. Powell, <u>The Explorations of the Colorado River and its Canyons</u>, 1895

Old cowboy inscriptions festoon the caverns along the river near Beaver Bottom's downstream terminus. Many of the names are of pioneer stock, as a glance in a local phone book will testify.

38.8 (R) This spur to Queen Anne Bottom marks the last call for swimming or water acquisition for treating/filtering. An old ferry used to take cattle across to Anderson Bottom from here.

43.5 (R) This pinchy canyon is the Holeman Slot, a bastion of shade, water (sometimes), and confined space in a sunny, arid, agoraphobic land. It provides great scrambling opportunities as well as smooth texture, graceful curves and glowing reflected light. The post marking the Wilhite Trail stands alongside the wash. This hiking trail, like the many other posted ones you'll see, accesses the Island's rim above the Wingate cliffs, and is a useful route to use in event of emergency.

45.7 (L) The Candlestick camp has only one site, and during a gale, it is not uncommon to see tents bivouacked to the outhouse! Candlestick Butte is the nearby monolith.

47.6 At the top of this pass, you can see Turk's Head, an isolated White Rim outcrop wrapped by the Green River. In just a few moments of geologic time, the Green will finish a shortcut west of Turk's Head and abandon the meander to leave a *rincon*. The rock around you is in the texturally fascinating Moenkopi formation, with cast examples of ripple marks, mud cracks, and rain drops, concrete evidence of this rock type's depositional origins in marine tidal flats.

48.5 (R) A visit to the Black Crack, a "keeper" joint fracture in the White Rim requires a short rimward walk. Please wait until you get to the point where the road nears bedrock before stopping. The use of wash bottom trails is second only to staying on rock for minimizing impact to fragile soils.

52.3 Before you is the first grunt on the way to mounting Murphy Hogback, the long, flat, saddle-interrupted feature extending from the point of the Wingate cliffs. The Hogback is a perfect example of the Mossback member of the Chinle formation, a conglomerate sandstone rife with petrified wood and bone. Debris from volcanoes in what is now New Mexico and Arizona buried forests here in mud, sand and ash. The suffocating lack of oxygen prevented the trees from rotting and decaying. Later, streams carrying dissolved silica and other minerals cut across the area, and their water penetrated the layer of buried forest, saturating the wood cells. The subsequent evaporation of this water crystallized the minerals as quartz within the wood. Weathering of this remnant or altered volcanic ash concentrates bentonitic clay in the Chinle, making for slippery roads when wet. Tire chains are a must in order to drive some of the Rim's hills when they are wet.

55.9 There is a school of thought which holds that if you flounder in a trail's crucibles long enough, one time, even if by accident, you're going to "clean" the crux move. This may be a necessary strategy at the final, super-steep climb onto the Hogback. There are three campsites at Murphy, with phenomenal views of the Land of Standing Rocks beyond the canyons below, which appear stamped into bedrock.

> Through the long desert day the sunbeams are weaving skeins of color across the sands, along the sides of the canyons, and about the tops of the mountains. They stain the ledges of copper with turquoise, they burn the buttes to a terra-cotta red, they paint the sands with rose and violet, and they key the air to the hue of the opal...they vibrate, they scintillate, they penetrate and tinge everything....

John C.Van Dyke, <u>The Desert</u>, 1903

Murphy Hogback, like Shafer, Lathrop, and Holeman Spring Canyons, was named after one of the cowboys who grazed stock out here. Cowboys of yore were known to spend great lengths of time alone with their animals, moving them from one pasture to another, protecting them from predators all the while. One of the Scorup brothers, of the Scorup and Summerville Cattle Company (once the second largest ranching operation in the States and now called Indian Creek Cattle Co; it is based out of Dugout Ranch near the Needles.), spent three years in the saddle, not once returning to the ranch. The myth of the cowboy as hero originates from efforts like this, though in this day of diverse pressures on public land, can the myth continue to justify government subsidized or "welfare" ranching? Will a traditional lifestyle prosper in an environment that it is willfully ruining or, at least, altering irretrievably?

60.0 (R) When you've finished the descent and regain the edge of the White Rim, the view from the nearby canyon head is called Vertigo Void. Crawl up to the lip and look over ... and under. White throated swifts and violet-green swallows perform in the updrafts along this sheer rim at speeds up to 100 miles per hour. On windy days, an edge like this can crack like a freshly laundered bedsheet.

(Above) Near White Crack Overlook

(Below) Monument Basin

51

63.6 (R) This is the spur 1.5 miles to White Crack Overlook, a must-see, perhaps THE "power spot," of the White Rim and certainly one of the most expansive viewpoints from the Rim. It is also a one-site camp, although the jasper chipping beds indicate that many prehistoric hunters have used this area. Lithic material at White Crack was deposited by humans as recently as 8,000 years before present.

65.9 (R) From the head of Monument Basin, you can see the cap-less Totem Pole, a 305-foot tall pinnacle. The formation beneath the White Rim—the Organ Rock Shale—is relatively soft, thus its accelerated erosion undermines the harder White Rim. Where the shale remains protected by caprocks above, you encounter huge "Nuts and Bolts"-like pillars.

This canyon is an important lambing area for the desert bighorn, an elusive and rangey animal. Once the country's most productive herd, the Potash herd has been crippled from exposure to domestic sheep diseases and live capturing to fortify herds elsewhere. They range freely at river level and on the White Rim, but are most at home on talus slopes, where their camouflage and agility insure their survival. The bighorn are a bio-indicator species; that is, their health is closely related to the wilderness qualities of the land. They are sensitive to recurring human intrusion, so please don't stalk these animals, even for a closer look. Thanks.

71.6 (L) Gooseberry Camp, with two sites. In the spring of 1988, the Park Service removed the natural shade and windbreak here—a stand of tamarisk trees. They came under fire for not publicizing their intent beforehand or informing the outfitters who used the area extensively. It all appeared to be part of a seemingly dogmatic tamarisk eradication project whereby, if a bulldozer could be gotten to the tamarisk, it would be plowed out. If not accessible, it remained, as it did along every waterway in southern Utah (arguably, more viable sources for the regeneration of tamarisks than an old earthen stock pond high and away from a rim), for removing tamarisk by hand is too labor intensive (and not disruptive enough) to be effective.

One positive outcome of this action was the contribution to the Park of some creative alternatives to plowing out the trees. The author's favorite was seasoned boatman Bego Gerhart's suggestion to prune the lower branches of the tree so that it develops a high canopy instead of a bushy base. In other words, "make the best of it." Be that as it may, progeny of the slain tamarisk have survived. If you have suggestions as to how the Park Service can better manage YOUR Park, let them know. A formal General Management Plan is reviewed periodically, and local environmental groups and chapters of national groups monitor and publicize comment periods on Park policy changes. Other comments can be directly addressed to the Park Superintendent of whichever Park is in question.

79.9 (R) There is walk-down access off the White Rim in this slickrock drainage. Both Washer Woman and Mesa Arches have been in view for the last mile.

82.5 (L) Spur to Airport camp.

83.0 (R) The sandy spur down Lathrop Canyon intersects the Colorado River in 3.5 miles where there is a picnic area commonly used by boaters.

90.9 (R) Traffic usually increases near the Musselman Arch turnoff, as most day trips are destined for the Arch. Riding your bike on or near the arch will result in an automatic fine if a ranger catches you. Surprisingly, cattle used to be driven down the Shafer Trail and off the White Rim near here, where they would ford the river and climb up to Chicken Corners, a three-foot wide ledge pasted 250 feet above the river, in order to get to Hurrah Pass and Moab. When cowboy Sog Shafer was asked how he got the cows to enter the river, he drawled, "I'd get 'em real thirsty."

91.1 (R) "Colorado River Overlook" marks the spur to the Walking Rocks, with its view of the Gooseneck (of the Colorado) and the subtle bulge in strata called the Shafer Dome. From here to the Park boundary at Shafer Canyon, the White Rim is roof to many "rooms with a view," which can be gained by chimneying down through some of the many joint fractures. The most notorious of these is Ottinger's Kitchen, a shady nook that until recently had rough furniture, an informal sign-in register, and a ladder stashed near its entrance.

Notice how there is an absence of the White Rim sandstone across the river. You are at the edge of the White Rim's lens-shaped deposit, having seen it at its thickest (250 ft.) near the Green River. The thicker this deposit, the more sheerly it tends to cleave off when undermined. That's why scrambling routes off the Rim are so few and far between from its first outcropping on the Green clear to Gooseberry and the Buck Canyon systems.

It is interesting to note that the recent increase in use of the White Rim Trail has attracted at least one pair of ravens. They swoop down as groups depart common stopping points to look for lunch scraps. This phenomenon has long occurred in the river camps, but was nonexistent up here. Whitewater rafters have reported that on their first trips of the season, ravens go as far as performing tricks to acquire food. While this is entertaining, it works to the animal's disadvantage, for it hinders its natural foraging skills, tending to make it somewhat dependent on the seasonal comings and goings of humans. Please take thoughtful precautions such as straining your camp's dishwater for organic matter and discouraging the disposal of even organic wastes anywhere but in the garbage bag.

93.1 (R) Please leave your bikes on the edge of the road or turnout if you take the half mile walk to the Gooseneck Overlook. A bike has never been stolen on the Rim, but if you're concerned, pop a rivet out of your bike's chain and reconnect it around the sign as you would a cable or chain lock. Again, all vehicle regulations apply to bikes, so be sure to keep it within the roadbed. The next mile offers much the same road condition the entirety of the Rim was in as recently as 1987. The ironic combination of dry years (just 4 inches of precipitation in 1989) and severe storms has wreaked havoc on its bearing surface.

94.4 (L) Information kiosk and **(R)** the spur to Potash (and Moab). Ahead is the "climb of reckoning" up the Shafer switchbacks. In 1955, local miners and cattlemen chased up what money and equipment they could to build the Shafer Trail, with some contributing manpower, their only wealth. The catskinner who upgraded it out of an existing cow track engineered much of the route by the seat of his pants. Ed "The kid" Johnson's overriding criteria for making so many tight switchbacks instead of a few long ones was the necessity

Granary, Canyonlands National Park

to limit the use of culvert pipes, which were in short supply. Therefore, he kept the trail "underneath itself," where runoff could do the least amount of damage.

They had to be tough, those people who made homes or searched for mineral treasure in this corner of the Canyon Lands. The prospectors, the oilmen and the Anasazi Indians all were tough, and clever, and brave, and persevering. But the land was tougher. Indifferently, the land tossed the men aside and held onto its treasure—which never was in the rocks anyway. The real treasure is the rocks: their massive shapes and subtle colors, their gorges and amphitheatres and secret fissures.

Jerome Doolittle, <u>Canyons and Mesas</u>, 1974

97.3 From this commanding position, you can see several Douglas firs ensconced in the northfacing Naturalist's Alcove across the canyon and above you. These trees are holdouts from a time when a significantly moister and cooler climate prevailed here, as recently as a thousand years ago. A pocket of aspen trees not two miles from here manages to hang on under similiar circumstances. It is rare to see an aspen or a Douglas fir at less than 6,000 feet in this latitude.
99.6 Continue left at the paved "T" intersection if you want to return to the visitor center.
100.6 Trailhead/-tail

Other Roads / Rides in the Island Area

Most of the unposted spurs from Highway 313 are marginally ridable, yet too sandy to be encouraging. Those to the highway's west tend to be out-and-backs which end at glorious canyon overlooks, while those to its east tend to interconnect near the rims of the Gemini Bridges area canyons, only two providing access to the canyons below.

Monument Basin's Totem Pole from above and below, an excellent example of the Organ Rock shale beneath the more erosion-resistant White Rim sandstone

Outtake #2   The Man Canyon

Major John Wesley Powell was a willful man–self-educated, self-motivated, and hardy to the point of hardbitten. The combined journal of his 1869 and 1871 voyages down the Green and Grand (Colorado) Rivers secured him the status of hero in the American mind.

The 5' 6" Powell lost much of his right arm in a Civil War attack that he had been forbidden to mount. As he raised his hand to yell "Charge!," it was pierced by a bullet. With the subsequent infection, most of his forearm was amputated, too. In retirement from the military, he became a university professor of geology, one of the first to use "field trips," some as long as six months. It was during a field trip to Colorado that Powell conceived of the idea of exploring the rivercourse from Green River, Wyoming, to the foot of the Grand Canyon. His influence with then-President Ulysses S. Grant helped him obtain from private grants the boats, supplies and passage necessary to embark on the trip.

As a youth, Powell had rowed nearly the length of the Mississippi River, a very tame water in comparison to the Green and Grand, yet this made him the most qualified boatman in his party of ten men. He sat in a wooden chair lashed to the deck of the Emma Dean, a flat keeled craft more suitable for a Sunday row on the lake than a whitewater experience. As it turned out, his party would have to portage or "line" the boats down most rapids. The "Ten Who Dared" emerged from a legendary unknown of "immense waterfalls, underground caverns, and hostile Indians" as the "six who persevered." One man fell sick and was left at a settlement; three others lost faith and climbed out of the Grand Canyon only to be killed by Indians who objected to their crops being stolen. Powell's party had been presumed dead for six weeks, and with scant supplies of moldy flour, fermenting apples and coffee, they came mighty close to abandoning the journey that would make them famous as the first men to descend and survey the "canyons of the Colorado."

One of the members of Powell's second voyage inscribed the initials of a major sponsor, the Colorado Explorers, into a rock in what is now Canyonlands National Park. Another sponsor sent a platted map of "Junction City" with Powell as a promotional stunt. And where do you think this city was to be sited? Naturally, at the confluence of the Green and Colorado.

The ever zealous Powell, a regarded scientist and philosopher, went on to help found several scientific institutions, including the United States Geological Survey (USGS) and the National Geographic Society. His warnings about the aridity of the west went unheard in Washington. The climaxing water debt that cities like Los Angeles, Phoenix, Las Vegas and San Diego continue to ignore could have been prevented if his sagacity had been honored. Nothing could displace the greed of pioneer America, however. And although Powell knew that reservoirs would be the only way to provide for population centers, he couldn't have imagined that the utter drowning of hundreds of peaceful side canyons, like the ones he named Music Temple and Cathedral in the Desert, would be given his name: "Lake" Powell.

The Major's imperious manner betrayed him later in life. As the second director of the USGS, he was determined incorrigible by a Congress that couldn't dismiss a man of his fame and distinction, so they merely voted not to appropriate funding for his salary. True to form, Powell stayed on in the position of authority for a full year—unpaid—and only the overwhelming pain of his reinfected arm kept him from remaining there.

Inscription from Powell's second expedition, Canyonlands National Park

The Rainbow Rocks Area

The "Rainbow Rocks" are mounds of Entrada sandstone slickrock that appear salmon colored until you get close, where pastel stripes of gray, white, yellow and blue are seen to be mixed throughout. They are indicative of this area; a sandy, rolling terrain punctuated by rounded ridges, mesas, and buttes of Entrada sandstone. Thus, it is an area with textures as diverse as its colors. Washes draining the area are shallow, and perenially wet only near springs. Riding surfaces are either clay hardpan, sand, or slickrock, and the obscurity of its hidden canyons is probably what has served to limit its use by mountain bikers.

The author riding the Bartlett Wash Slickrock

The Monitor and Merrimac on maneuvers

MONITOR AND MERRIMAC

Type: Loop
Length: 16.5 miles
Difficulty: Physically moderate to difficult / Technically moderate
Best Seasons: Spring and fall, especially after rainfall, unless the clay-soiled trailhead area is slick.
Elevation: Trailhead/-tail—4,450 ft., High—5,150 ft., Low—4,400 ft.
Land Agency: BLM
Route Summary: Any non-slickrock ride in this area is going to be sandy. The layout of the Monitor and Merrimac route not only avoids the sandiest roads, but it orienteers all over Courthouse Pasture, keying on and circling one landmark after another, but only twice actually retracing itself (for a total of 2.3 miles). The pasture area is entered via Mill Canyon and exited via Courthouse Wash, which are just parallel drainages split around the small mesa called Mill Rock.
Options: Spurs off of the described route access Highways 191 and 313 via the graded Cotter Mine Road and a sandy doubletrack across Seven Mile Canyon respectively. Another spur accesses Tusher Canyon, but it is prohibitively sandy for a mile before reaching the Tusher Canyon Slickrock trailhead (which is itself another 1.2 sandy miles from the nearest universally-ridable road).

Attractions: The views from the base of the Monitor include Arches National Park, Castle Rock, and Seven Mile Canyon. It's unusual to be able to perimeter a butte or monolith, and this route partially or totally circles five of them, staying either on roads or bedrock. An excellent hike onto Mill Rock is recommended.

Riding Surface: Hardpacked sand and sediments and an unavoidable encounter with deep sand on jeep trails and two-laned dirt roads, except for line-of-sight orienteering across slickrock surfaces.

Geology: Three members of the Entrada sandstone are identifiable on this ride. The relatively thin, whitish layer high upon the tops of every landform in sight is the Moab Tongue. The massive, burnt orange cliffs that show slickrock rims are of the Slickrock member, which is also composed of wind-deposited sand. And the wavy, crinkly brown rock at the very base of the cliffs is the Dewey member, its tidal flat-deposited mudstones and siltstones contorted by slumping which must have occurred when they were still soft.

Logistics: No shuttle or permit is necessary.

Trailhead Access: Almost 16 miles north on Hwy. 191 out of Moab (Main x Center St.'s), after mile mark 141, there is a dirt road left, which immediately crosses the railroad tracks. Park in turnouts on either side of the tracks to begin your ride through what locals affectionately call "stinking desert," and follow the signs towards Mill Canyon.

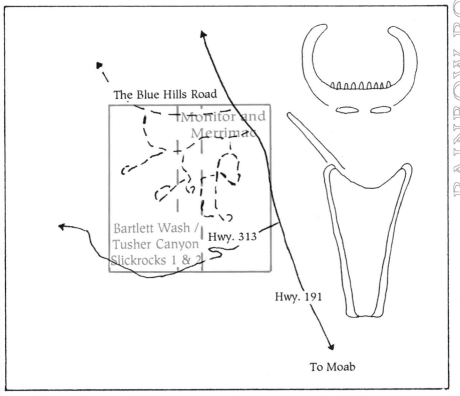

The Blue Hills Road

Monitor and Merrimac

Bartlett Wash / Tusher Canyon Slickrocks 1 & 2

Hwy. 313

Hwy. 191

To Moab

Mileage Log and Route Description:
0.0 Continue west by bike on the dirt road.
1.1 Turn right, on the spur to Mill Canyon, where you'll soon see the colorful clay hills of the Morrison formation. Its hues range from magenta and slate blue (most commonly) to apple green, yellow, purple, orange, pink or brown—not a good place for a withdrawn chameleon...
1.8 (R) Short spur to the trailhead register box for the Mill Canyon Dinosaur Trail, a self-guiding trail to the petrified bones and fossilized plant remains in the wall across the wash.
2.1 (R,L) A seam in the rock walls provides scrambling access onto the mesa tops. Mill Rock, on the east, offers particularly nice exploring.
2.7 (L) Upon descending the brief hill into a narrow, cottonwood-shrouded wash, you'll notice an acute spur to the left. If you follow this route description, you'll end up back here in order to take this spur, but for now, continue straight up to Courthouse Pasture.
3.9 (R) Spur to Determination Towers. You'll be seeing this intersection again, too. Shortly, a view back over your right shoulder will reveal the gap in the wall where Tusher Canyon drains the pasture.
5.8 This slickrock plaza area between the Monitor and Merrimac is the crossing point for a giant figure "8." The pinkish-white quartz strewn about is called chert, and it has eroded out of softer rock above. The most expedient route around the Monitor stays as close to its vertical apron as possible.
9.7 After rounding the northern periphery of the Determination Towers, drop off the slickrock to take a sandy road right, away from the gap into Tusher.
10.2 (previously mile 3.9) Go left to backtrack for a ways.
11.5 At the cottonwood, **previously mile 2.7**, take the obtuse right, up the sandy road towards the (unofficially named) Macroneurotic Butte.

> The days of wandering alone in a lonesome land and calling topographical features what you please are gone... I am not eager to splash names around the remaining few wild canyons, but once in a while a name helps a person find his way.

> Kent Frost, My Canyonlands, 1971

11.8 (L) At halfway along the butte's flank, check out where the large natural arch collapsed in early spring of 1988. It was long but relatively flat, which probably taxed its support more than if it had an evenly radiused arch. The highest white curb of slickrock provides a ridable approach to it.
13.4 Look for the vague road into Courthouse Wash's west side.
15.1 (L) The "Halfway" station for the old Moab to Thompson stagecoach, a 35 mile trip that took eight hours in 1883.
16.5 Trailhead/-tail

MONITOR AND MERRIMAC

Courthouse Pasture from on high

TUSHER CANYON SLICKROCK #1

Type: Out-and-back
Length: At least 3.5 miles
Difficulty: Physically moderate / Technically difficult
Best Seasons: Spring and fall.
Elevation: Trailhead/-tail/Low—4,600 ft., High—4,950 ft.
Land Agency: BLM
Route Summary: For those without a four wheel-drive vehicle, there is a 1.2 mile trudge up the "user-unfriendly" sand wash of Tusher Canyon just to get to the trailhead. But from there, a mostly sidehill slickrock ascent takes you up to an outrageous playground of spillways and turrets overlooking beautiful Courthouse Pasture. The descent back offers only the slightest variation from the route up.
Attractions: Freeform route playing and nice panoramas from a high bluff.
Riding Surface: This route follows the Entrada's Slickrock member, which is textured with abruptly terminated or cross-bedded planes, or "waves," that make descending on it seem like surfing one continuous breaker.
Geology: This route starts where the Slickrock member angles upward out of the ground from a northwest-southeast trending fault. At the ride's highest point, the Entrada's white Moab Tongue caps the mesa. The bedding planes in the Slickrock member show their graceful origins as windborne sand dunes.
Notes: The vertical exposure on this oblique route is deadly. Make sure your bike is operating well.
Logistics: No shuttle or permit is necessary.
Trailhead Access: Almost 16 miles north on Hwy. 191 out of Moab (Main x Center Streets), after mile mark 141, there is a dirt road to the left which immediately crosses the railroad tracks. It has a clay content which makes it slippery when wet. Continue onward, taking a right towards Tusher at the "T" intersection in 0.6 of a mile, and before another two miles, you'll see the deep sand of Tusher's wash bottom. It's probably not wise to continue further by vehicle unless you've got four wheel-drive. (If for some reason you get stuck, the wadding of rocks, boards, bushes and even—okay ... especially—this guidebook under the digging tire can give you the traction to pull out. Also, reducing the air pressure in your tires can assist traction.) From here, stay in the wash, avoiding the road's continuation up the hill. In a mile, the land on either side of the now-constricted wash rises (allowing the first up-close views of the salmon and gray banded Slickrock member), and after a bend to the right, you gain a view of the larger canyon. The (unposted) trailhead is on the left in about a hundred yards, where a decrepit roadbed spurs acutely out of the wash up onto a low bank.

Mileage Log and Route Description:
0.0 From the dirt flat on the hill, portage up to the slickrock this side of the white-on-red rockslide. Hike-a-bike your way across the upper part of the slide, resisting the temptation to take the obviously ridable lower gray slope. Once around the corner on this high ledge, you'll see the logic of it, as you need to make two more "upclimbs" to keep from becoming rimmed out.
1.0 As you level out near the point of the rising mesa, the Determination Towers, the La Sal mountains, and other landmarks come into view. Congratulations. You've survived the tedious. This multi-acre rim area offers challenging technical routefinding for the frolicsome.
1.3 You'll find that the slickrock gets vertical as you contour along the Mill Canyon rim to the north, so when you're ready to return, use the white Moab Tongue ledge as long as it remains clear, then drop back onto the Slickrock member for the cruise back. Please avoid tracking up the occasional soil deposits in the Moab Tongue member in order to maintain the pristinity of the area.
3.5? Trailhead/-tail

Dodging the solution pockets

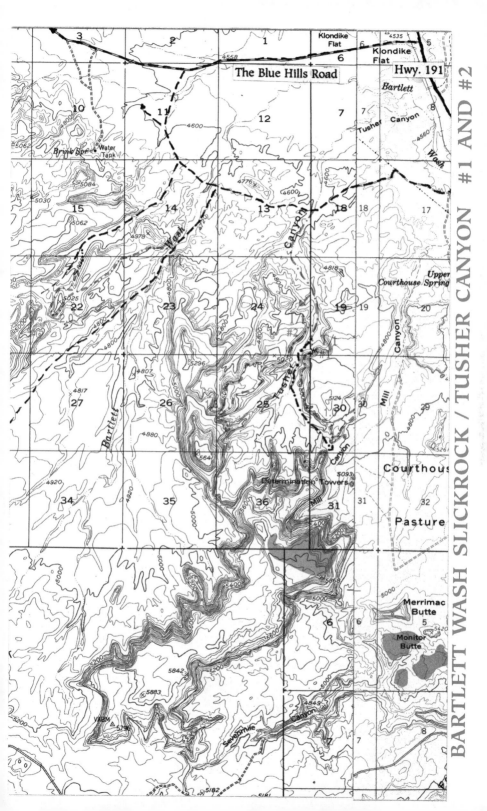

TUSHER CANYON SLICKROCK #2

(Background information for this ride is identical to Tusher Canyon Slickrock #1, with the following exceptions:)

Best Seasons: Spring and fall, but with its solar exposure, this also makes a great winter ride (and the sandy approach to the traihead is usually frozen).

Route Summary: The ascent up the tilted slickrock on this side of the Canyon offers a greater variation of routes than Tusher #1. Where the route variations start to thin out, a cairned route through a mini pass takes you to another fork of the Tusher system, where you can ride its slickrock rim in a short loop to connect back to the initial route for your return.

Options: As mentioned, one can do a little loop at the far end of the out-and-back which circles an outcrop of the Entrada formation's Moab Tongue member. Also, an exposed hike-a-bike to the head of Tusher Canyon ramps over a saddle to the Bartlett Wash side of the dividing mesa, where a frequently interrupted descent (to portage across rock slides) on its slickrock can set you up to close a loop.

Trailhead Access: Same as Tusher Canyon Slickrock #1, except after the wash's "bend to the right," look to any of the several gullies to the right for a portage up to the slickrock.

Mileage Log and Route Description:

0.0 Once you've reached the slickrock, try to gain a layer in the cross beddings that won't soon pinch out. There are two broad bowl areas within the mile of direct ascending before the whole slickrock layer begins pinching up to a very narrow ledge.

1.3 (R) Just after the second bowl, a ridable route up to the white rock above leads to a cairned single track which crosses a mini pass into another distinct fork of Tusher Canyon that is much like the one just left. A short loop can be closed by heading downcanyon on the contact layer (between the white and red formations) and taking the first possible option back over to the canyon rim you ascended.

3.5? Trailhead/-tail

BARTLETT WASH SLICKROCK

Type: Out-and-back
Length: At least four miles
Difficulty: Physically moderate / Technically difficult
Best Seasons: Spring and fall, but winter is good, too, because of the solar exposure
Elevation: Trailhead/-tail/Low—4,620 ft., High—5,000 ft.
Land Agency: BLM
Route Summary: This route is the finest Entrada Slickrock ride in the area, from the standpoints of surface quality, route variety and environmental soundness. (The author suggests you avoid the "Hidden Canyon Rim Trail" as outlined in another canyon country mountain biking guidebook, for not only is it a fraction as rewarding as the Bartlett Wash Slickrock ride, but its difficulty to follow has caused a great deal of damage to a once-pristine environment. Take this advice for what it's worth.) Non-four wheel-drive vehicles have direct access to the trailhead, which is a stone's throw from eminently smooth and ridable slickrock. Beginning at a fault, where the slickrock emerges to angle skyward, one can wiggle and giggle through an array of wild freeform routes, with spiralling climbs, wicked sidehills, and enormous spillways to "transcend" and descend. One 300 foot hike-a-bike across a sand dune is the only obstacle to relentless family fun.
Options: From the turnaround point, you can descend into Hidden Canyon, where a sandy road connects to the trailhead access route to close a loop.
Attractions: The wave-like quality to the rock's bedding planes is visually and technically a very pleasing place to "surf" a bike. The view into the intricate Hidden Canyon is compelling, too.
Riding Surface: slickrock
Geology: The salmon and gray Slickrock member of the Entrada sandstone formation exhibits the signs of its wind-deposited origins in obvious, sweeping, bedding planes. The Entrada's two other members are visible, too: the Moab Tongue is the white layer above the Slickrock, and the dark brown, crinkly-surfaced Dewey member lines a sheer-walled length of Bartlett Wash near where it drains out of Hidden Canyon. A very graphic fault crosses the wash right next to the trailhead, as displayed by the abrupt subduction of the colorful Entrada to the nondescript, boulder-strewn Morrison shale.
Notes: Severe vertical exposure can make for "the fall of a lifetime." Make sure your bike is functioning perfectly.
Logistics: No shuttle or permit is necessary.
Trailhead Access: (Although you can get to Bartlett Wash by continuing on the same road which leads to the Monitor and Merrimac and Tusher Canyon rides, the way described here is accessible to all but sports cars.) About 17 miles north of Moab (Main x Center St.'s) on Hwy. 191, just shy of mile marker 143, the dirt Blue Hills Road turns left off the highway. (It is a

treacherously slick road when wet.) In 2.2 miles, just after the road bends right, take the doubletrack that spurs left. You'll come to a three-way intersection in another 0.8 of a mile, where again you should bear left. Bypass the spur right, to Hidden Canyon in another 0.2 of a mile, and at the sandy crossing of lower Bartlett Wash, use your momentum to blast through the sand. If you have misgivings about trying to cross it, by all means, park it and pedal, for it's just 1.3 miles to the trailhead. As you crest the hill out of the wash, take the spur right, which ultimately descends into Bartlett Wash. Scout the road ahead where it reenters the wash. The (unposted) trailhead is just on the other side of the fence, on the right side of the wash.

Mileage Log and Route Description:

0.0 (Pedal?) or carry your bike up the ramp next to the little juniper tree and take a left. From here, you're on your own. You'll soon discover that the gray patches of slickrock don't hold a tire as well as the salmon patches, probably due to its lack of oxidized minerals, which are known to bind sand grains together. Familiarize yourself with this rock, which is less "sticky" than the Navajo sandstone slickrock (like the Slickrock Bike Trail), before attempting any exposed moves. And try to stay centered laterally over the bike when angling up the rounded curbs of rock.

2.0 (at least) From the apex of the mesa, you could descend into Hidden Canyon down the alter ego to the route you just climbed, and the sandy road out of it could connect you back to your vehicle, but the return ride down the rim of Bartlett is just too fun to miss. Hidden Canyon is an interesting feature, and if you study it closely, you'll realize that its upper drainage diverts into Bartlett beneath this point, and its lower half flows parallel to Bartlett down its own course, as you'd expect.

4.0 Trailhead/-tail

Other Roads / Rides in the Rainbow Rocks Area

Some sandy, but ridable, roads here include: the Dubinky Well Road, from Highway 313 to the Blue Hills Road; the Bartlett Wash Road, from the Dubinky Well Road to the Blue Hills/Mill Canyon connector; the Cotter Mine Road, from Courthouse Pasture to Highway 191; and the Seven Mile Canyon North Fork road, from Highway 313 to the Monitor and Merrimac. The remaining roads in this area are too sandy to be enjoyable, but there are other Entrada bluffs north of the Rainbow Rocks proper that might offer lengthy rim traverses.

Joe's getaway car

The Labyrinth Canyon Area

The labyrinthine meanders of the Green River are scotched deeply into a vast redrock desert where it nears its confluence with the Colorado. The only ride representing this area is somewhat "forced" through the sheer gorge of Labyrinth, as a portage is necessary to escape its confines and close a loop. Like the White Rim Trail, Labyrinth has that unsubtle quality about it that allows you to ride directly up to "the edge of eternity" before realizing that a canyon is gashed into the terrain before you. Overlooks are many, but ingresses to the canyon are few.

THE RIVERSIDE LOOP

Type: Loop
Length: 33.2 miles
Difficulty: Physically difficult / Technically moderate
Best Seasons: Spring and fall, and not too soon after a rain or high river flow, as the trail next to the river can flood and has a clay content that holds rainwater on the surface a long time
Elevation: Trailhead/-tail, High—5,310 ft., Low—3,960 ft.
Land Agency: BLM
Route Summary: From a vast, rolling desert, this route descends rapidly to the mouth of Spring Canyon on the Green, where it parallels the river upstream to Hey Joe Canyon. A rugged portage out of Hey Joe reaches the Spring Canyon Point Road, which loops back to the trailhead via the Dubinky Well Road. The majority of the ride can be fast paced, for it travels across open desert on predictable roads.
Options: From the mouth of Spring Canyon, one might be able to take abandoned mining roads down along the Green River to Hellroaring Canyon, and on to the Horsethief Trail towards closing a loop, but it would involve a great deal of off-bike work, and should only be attempted with the Green at a low water level.
Attractions: The part of this trail near the river has seen very infrequent use by jeepers, and probably even less by mountain bikers. The Green River is easy to swim/walk across most times of the year, and the mining camp artifacts that abound offer an unsanitized glimpse into this desperate occupation (double entendre intended).
Riding Surface: Hardpacked sediments, rock-studded sediments, clay and sand on jeep trails and two-laned dirt roads
Geology: The white, domey slickrock near the trailhead is Navajo sandstone, a windblown dune deposit. Near the rim of Spring Canyon, you encounter the ledgy, buff-colored Kayenta formation, which is the hard layer that protects the massive orange Wingate cliffs from receding as fast as they might. At the base of the Wingate, at the bottom of Spring and Labyrinth Canyons is the

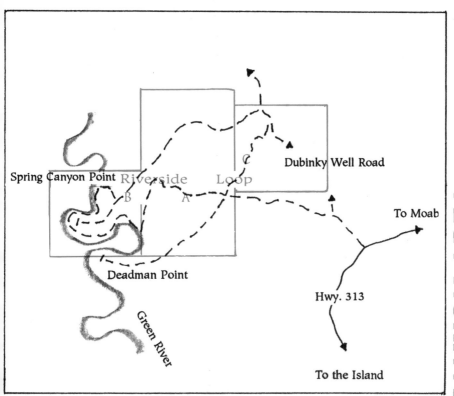

Chinle, a slope-eroding soil that is high in altered organic compounds. As will become apparent to you with time spent in canyon country, the Chinle was a "hot" item amongst miners, for it contains radioactive minerals that when refined could produce explosive effects. In the wildcat days of the 50's and 60's, pilots would fly low enough to pick up readings on a Geiger counter, and they'd drop a sack of flour onto a promising site for the hapless prospector to locate. Needless to say, the toil's spoils have benefitted us. Who would have thought that in just a quarter of a century, people would leave the comfort and security of their homes expressly to be in country like this, and on bicycles, even?

Logistics: No shuttle or permit is necessary.

Trailhead Access: The turnoff to Highway 313, the road to Island in the Sky and Dead Horse Point, occurs 12.5 miles north of Moab on Highway 191. Another 8.5 miles on 313 brings you to a signed dirt spur road right, to Dubinky Well. Take this road for 6 miles, bypassing all spurs (one of which is the actual route to Dubinky Well), and park somewhere near the high, open area where spurs right and left intersect the road almost directly across from each other.

Mileage Log and Route Description:
0.0 Continue straight on this road, which crests a hill, then descends rapidly to Spring Canyon.
6.5 (R) What looks like the sculpture of a giant toeclip is in actuality the mooring for an old ferryboat. The next eight miles along the river use an abandoned mine access road that is occasionally flooded, but always overgrown and rock-strewn, guaranteeing a degree of exclusivity to mountain bikers, hikers, and river users.

> The canyon curves deeply to the left and right, sinuous
> as a snake, no more willing to follow a straight line than is
> anything else true and beautiful and good in this world.

> Edward Abbey, Slickrock, 1971

14.4 The mouth of Hey Joe Canyon is evidenced by the giant yellow "paperweight" on the hill. Take any of the road cuts up canyon to the mine, where they terminate. The portage to the south or righthand rim takes off past the shafts and works back toward the head of the short tributary you passed. This tributary has a significant jump above which you should stay, and as the terrain levels out, you'll connect to a spur of the Spring Canyon Point Road.
24.9 (R) At Tombstone Rock, the doubletracks on either side of the cattle guard spur to an interesting feature in less than a mile called the Dellenbaugh Tunnel, a 110 foot-long conduit starting near the canyon's rim. (When you intersect a wash, turn down it to the rim.) Continue past the Tombstone towards Dubinky Well's windmill.
27.5 (R) Leave the better established road to take the spur right, at this triangulated connection.
33.2 Trailhead/-tail

Other Roads / Rides in the Labyrinth Canyon Area

There are many tremendous Green River overlooks accessed by spurs to the Spring Canyon and Spring Canyon Point Roads, but with the exception of the actual rim areas, they are too sandy to ride. (If you want a rim view of Labyrinth Canyon, it is suggested that you follow either the Dead Man Point, Spring Canyon Point, or Ten Mile Point roads to their conclusions.) Ten Mile Canyon is a beautiful tributary of the Green north of Spring Canyon, but the Dripping Springs connector from the Point Road north to Ten Mile is also too sandy. However, the Dubinky Well Road proceeds north to the Blue Hills Road, and a turn off of Blue Hills goes to Ten Mile Point via a hardpacked clay road. Of interest to wintertime riders is this road's access into Ten Mile Canyon, which when frozen makes a nice route to the Green via a Navajo sandstone-walled corridor reminiscent of lower Courthouse Wash in Arches National Park.

Battered mining road by the Green River

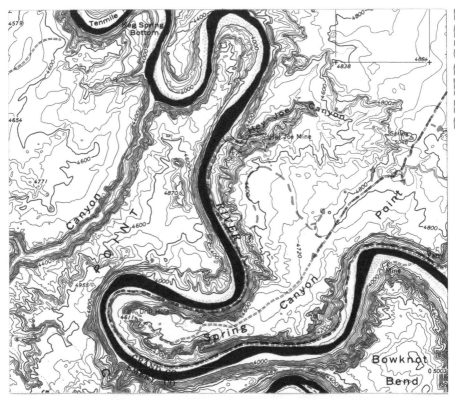

RIVERSIDE LOOP A

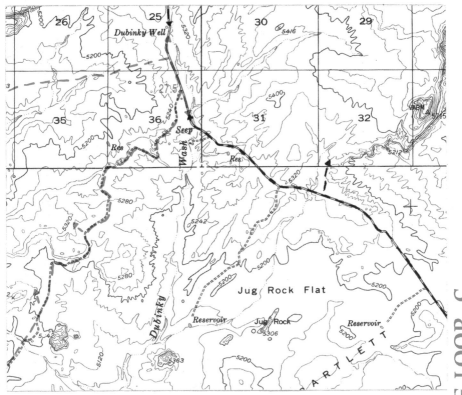

Three Gossips and Sheep Rock by night

Outtake #3 Gonzo-Abusive Memories

It's funny to think back on it, but just a few years ago we only had a dozen regular rides around Moab. Perhaps only five or six year-round residents even rode their mountain bikes extensively. Then riders like Todd Wagner, Lu Warner, and Hank Barlow began visiting Moab and started sniffing out presumed dead end routes, pushing the occasional one through. They've put some excellent routes on the map, but more importantly, they've kept some routes off.

The skill and strength necessary to "clean" some of a route's finer moves is inspiring. A lesser rider might balk and crash, damaging environment, bike and/or self, but Lu would bawl, "Check out this wiggle." Todd might laugh in that disturbing manner of his that you know spells D.A.N.G.E.R., and Hank—he'd wait until later to "wane" poetic about the essence of friction or something. All three men show incredible oneness with their bikes in the way they interpret the environment.

I used to call unlikely or difficult rides "gonzo"—a word invented, I think, by Hunter S. Thompson. I'd find just an awful seam in a Wingate cliff somewhere near one of the doubletracks, and scout it to determine "portageability" to the canyon below or rim above. My friend and mentor John Groo could usually be convinced to accompany me on an epic ride, so off we'd go, he periodically subjecting his custom-built bike to a verbal arsenal of booming deprecations, insinuations and vituperations, and I cooing none but pleasantries over my "brass barbell," the heavy—therefore heavy-duty—bike.

Back then, John didn't wear lycra (having just recently graduated from leathers), so his usual cursing wasn't so much about torn shorts from sliding down talus slopes as it was the discomfort of shouldering his bike up a thousand-foot cliff in 90° heat. One afternoon, as we were cooling down from just such a ride, I rashly suggested another gonzo route. I can still remember the bugeyed expression on his face as he slammed down his Thirst Aid and spluttered, "That's not gonzo—that's abusive!"

With the mating of these two adjectives, the supreme difficulty level of riding was coined, a level beyond slickrock, beyond ridable, and yes, beyond necessary.

Now, there aren't a lot of places near Moab that haven't been cycled, regardless of whether or not they are actually very ridable. And because talus slopes and sand limit how easily a bike can travel over them, their inefficient surfaces are gonzo-abusive routes, almost by definition. Furthermore, indiscreet tracking on gonzo-abusive routes has the capacity to cause irreparable harm to microbiotic crust. The maker of such tracks risks a verbal shellacking at the hands of John Groo, if not worse. Some turkeys have even forged through roadless parts of Wilderness Study Areas—and lived to regret it.

...Have you ever heard of a Gonzo-Suicidal ride?

The Arches National Park Area

The Arches area is a true "holey land," with over 1,500 known arches. (Arch-finders use different parameters to define an arch, such as the ability to throw a football through, climb through or measure a minimum diameter of three feet across its narrowest part.) Dirt roads are few in the Park, but several mountain biking routes skirt its boundary, the vestige of wildcat mining days. Central to Arches' topography is long, cliff-hemmed Salt Valley. Its cliffs are deeply creased and corraded by erosion into elongate slickrock fins that beckon to be explored. The rider willing to leave the bike for an hour will discover unlikely passageways through these fins and the various slickrock "parks" nearby.

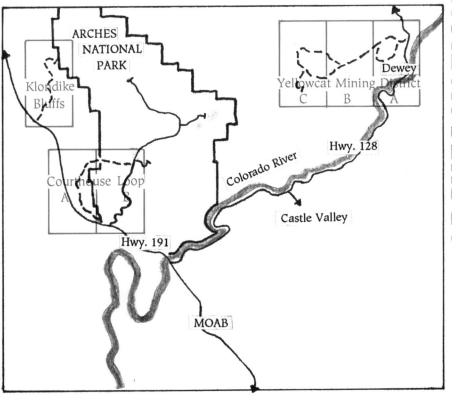

THE COURTHOUSE LOOP

Type: Loop
Length: 25.2 miles, 9 on pavement
Difficulty: Physically moderate / Technically easy
Best Seasons: Spring and fall
Elevation: Trailhead/-tail/Low—4,220 ft., High—5,040 ft.
Land Agencies: NPS and BLM
Route Summary: This route ascends the broken old highway that predated Highway 191 to where it crests the hill out of Moab Canyon. It then goes to near the rim of Courthouse Wash, a pretty, cottonwood-lined canyon with perennial flow near its springs. After swinging around a tributary canyon's "jump," a pipeline road crosses a sandy highland, then Courthouse Wash, to connect with the Willow Spring road to Balanced Rock on the Arches Entrance Road. From here, the pavement assists a fast and furious downhill which bridges Courthouse to perimeter Park Avenue and descend to the Park entrance, where a short stint on Highway 191 returns you to the trailhead.

The strength of this route is that it minimizes both actual and visual contact with Highway 191 while securing access to Courthouse Wash.
Options: From Balanced Rock, the five minute ride out the Windows spur has more than its share of scenic splendor, making it seem more like a movie set than a "play" of nature.
Attractions: Any of three suggested hiking routes into Courthouse reveal this wonderful, verdant canyon. After touring its backcountry, the ride ends with the "standard" tour of Arches, though unfiltered by windshield. Many of the arches defy imagination by their manmade-seeming perfection and "ostentatiousness."
Riding Surface: Broken asphalt, hardpacked sediments, drift sand, and pavement on jeep trails, two-laned roads and highways
Geology: At mile 3.7, the white sandstone that is furrowed by Courthouse Wash is the Entrada formation's Moab Tongue layer, probably named after the "tongue" of it that approaches the Park's visitor center from the north. (Sounds like a horror flick, huh?) The pink or salmon-colored slickrock beneath the Moab Tongue is seen deeper in the wash, and it corresponds to the towering walls, standing rocks, perforated fins and slickrock park areas that become prevalent later in the ride. It is the Slickrock member of the Entrada, and by mile 15.4, you'll have seen some scattered examples of it, but in another 0.8 of a mile, you'll be overwhelmed by the sight of it. The "petrified dunes" occupying the expansive mesa between here and Moab Valley are in the Navajo sandstone, and you can spot where the Navajo's Slickrock Bike Trail is from here, across an unseen river. Behind the Rocks and Poison Spider Mesa bare their Navajo fins to the valley, also, fixing this geologic formation to the collective Mountain Bike Psyche.
Notes: You may be asked for proof of having paid an entrance fee at any

Riders at Looking Glass Rock

time while in the Park, so carry at least $3.00 with you if you haven't a receipt.

Logistics: No permits are necessary for daytime use.

Trailhead Access: 6.0 miles north of Moab (Main x Center St.'s) on Highway 191, and not far past the entrance to Arches, a gravel turnout right makes an opportune parking area and (unposted) trailhead.

Mileage Log and Route Description:

2.6 Take the first spur right, after the broken asphalt highway gives way to dirt.

3.7 Make the obtuse left onto this prominent road which fronts Courthouse Wash. It stays at the interface of the white rock and the red soil. A very unlikely route into the nearby finger canyon of Courthouse provides deft scramblers a route down.

5.7 (R) This recommended spur road on a soil fill bed strikes out towards the confluence of Courthouse and Seven Mile Canyons, to which you can nearly ride before reaching the Park boundary. Remember, riding "cleanly" is neither dabbing nor leaving track in soil when there's ample rock around.

> You are stretched out like a string all over the place. The end of the string is here, the rest is there and there, back there in the mountains, on the other side. You must reel in the string, you must roll yourself up in a ball and then unravel yourself out here where you have the room and clear light to study the condition of the threads.
>
> Barry Holstun Lopez, <u>Desert Notes</u>, 1976

7.2 At this "T", go right to follow the buried pipeline notices for the next 2.6 miles.

7.5 The abrupt rim of Seven Mile Canyon is broken on the south side by a cattle trail. This is a nice walk to Courthouse anytime except May through August, when the motion flies can gang up to put the bite on you. Loose fitting, longsleeved and -legged clothing is a must for bug season excursions here. The wash crossing above the "jump" prepares you for the initial struggle up the hill.

9.1 The road bends left where the pipeline drops off the hill, but a clean descent can be made crossing the berms to track straight down the hill for the crossing of Courthouse Wash.

9.8 From the pumphouse on the north side of the wash, take the prominent dirt road that angles 30° to the right from the continuing pipeline road. This is the Willow Spring road, the old entrance to Arches National Monument.

12.0 (R) At the "Road Closed" sign, a nice hike to Courthouse Wash bypasses Willow Spring.

14.8 (L) This spur to Klondike Bluffs becomes sandier than sin after passing Herdina Park.

15.6 A turn left onto the Entrance Road can detour you to the Windows.

25.2 Trailhead/tail

Corona Arch sightseeing

Looking Glass Rock near the Canyon Rims Area

THE COURTHOUSE LOOP A

Hwy. 313

Hwy. 191

The Old Highway

Dalton Well Wash

Cedar Ridge Well

Cedar Ridge

Canyon

Courthouse Wash

Moab

Chinarump Mines

Corral Canyon

RIO GRANDE AND WESTERN

PIPELINE

Tunnel

Pit

Tunnel

Court

BM 4412
BM 4465
BM 4484
BM 4583
BM 4563
BM 4222
VABM 5701

22   23   24
27   26   25   30
34   35   36   31
3   2   7.5   5.7   6
      7.2
      4610
10   11   12   2.6
15   14   13   18   7
22   23   24   19   17

9.8   12.0
9.1

Willow
Spring

Willow
Flats

Balanced Rock

Ham
Rock

Cove Arch

Double Ar

NATIONAL

ARCHES

Courthouse

Sheep
Rock

Tower of Babel

Courthouse

Three
Gossips

The Organ

Towers

Park
Avenue

LaSal Mts
Viewpoint

Wash

Monument Hdqrs

Water

Canyon

BM
4120

BM 4021

VABM
5373

Substation

Ore Reduction
Plant

Matrimony
Spring

4828

5002

4800

5120

5120

4906

4602

4160

4503

4770

4800

4347

4537

4537

4320

4480

4800

4982

4698

4400

128

279

YELLOWCAT MINING DISTRICT

Type: Figure "8" Loop
Length: 34.3 miles
Difficulty: Physically moderate / Technically moderate
Best Seasons: Spring and fall, but avoid when wet
Elevation: Trailhead/-tail/Low—4,100 ft., High—5,300 ft.
Land Agency: BLM
Route Summary: From its trailhead on Highway 128, this route utilizes the Kokopelli Trail to access the rim of Squaw Park, a slickrock-walled basin near the settlement of Dewey on the Colorado River. Upon deviating from the Kokopelli Trail, the ride traverses over to Owl Draw, whose drainage it parallels southwest to the Highlands, a modest bluff that functions as the recrossed ground in a huge figure "8." The route continues west, coming to a spur to the Lost Spring Canyon Wilderness Study Area (WSA). From here it veers north to tour some of the colorfully-soiled country that was mined so intensively years ago, nothing but yawning mine shafts, hulking equipment and a web of roads to speak for it now. The route then recrosses the Highlands to descend all the way back to the river via Owl Draw.

This route has been pieced together thanks to the efforts of the indefatigueable John Groo. It strategically avoids the many sand and rubble roads while navigating through a veritable nerve center of possibilities.

Options: The aforementioned spur to Lost Spring WSA offers access to that colorful canyon, and for the hardy, innumerable rugged spurs wander from the heart of the mining district to outlying areas.

Attractions: For desert rats, this is a fascinating place, full of castoff machinery, roofless buildings, dinosaur bone, petrified wood and open space. Canyon walls sometimes feel like blinders, as if they insulate you from the larger world stage (besides making it difficult to get reception). The wide open, vaguely threatening Yellowcat area will remind you why you live indoors.

Riding Surface: Hardpacked sediments, clay soils, and packed sand all on jeep trails

Geology: Much of this trail is in the contact between two layers—the Moab Tongue Entrada and the clay-rich Morrison formation. The Morrison shales are remnants of a coastal floodplain, and they occur in banded colors of purple-brown, pink, red, and blue-green. Fossilized plants are indicative of uranium-bearing formations, because these plants "reduce" or attract uranium from overlying layers of both volcanic ash fallout and stream-carried uranium from granite sources such as the La Sal Mountains.

Notes: Do not enter mine shafts. The breathing of radon gas has caused lung cancer in miners who have worked in unventilated uranium mines.

Logistics: No permit or shuttle is required.

Trailhead Access: Take the "River Road," Highway 128 from near Moab 34.2 miles through Dewey and out to a brief asphalt spur where the highway has begun climbing away from the river. (This spur left is just after mile marker 34.) A brown "grape stake" or Carsonite marker indicating the Kokopelli Trail may be posted to the telephone pole here.

Mileage Log and Route Description:
0.0 Upon climbing the first hill from the trailhead, a spur right is encountered in a half mile. You will be returning along this road at ride's end, but for now continue on the Kokopelli Trail.
2.3 Take a left at the fork upon descending from the low pass.
4.0 (L) This obtuse spur is the Wood Road, which connects to the River Road near Dewey.
4.9 At this 4-way intersection, the Kokopelli Trail goes left to cross the prohibitively sandy Squaw Park, but your move is to continue across and up the road on the edge of the bluff ahead.
5.4 After a "cogs too spare" hillclimb, take the spur right, from its top.
7.2 Turn left onto this sandy doubletrack (before cresting the hill). It ascends plates of broken bedrock to the old Squaw Park Claims Office.
8.3 Bear right as you pass the claims office (Looks like that fire insurance wasn't necessary, after all...), and stay right at all opportunities for the next half mile.
8.8 Go left from this sandy three-way intersection in Owl Draw to climb yet another uplift.
10.5 A cairn may denote this obtuse spur **(R)** where the road begins to flatten and angle away from the rim. This spur is the critical move for the return route, for it will be easy to miss, what with the head of steam you'll likely have. (If you do miss it, the sandy road down Owl Draw from the three-way connects to it.) Continue on up to the Highlands.
12.1 Bear right upon intersecting this prominent, graded road to Auger Spring. This is another easy-to-miss junction on your return.
13.2 Turn left at this ungraded spur which triangulates to the Highlands Road.
17.4 From the "T," this wide, graded road goes left to a recommended out-and-back detour to the removed Lost Spring WSA. (Stay on the little-used ridge trail to view the intersection of Lost Spring with Salt Creek.)

> ...and you can't assign a dollars-per-capita value to space or solitude. Neither can you measure silence on a slide rule—except as zero decibels, and that misses the point with a quite consummate engineering skill.
>
> Colin Fletcher, <u>The Man Who Walked Through Time</u>, 1973

Go right to continue up to the Poison Strip and the most intensely mined part of the Yellowcat District.
23.0 Take the fork right, at this splendidly graded triangulated intersection.
26.7 (previously mile 12.1) Don't miss this spur left, off the graded road.
28.3 (previously mile 10.5) And don't miss this acute spur left, onto this

discreet, cairned road.

30.5 The washed out roadbed descends the smooth bedrock of a narrow wash. Hike-a-bike through, getting out of it to the right on an old road bed turned singletrack. The track is confused by several old splayed roadbeds, but if you stay right, against the hill, you'll drop into another, more navigable arm of Owl Draw. Go left here to continue down the streambed.

32.7 The last crossing of Owl Draw turns you towards the home stretch, but not before passing a springfed stocktank and intersecting the Kokopelli Trail at previous mile 0.6.

34.3 Trailhead/-tail

Highlights of the Loma-to-Moab Kokopelli Trail

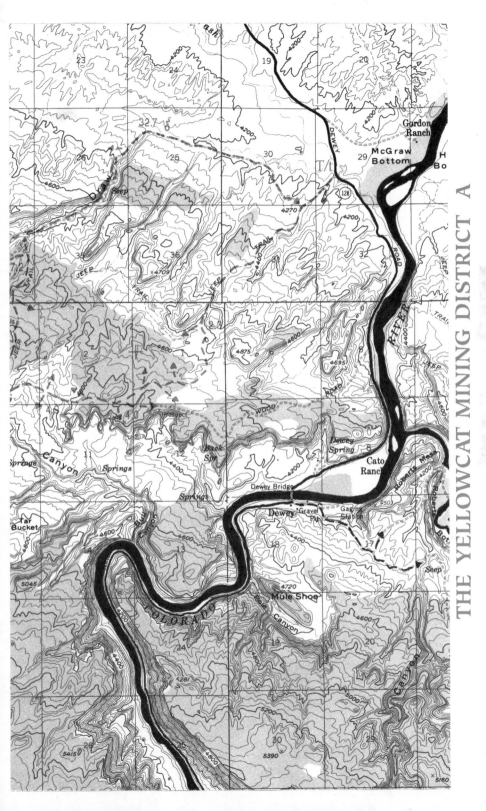

THE YELLOWCAT MINING DISTRICT A

THE YELLOWCAT MINING DISTRICT C

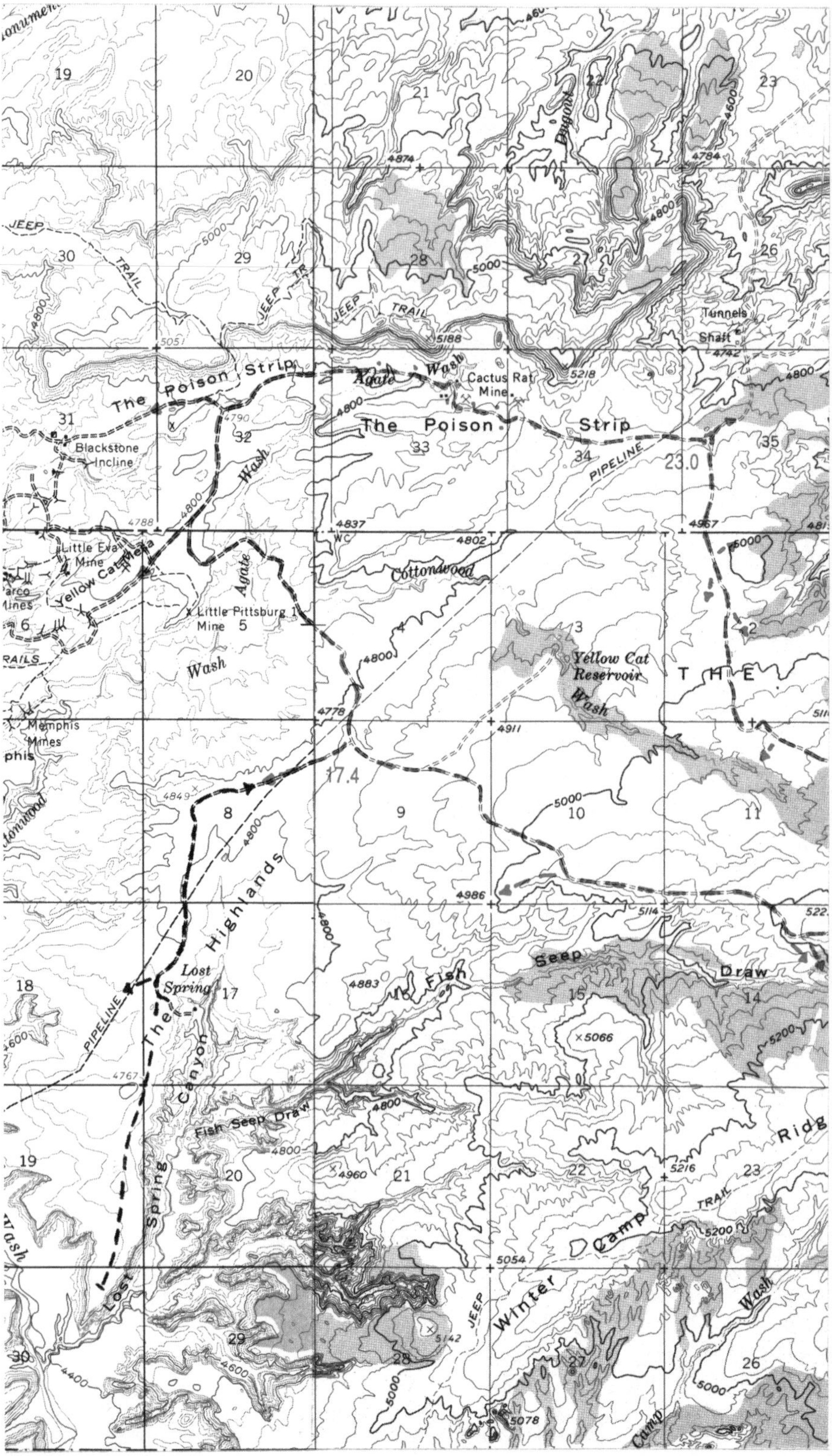

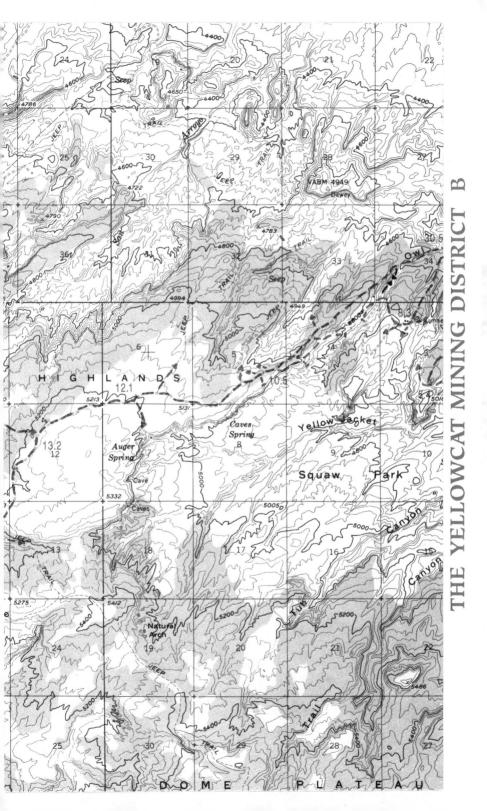

THE YELLOWCAT MINING DISTRICT B

KLONDIKE BLUFFS

Type: Out-and-back
Length: 15.6 miles
Difficulty: Physically easy / Technically moderate
Best Seasons: Spring and fall, but not after rain
Elevation: Trailhead/-tail/Low—4,550 ft., High—5,380 ft.
Land Agencies: BLM and NPS
Route Summary: The first few miles of this route weave through the bleached, clay hills of a sterile landscape. Upon turning to Little Valley, evidence of life in a renegade band of cottonwood trees earmarks the canyon that is the gateway to a broad, tilted plane of slickrock. When you reach this plane of white rock, you'll find that it is jointed and fissured, a fact that actually limits and makes easier the routefinding across open rock. Cairns are often in place to mark the route ahead. After gaining a soil roadbed, the route nearly doubles back on itself as it climbs up to the Klondike Bluffs proper.
Options: Many "gateway" canyons have incurred mining roads hereabouts, and these might be of interest to dinosaur track hunters, for tracks abound here. A spur near the Bluffs offers ingress to Salt Valley, the geologic feature responsible for the slickrock plane's tilt.
Attractions: This is an excellent beginner's route, as varied riding surfaces serve to gain less than a thousand feet of elevation, and the culminating view

Colorful Morrison formation hills

92

is wonderful. On-foot exploration from the overlook is encouraged. The search for dinosaur tracks enroute can keep fast riders occupied while slow riders get their bearings.

Riding Surface: Hardpacked clay sediments, slickrock and coarse sand on two-laned dirt roads and jeep trails.

Geology: The low hills of Morrison shale- and sandstone lap at the tilted slickrock of the Entrada's Moab Tongue layer, a coastal dune deposit of windblown sand. The tilt is a reminder of the forces that created the canyonlands as we know it. Evaporated salt from receding seas became trapped under thousands of feet of sediments washed down from the ancestral Rockies. Under pressure, the salt flowed like wet putty out from underneath the sediments, finding faults to vent through. Salt Valley, Castle Valley and Moab Valley are along fault blocks that were bulged, then pierced by the pressurized salt flow. Brittle surface rock was fissured, some of it slumping into the widening valley, and some of it remaining, tilting away from the rim. As surface moisture dissolved the salt, the valleys became ever deeper and wider as they undermined the walls that defined them.

The dinosaur tracks were made by a relatively small animal that could walk across wet mud without bogging down under its own weight. Track densities near Arches have been reported at as many as 2,300 per acre, a fact that bespeaks dinosaurs as gregarious beasts.

Logistics: No permits or shuttles are necessary.

Trailhead Access: About 16.6 miles north of Moab (Main x Center St.'s) on Highway 191 (0.4 of a mile north of mile marker 142 and just before a concrete embanked bridge), a dirt spur right passes through a fenceline. This is the (unposted) trailhead.

Mileage Log and Route Description:

0.0 Continue by bike towards Klondike Bluffs.

2.7 Flare left off of this sweeping right turn.

3.8 Turn right, at the "T" after the cottonwood grove to enter a short canyon, avoiding the fork left.

4.5 Stay low, close to the red sediment slope as you traverse the plane of white slickrock.

5.2 (L) A nice "track record" of dinosaur tracks looks like giant bird prints. At the following crest, where there's a huge cairn, strike out straight across the rock instead of dipping down on the road. A string of cairns is usually in place starting from this point, as the route descends, then climbs acoss opportune plates of rock. The fractures separating these plates are widened by delving roots and mild acid releases from plants.

6.4 Well after regaining a soil roadbed, take this obtuse spur right, to avoid the connector up and over to Salt Valley.

7.8 As you gain the view of the white-capped Klondike Bluffs, further travel on bike becomes inconvenient. Nice textures embellish this area—lichen patterns and ironstone concretions, plus beds of chert flakes studding the soil.

KLONDIKE BLUFFS

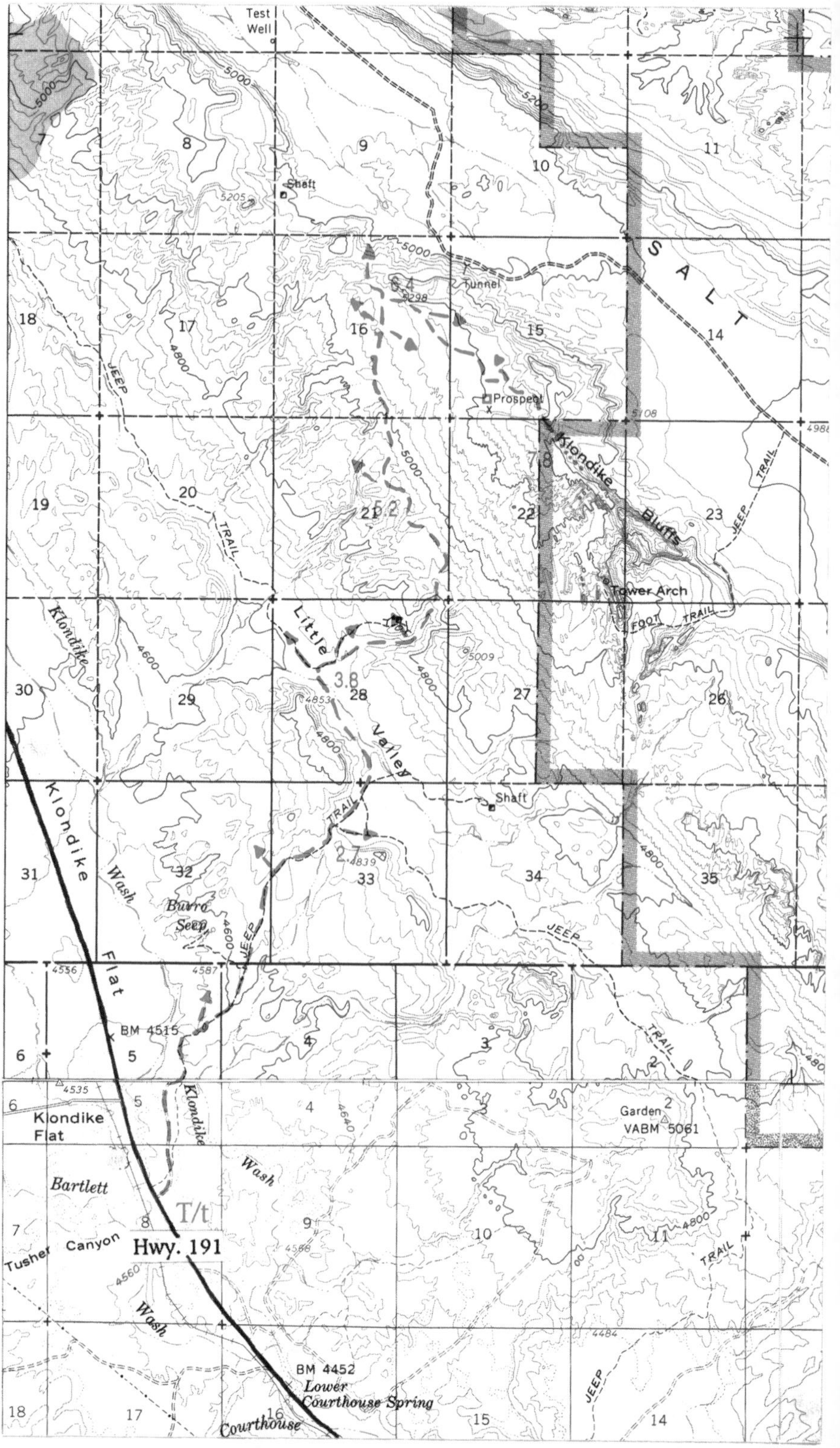

SALT

Hwy. 191
T/t

Test Well
Shaft
Shaft
5205
Tunnel
Prospect
Klondike Bluffs
Tower Arch
FOOT TRAIL
JEEP TRAIL
Little Valley
Klondike Wash Flat
Burro Seep
BM 4515
Klondike Flat
4535
Bartlett
Tusher Canyon
Wash
Garden VABM 5061
BM 4452
Lower Courthouse Spring
Courthouse

7 8 9 10 11
18 17 16 15 14
19 20 21 22 23
30 29 28 27 26
31 32 33 34 35
6 5 4 3 2
6 5 4 3 2
7 8 9 10 11
18 17 16 15 14

Dinosaur tracks on the Klondike Bluffs Trail

The Bluffs are fun to explore, with narrow passages, balconies, and arches in and amongst its domes. The route back crosses the identical terrain as the approach.

Other Roads / Rides in the Arches Area

Unfortunately, there are more routes to dissuade you from than to recommend to you. These include the sandy Klondike Bluffs road from Herdina Park to Klondike Bluffs, the chronically washboarded Salt Valley Road, the sandy roads around Winter Camp Ridge and Squaw Park south of the Yellowcat ride, and the sandy road onto Dry Mesa east of Delicate Arch (although a hike-a-bike up Cache Valley to a river overlook can be enjoyable). The entire northern boundary of Arches National Park would be of interest to passionate explorers, and various dead end spurs shoot like roots from the Yellowcat through-road that connects Highway 191 to Highway 128.

The Klondike Bluffs

One yawning dawn finds two lanky characters trit-trotting along a dry wash bottom, nearly too played out from the night's misdeeds to scent or scent upon. Coyote, renowned for his licentious ways, has stopped to eye a track. "Look here, friend. Wheels have passed."

"Indeed," remarks Iktome, blinking his bloodshot eyes. "What's a *wasichu* doing out here, and on a bicycle, even?"

"Lost—and weary, by the looks of that wobble. We'd better find him before the buzzards do," grins Coyote. "Got some hungry pups at home."

The two tricksters hasten to follow the tire tracks, which cross the wash and continue roughshod across the desert. "Look at that hawk, Ikto. It must have quarried a rabbit. You should go take a look."

"Yes, friend. You ought to relax in the shade of this juniper while I fetch it." And so it went, each in a like deviousness trying to distract the other from the wayward cyclist's tracks.

But the mountain biker's tracks were easy to follow, as they tore through gardens of microbiotic crust, cactus patches and brittle old blackbrush in an almost straight line cross country. Never did the *wasichu* contour along slickrock benches or travel in the drainages.

After awhile, Iktome grew uneasy. "You know how the Earth Mother hates her skin prickled like this. That *wasichu* flea's going to get swatted."

"You don't believe that fable, do you, Ikto, that tomfoolery, that nonsense about needing to travel in Earth Mother's wrinkles and on her calluses or else get disciplined by her hand? None of our people ever got it."

"Yes, but ..."

"... And none of our people ever did see it happen, either. It's like those defaming things they say about us coyotes." Coyote noticed Iktome fall off the pace some, a reluctance born of gullibility, no doubt.

From a low bluff, Coyote stopped to survey the landscape. There, weaving in and out of the junipers, was the *wasichu*. As he squinted to narrow his focus, Coyote's golden eyes reflected a biker dismounting and struggling across obstruction after obstruction. There were no water bottles on his bike, no pack on his back, not even a visor on his head. And Coyote could smell the fear. Whiskers flattened back along his nose, he loped off toward Opportunity.

Iktome, disinterested in the pursuit now, found a beautiful jasper arrowhead in the wash bottom. He made a shrine for it in a pocket on a nearby rock face, then bent to the heavenly scent of a cliffrose. As was his habit, he sidestepped or step-stoned his way through areas with microbiotic crust so not to violate this "building block of the desert" with telltale tracks. Even his limited animal reasoning allowed him the realization that this black carpet is the base of the food pyramid upon which his own life depends. It fixes nitrogen, stabilizes soil against erosion, and sponges up water—all factors in helping establish larger, more nutritious plants that, let's say... rabbits, might

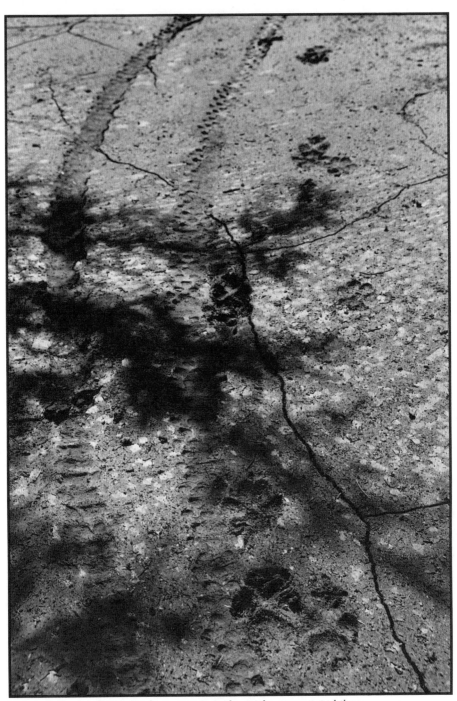

Critter tracks — coyote and wasichu mountain biker

eat.

Iktome looked with dismay at Coyote's prints tracked indiscreetly beside the *wasichu*'s distressed and flailing trail. As Iktome arrived at the low bluff, he saw Coyote closing in on the unsuspecting *wasichu*, but his attention was carried by a blue-black cloud moving swiftly from the west. Dark and angry fingers from the cloud suddenly cowled the sunny day. A quiet and ominous pall stilled the wind, and even the few trees looked to be hunkering down in expectation.

Two parallel blue shafts of electricity dropped, drilling both the *wasichu* and Coyote dead.

Horrified at the sight, Iktome shuddered, blinked, untensed, then actually smiled to himself, thinking how much Coyote's beautiful and voluptuous *winchinchala* would cherish the heap powerful gift of a mountain bike.

Hummingbird in the iris meadows

The La Sal Mountains

These "inverted canyons" that bless Moab are more than just a pretty backdrop for the Slickrock Trail. They complement the canyons as naturally as green complements red and cold complements hot. By benefit of trail work, many heretofore unridable, nearly unfindable trails have been cleared in the last few years. As mountain bikers continue to "push" the prime riding seasons, the La Sals are seeing increased summertime use. Like the Abajos, the La Sals are an "island" range or would-be volcano that never vented, solidifying into a hard mass which was later exhumed by erosion.

The La Sals have two prominent passes over 10,000 feet, both visible from Moab. This book describes rides that encircle the peaks using these—Geyser Pass and La Sal Pass—and other, less prominent ones. Although its singletracks aren't as groomed, as abundant or as long as those in Sun Valley or Crested Butte, La Sal tracks can offer immediate gratification as an escape from the oppressive heat that shimmers over the slickrock. Sunsets as viewed from the range are wonderful, with distant desert mesas that recede in ever-softer steps of lavender. Hummingbirds dogfight amongst the wild irises, and the deciduous/evergreen contrast of aspen and fir is always picturesque. Mormon missionaries to the Moab Valley in 1855 named them the Elk Mountains, and elk continue to roam the La Sals in herds one hundred head strong. The early Spanish explorers (circa 1670) dubbed them, the "Mountains of Salt."

Mill Creek's South fork leaves the mountains for the desert

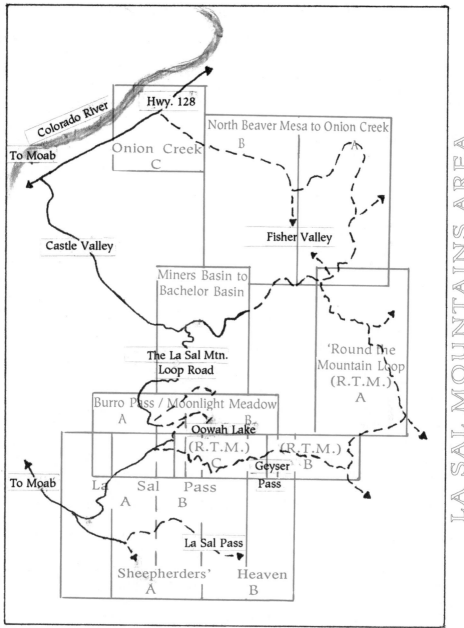

Colorado River

Hwy. 128

To Moab

North Beaver Mesa to Onion Creek

B

A

Onion Creek

C

Fisher Valley

Castle Valley

Miners Basin to
Bachelor Basin

The La Sal Mtn.

Loop Road

'Round the
Mountain Loop
(R.T.M.)

A

Burro Pass / Moonlight Meadow

A

B

Oowah Lake

(R.T.M.)

(R.T.M.)

To Moab

La

Sal

Pass

C

Geyser

Pass

B

A

B

La Sal Pass

Sheepherders'

A

Heaven

B

NORTH BEAVER MESA TO ONION CREEK

Type: One-way
Length: 25.6 miles
Difficulty: Physically moderate / Technically moderate
Best Seasons: Spring and fall, "squeezing" summer
Elevation: Trailhead—8,050 ft., High—8,175 ft., Trailtail/Low—4,210 ft.
Land Agencies: BLM and USFS
Route Summary: This mostly downhill ride begins near the head of Fisher Valley with a view of the distant Fisher Towers near the Colorado River. Before dropping to Polar Mesa, an unlikely turn swings out to Cowhead Hill, the point of a ridge which divides Thompson Canyon from Hideout Canyon. The route then spirals around Cowhead Hill on its descent to Hideout Canyon, which it crosses to burst into Fisher Valley by way of a short and steep, "thrust or bust" hill climb. The flats of broad Fisher Valley are syphoned into Onion Creek, a perennial flow through a narrow, colorful canyon that is home and haunts to "ten thousand strangely carved forms" (in the words of Major Powell). Onion Creek surges through a dramatic narrows to flow into the Colorado River, bypassing an amphitheatre of immense, brick-red towers—the no-longer-distant Fisher Towers—and the ride terminates at the River Road.
Options: A mega-, ultra-, gonzo-abusive option to descend the cow track at the head of Fisher Valley exists, but may only appeal to masochistic trials riders.
Attractions: A descent of almost 4,000 feet takes you from a ponderosa/aspen community through pinyon/juniper to sagebrush. Views down Thompson Canyon glimpse the rounded slickrock walls of the Dolores drainage, a river that starts near Telluride, Colorado. Onion Creek Canyon offers some outstanding scrambling opportunities up labyrinthine corridors with access to the rim above, which happens to be a narrow ridge overlooking the stately Fisher Towers. The road splashes across the creek over thirty times, a fact that convinces some cyclists to ride down the creek bottom itself. While the shuttle vehicle is being retrieved, the bulk of your party can swim or skip rocks in the river.
Riding Surface: Hardpacked sediments, rock-studded sediments, duffy sand, and coarse sand on jeep trails and two-laned dirt roads
Geology: Fisher Valley is another salt valley, like Castle and Moab Valleys. (For elaboration on its forming process, consult the Geologic Summary.) Its obvious similiarities are its north-south orientation and its sheerwalled confines. Oddly enough, it drains out via Cottonwood Canyon to the Dolores, even though Onion Creek's perennial flow to the Colorado would lead you to believe otherwise. (Onion Creek is fed by Stinking Spring and others.) The pressure of the uplifting salt beneath the valley dispersed drainage to the two separate rivers over sixty-five million years ago, but Onion Creek Canyon exhibits the earmarks of a "young," notched canyon, as erosion there could

only be as recent as the rise of the entire Colorado Plateau—ten million years, give or take a few leap days. The head of Onion Creek (mile 17.0) shows massive slumping where the contrary tendencies of uplift and erosion face off. Springs in the vicinity tend to exacerbate this clash, and their suspended brine frosts much of Onion Creek. Just how high the Fisher Valley floor has risen is displayed by the fact that Onion Creek was carved from Cutler sandstone, the first layer of sediments deposited on top of the salt before others buried it deeper. The Cutler in Onion Creek is several hundred feet lower, and may be just the tip of a 3,360-foot deposit.

Notes: Fenders might be useful in keeping you stripe-free. It's hard to keep from whaling through the stream crossings, as their subsurfaces are fairly predictable. Stay in the tracks of preceding vehicles, to be safe, as flash floods commonly furrow or wash debris into the stream's course. This entire route includes optional segments of the Kokopelli Trail.

Logistics: A shuttle vehicle needs to be left at the Onion Creek road where it intersects Highway 128.

Trailhead Access: Go north on Highway 191 out of Moab to turn on the River Road, Highway 128. In 15.5 miles, take the spur to Castle Valley. In another 18.6 miles, well after passing the La Sal Mountain Loop Road spur, the now-gravel road will head around deep Bull Canyon and come to a 3-way junction. This is the (unposted) trailhead, the left turn to North Beaver Mesa.

Mileage Log and Route Description:
0.0 Descend towards the mesa, visible across the way.
0.3 The road crosses a diversion ditch that starts five miles away, at Don's Lake, to irrigate the fields in Fisher Valley below.
0.5 (L) An obscure ATV track marks the trials ride down Fisher Creek, a route that connects to the mesa route in 5.5 miles at mesa route mile 15.2.
4.2 *Downhillus interruptus.* Take this spur left, to Fisher Valley before reaching the white cliffs of Polar Mesa.
6.2 (R) The views of the Dolores River drainage beyond Thompson Canyon are themselves a foreground to the Uncompahgre Plateau, the ancestral Rocky Mountains.
7.9 (L) An overhanging shelf of rock next to the road offers the classic view of Hideout Canyon, Fisher Valley, and the red-brown rock figures in and around Onion Creek. Can you guess which one is Mother and Her Baby Stroller?
13.4 (L) The so-named hideout is just up the creek at this second crossing.
14.1 This short kneeknocker is a delight to us fast-twitch types.
15.2 Careful of the washouts as you descend to the "T" at Taylor Livestock Ranch. This is where the optional route reconnects. A right turn towards Onion Creek will see you through without any too-distracting spurs.
16.2 (R) This spur goes to Dewey via a road once described as, "It may be steep and loose, but that ain't nothing can't be made up for by its overall ruggedness." It is the most specious segment of the Kokopelli Trail. Get ready for the fast, splashing descent through Onion Creek. Get wet. Go.

20.8 (R) Just before you enter the Narrows, a defile on your right offers on-foot access to the Fisher Towers, perched out of sight some 750 feet above the canyon floor.

As you might suspect, Onion Creek sees some nasty flash floods. People often sense flash floods by the earthy, necrotic smell that precedes them. A slurry of pinyon needles and juniper berries noses down the wash, first wrapping around, then flowing over boulders in its way. The flow crescendos rapidly, smashing the outer walls of each bend, spraying them high up with a silty deposit that will tell future travellers of its ferocity. Logs and whole trees carried down will become lodged in the narrowest corridors, sometimes causing tons of detritus to jackstraw up behind them. Days may pass before the creek flows clear again. Clay basins along the channel then dry up, shrink, and crack into fanciful geometric shapes, curling up at the edges to provide crackling accompaniment to the rare hiker.

25.6 Highway 128, just a few miles from the Castle Valley Road. (The best river access spurs less than a mile northeast on the highway.)

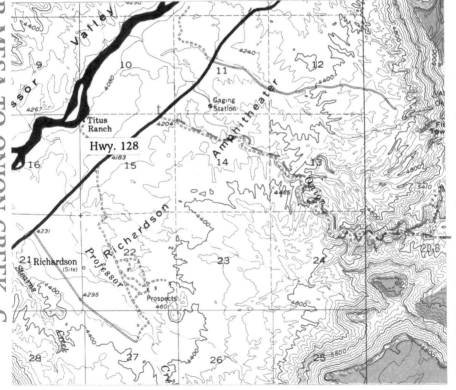

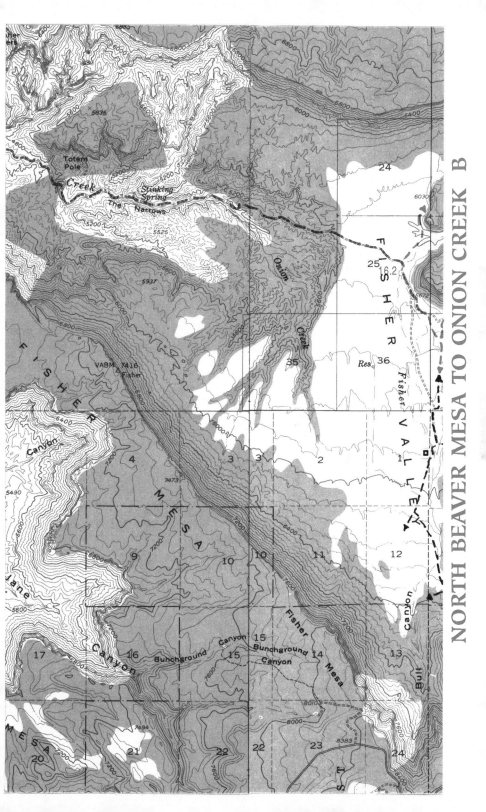

NORTH BEAVER MESA TO ONION CREEK B

NORTH BEAVER MESA TO ONION CREEK A

A view of the Colorado from near Fisher Towers

Colorado's distant San Juan Mountains as seen from La Sal Pass

107

'ROUND THE MOUNTAIN LOOP

Type: Loop
Length: 50.1 miles, including 17.4 miles on pavement
Difficulty: Physically difficult / Technically easy
Best Seasons: June through October
Elevation: Trailhead/-tail/Low—6,490 ft., High—10,550 ft.
Land Agencies: USFS, State Forest and private land with travel easements
Route Summary: From the head of Castle Valley, this ride circles the northern group of peaks. The climb up the Castleton-Gateway Road spurs to Taylor Flat, a pastoral area peppered with aspens, then skirts the mountain before climbing 1,500 feet to Geyser Pass. The Geyser Pass Road ends at the Loop Road, where a substantial, paved warmdown returns you to the trailhead/-tail.
Options: If you can arrange to be dropped off somewhere on the route, you can coast all the way down to Moab from Geyser Pass, a loss of 6,500 feet. It can also hook up to the Moonlight Meadow or Burro Pass rides from near Geyser Pass.
Attractions: This is a great endurance ride, mostly on roads suitable for a passenger car. It offers grand views of redrock canyons and snow-clad mountains, including ranges in Colorado and New Mexico. Views of Sinbad Valley, a salt valley that aligns with Fisher Valley north of the La Sals, verify that they were created along the same fault block, and would be a continuous valley if not for the upthrust mountains in between.
Riding Surface: Packed sediments, rock-studded sediments, and pavement on jeep trails and two-laned roads
Logistics: No permit or shuttle is necessary, but a shuttle or drop-off can tailor the ride to your specifications.
Trailhead Access: Go north on Highway 191 out of Moab to turn on the River Road, Highway 128. In 15.5 miles, take the spur to Castle Valley another 10.8 miles to the intersection with the Loop Road, the (unposted) trailhead.

Mileage Log and Route Description:
0.0 Bike east on the Castleton-Gateway Road.
7.8 After heading Bull Canyon, stay right at the 3-way intersection towards Gateway.
12.7 Go right, at this fork, towards Sally's Hollow.
18.1 Turn right, towards Buckeye Reservoir.
22.9 Turn right, onto this doubletrack just before the road passes through a corral to begin the challenging climb to Geyser Pass.
35.0 (L) This spur on F.S. Rd. 68 might offer some extra fun to those descending to Moab instead of taking the Loop Road back to the trailhead/-tail. Otherwise, the Loop Road provides straightforward access back to the trailhead/-tail.
50.1 Trailhead/-tail

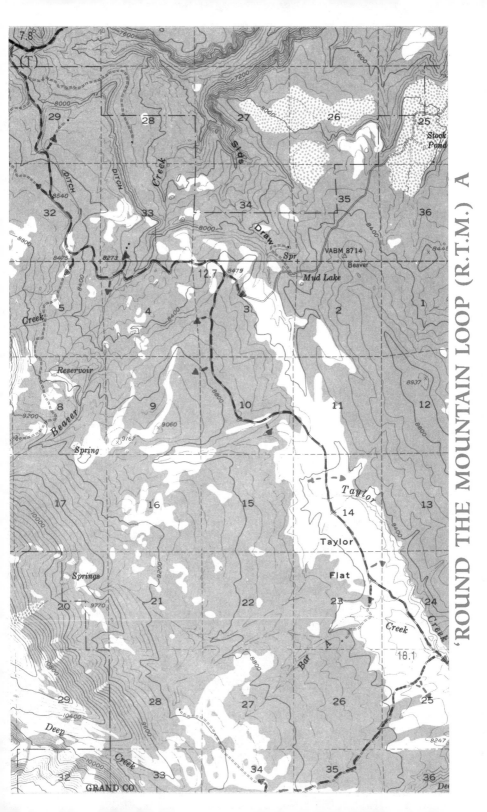

'ROUND THE MOUNTAIN LOOP (R.T.M.) A

SAN CO
36
31
32
33
34
Deep
11200
10752
MANTI-LA SAL
NATIONAL FOREST
6
5
10000
4
9200
3
BOUNDARY
Sawmill
Geyser
22.9
10400
Blue Lake
19

SAN JUAN CO
SAN JI
32
Boren
33
34
Haystack Mtn
35
8562
Mesa
10800
8000
11642
Horse
8800
10400
35.0
Geyser
Pass
G E
5
4
Creek
3
Sprin
9970
2
Creek
Spring
10000
Spring

A view from the La Sal Mountain Loop Road

MINERS BASIN TO BACHELOR BASIN

Type: Loop
Length: 15.6 miles, including 6.1 on pavement
Difficulty: Physically difficult / Technically difficult
Best Season: Mid-June through October
Elevation: Trailhead/-tail—7,880 ft., High—10,735 ft., Low—6,490 ft.
Land Agency: USFS
Route Summary: A pavement climb precedes a steep climb on a tricky cobble road that ascends past a lake and rustic cabins to a high pass. Remnants of a gold mining community, which had as many as fifty residents at the turn of the century, are everywhere in both basins. Many claims are still worked with new, efficient mining technology. The descent from Bachelor Basin is on deteriorated roadbeds and single track. It intersects the Castleton-Gateway Road for a short ways to reach the trailhead/-tail.
Attractions: This is a short, strenuous ride through aspen and fir forests that offers you a chance to collate the sometimes romantic, sometimes sordid history of alpine gold mining.
Riding Surface: Cobble-studded sediments, shale, hard packed sediments, and pavement on jeep trails, singletrack and two-laned roads.
Trailhead Access: From Moab, head south on Highway 191 for 7.9 miles to take the signed spur left to the Loop Road. A right turn from the next intersection, a "T," will mark Spanish Valley Drive. The Loop Road climbs past the Pack Creek Picnic Area spur, and after much meandering, you'll reach the trailhead/-tail at the "T" intersection of the Loop Road and the Castleton-Gateway Road at cumulative mile 33.8 from Main and Center streets in Moab. You will pass the sign for Miners Basin 4.7 miles before reaching the trailhead. Disregard it until you return via bike. The drive back to Moab via Castle Valley and Highway 128 is recommended.

Mileage Log and Route Description:

0.0 After parking discreetly off the road in an already impacted area, a quick twenty jumping jacks will warm you up for the nine mile pull up to Miners Pass.
7.7 After passing the lake, two spurs (R) access primitive campsites and the rocky road-trail that passes over to Schuman Gulch and Warner Lake.
9.1 There is one absolute widowmaker on the road to Miners Pass, but once there, you have unrestricted views across Bachelor Basin to Mount Waas, the highest peak in the northern cluster. From the pass the route dives left onto a shaley switch back, as the dead end spur to the now-decrepit "Bachelor pads" continues straight. This shaley old road will thin to a single track once before intersecting the perfectly drivable road down to Willow Basin.
11.5 Take the acute spur left onto the singletrack.
15.6 Trailhead/-tail.

MINERS BASIN TO BACHELOR BASIN

The La Sal Mtn. Loop Road

BURRO PASS

Type: Loop
Length: 18.7 miles, including 0.6 of a mile on pavement
Difficulty: Physically difficult / Technically difficult
Best Season: July through October
Elevation: Trailhead/-tail—7,950 ft., High—11,180 ft., Low—7,665 ft.
Land Agency: USFS
Route Summary: Burro Pass is the highest (potentially) all-ridable pass in the La Sals. Upon climbing to Geyser Pass, it is only a mile up to Burro Pass, and after the steep descent into the beautiful Wet Fork of Mill Creek, a doubletrack takes you across to Warner Lake, where this ride's *coup de grâce* singletrack descends the Shafer Creek Trail to Mill Creek. A swift descent with a final short thrust back to the trailhead/-tail closes this loop.
Attractions: The terrain covered is much like that seen in Colorado's Rockies, with wildflower meadows, quiet creeks, and gorgeous aspen stands.
Riding Surface: Gravel, rock-studded sediments, loam and pavement on singletrack, doubletrack, and two-laned roads
Logistics: No permit or shuttle is required.
Trailhead Access: 7.9 miles south of Moab on Highway 191, there is a signed spur left, to the Loop Road. After taking this, and the right turn from the "T" in half a mile, Spanish Valley Drive climbs steadily towards the mountains to become the Loop Road after passing the turnoff to the Pack Creek Picnic Area. At cumulative mile 20, a turn onto the (signed) gravel Geyser Pass Road provides a parking turnout a hundred yards up on the left.

Mileage Log and Route Description:
0.0 Begin the eight-mile climb to Geyser Pass.
7.9 Take the left fork at shady Geyser Pass. Beware the deceptively deep mud bogs, like the one that forced John Groo to plead for help off of his augered, front-wheel-standing bike. (We were laughing too hard to do him much good.)
9.1 An unposted doubletrack to the left up across a clearing is the critical turn to Burro Pass.
9.6 At the gate, you can choose either the road or the singletrack, as they merge soon. The trail twice splits briefly before achieving the pass.
10.5 From Burro Pass, the scree scramble to the ridge on the south is worth the view of the desert below. Make sure your brakes are functioning properly before descending to Mill Creek.
12.3 Where the creeks join, the trail **(R)** up Dry Fork is soon unridable.
13.9 After going through the gate, look for the trail which starts immediately after the dirt road intersects from the left. An old post may indicate where the Shafer Creek Trail sign once was. Before riding this fun singletrack, take a minute to view Warner Lake, which is just a few hundred yards ahead.
16.8 After crossing the Wilson Mesa Ditch and fording Mill Creek, a quick grunt gets you to the Oowah Lake Road. A sometimes w-w-washboarded

descent finds you at the Mill Creek bridge. It spans a narrow, Entrada-rimmed gorge, the hiking of which is fraught with hazard. If the devil's club, stinging nettle and wild currant doesn't stop you, the icy cold waterfalls might.
18.7 Trailhead/-tail

Mountain Magic

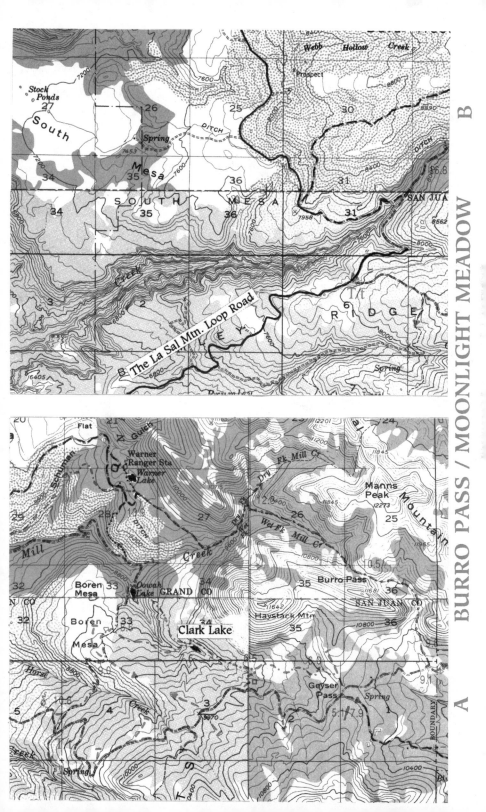

A   BURRO PASS / MOONLIGHT MEADOW   B

Bleeding aspen

MOONLIGHT MEADOW

Type: Loop
Length: 11.0 miles
Difficulty: Physically difficult / Technically difficult
Best Seasons: June through October, but not directly after rainfall
Elevation: Trailhead/-tail—8,990 ft., High—10,575 ft., Low—8,835 ft.
Land Agency: USFS
Route Summary: Upon climbing the road to Geyser Pass, this route flares into Moonlight Meadow to begin the 5.7 mile-long singletrack down the mountain. Upon reaching Clark Lake, the suggested route works across to Boren Mesa, then descends across Horse Creek to the trailhead/-tail on the Trans La Sal Trail, a pearl necklace strung around the Moab side of the La Sals.
Options: From Clark Lake, you can choose from at least three options. 1) Instead of heading towards Boren Mesa, you can descend a steep singletrack to Oowah Lake. 2) You can head towards Boren Mesa, then take the Trans La Sal Trail to Oowah Lake. 3) From either of these two options, you can descend along Mill Creek to the Loop Road or portage part-way up to Warner Lake on the continuing Trans La Sal Trail for the singletrack descent of Shuman Gulch.
Attractions: Beautiful forests, meadows and lakes frame this, the longest continuous singletrack in the La Sals. Fraught with the usual obstacles—deadfall, steep chutes, and tight turns—singletracks offer to mountain bikers willing to carry tools, lunch and possibly even their bikes the gift of wilderness-like seclusion in a day ride.
Riding Surface: Loam, gravel, rock-studded sediments and pavement on singletrack and two-laned dirt roads
Logistics: No permit or shuttle is necessary.
Trailhead Access: 7.9 miles south of Moab on Highway 191, there is a signed spur left, to the Loop Road. After taking this, and the "T" to the right in half a mile, Spanish Valley Drive climbs steadily towards the mountains to become the Loop Road after passing the turnoff to the Pack Creek Picnic Area. At cumulative mile 20, turn right, onto the (signed) Geyser Pass Road and drive another 2.8 miles to the (posted) trailhead for the Trans La Sal Trail at a pullout (right).

Mileage Log and Route Description:

0.0 Continue up the Geyser Pass Road by bike.
5.1 After cresting the pass, take the left fork, then the immediate acute doubletrack left. Where Moonlight Meadow begins to open up, take the singletrack across it to skirt the lower edge of the meadow at its aspen fringe.
6.0 Switchback past the half 55-gallon drum (cattle salt) across the meadow below to a solitary pine that splits into two parallel trunks about three feet above the ground. Beware the grassily overgrown, wheel-stuffing channel

117

twenty feet before the pine. From the pine, it's best to stay on the fringe of the trees, not getting enticed into them.

6.5 After the sweeping traverse of the huge, open area, the descent takes you adjacent to a creek. An "escape route" up to the Geyser Pass Road (0.3 of a mile) spurs from here, but the route continues downstream along the creek.

7.6 At the wood and wire fence past Clark Lake, take the obtuse switchback down to the Lake. This point is Decision Making Central. The quickest way out is to descend to Oowah Lake directly. The longest way is to traverse to Boren Mesa (on the route described below), then double back to Oowah. The third, described way gives you the most singletrack time.

Just 100 feet downstream from the lake, an inconspicuous gate provides access through the fence and across the creek to an obvious track. Beware the washout ahead.

8.6 As you break out of the trees into this iris-studded vale, a Carsonite marker denotes the Trans La Sal Trail, which you can ascend left onto Boren Mesa or descend to Oowah Lake. Again, the described ride goes up to Boren Mesa from here, staying left on the woven trails.

9.0 The doubletrack you've run across connects to, you guessed it, the Geyser Pass Road. Carsonite markers (if not shot to bits) will direct you off the abrupt south side of the mesa by continuing straight across the doubletrack on a now-obscure, grassy singletrack.

10.8 The trail continues through this campsite clearing on an old roadbed.

11.0 Trailhead/-tail

Lee Anne Truesdell and Dave Clark at Medicine Lake

SHEEPHERDERS' HEAVEN

Type: Loop
Length: 26.0 miles
Difficulty: Physically difficult / Technically difficult
Best Seasons: Mid-June through October
Elevation: Trailhead/-tail/Low—8,970 ft., High—10,120 ft.
Land Agency: USFS and State Forest
Route Summary: This complicated route perimeters the middle set of peaks in the La Sals, utilizing 5.7 miles of singletrack in the process. After climbing to Geyser Pass, it takes the righthand fork towards Blue and Dark Canyon Lakes, though it bypasses them in its contouring of Mts.Mellenthin and Peale. It catches a rarely used singletrack across a "beaver-ized" slope to intersect the La Sal Pass Road near some private cabins. A short climb to Medicine Lake and La Sal Pass precedes the descent down to where the Trans La Sal singletrack returns to the trailhead/-tail.
Options: A detour into a pretty meadow below Mount Peale makes a great lunch stop. Also, it's convenient to incorporate part of the La Sal Pass figure "8" ride—including its 3.9 mile singletrack section from near La Sal Pass down to the Pass Road on a part of the Trans La Sal Trail the Sheepherders' Heaven ride doesn't use.
Attractions: This route crosses open, sloping terrain pocketed by aspen and pine into scenic, pond-stippled parks. Long distance views of the Sleeping Ute, the San Juan Mountains, the Uncompahgre Plateau and Paradox Valley, another sheer, redwall-lined salt valley round out the scenic appeal. Complexities in following the trail will challenge even the best routefinders.
Riding Surface: Rock-studded, hardpacked sediments and gravel on two-laned dirt roads and singletrack
Notes: Both of the singletrack lengths require above average map and trail reading skills. They alternate from scrub to forest to meadow and back, defying predictibility.
Logistics: No permit or shuttle is necessary.
Trailhead Access: 7.9 miles south of Moab on Highway 191, there is a signed spur left to the Loop Road. After taking this, and the "T" to the right in half a mile, Spanish Valley Drive climbs steadily towards the mountains to become the Loop Road after passing the turnoff to the Pack Creek Picnic Area. At cumulative mile 20, turn right on the (signed) Geyser Pass Road and drive another 2.8 miles to the (posted) trailhead for the Trans La Sal Trail at a pullout (right).

Mileage Log and Route Description:
0.0 Continue up the Geyser Pass Road by bike.
5.1 After cresting the pass, take the right fork towards Blue and Dark Canyon Lakes.

8.9 The peak ahead of you with the columnar escarpment is Mt. Peale. During this descent, the spur road to the right enters an old logging area that has some extraordinary alpine beauty. (The noisy water pipe buried beneath this road led the author to wonder about the origins of the name, "Geyser.")

10.8 Bear right, onto the acute, cobbly doubletrack. The Carsonite marker on the continuation indicates the Mt. Peale Loop, a long, all-road tour over both Geyser and La Sal Passes laid out by the Forest Service's Pat Spahr.

12.0 (R) A prominent acute singletrack parallels the road for half a mile, if you feel like taking it.

12.5 Both routes "T" at a graded gravel road. Go downhill from here.

13.0 An obtuse doubletrack to the right is the critical spur to Sheepherders' Heaven, and you are entitled to pass through the drift fence and the encampment beyond to pick up the singletrack around Mt. Peale.

13.9 The track "T's" into another track near a drift fence. Take it right, through the pole-sliding gate and out into the "beaver-ized" zone of muddy lakes. Peel left, onto a very discreet singletrack in about 0.3 of a mile. (If the track crosses the gash in a shallow old earthen levee, you've gone 100 feet too far. Rocks on the levee may direct you correctly the first time.)

14.7 Stay right, as the trail forks to ascend a low hill and enter the aspens. Herds of elk glory in country like this. Chafe marks on the aspen are signs of velvet rubbing off of developing antlers, but the obvious tooth-gnawing gouges on the aspen reflect the elks' ability to get their chlorophyll during the winter when snow covers the forage. Where you come to another gate, a ranch is visible ahead. After passing through, stay to the right of the aspen-log drift fence to circumvent the ranch, crossing gullies as necessary. Pick up the doubletrack (the ranch access road) over to its "T" at the La Sal Pass Road (mile 15.7).

18.4 From La Sal Pass, the rocky road descends to the Trans La Sal Trail for the final singletrack leg of the route. (An option that still-fresh riders might want to explore is the singletrack that connects to the Trans La Sal. It is reached by going left on this doubletrack (F.S. Rd. 237) and can be followed in the Route Description of the La Sal Pass Figure "8" ride.)

20.2 Avoid the old switchbacks of the La Sal Pass Road by following the sign right, towards Pack Creek.

21.7 (L) Discreet obtuse singletrack forged into the oakbrush is where the optional singletrack emerges.

21.9 At a steep meadow on the right, an obtuse doubletrack cuts up into the forest. A "TRAIL" sign may indicate this spur to the Trans La Sal Trail.

After crossing two springfed creeks, the doubletrack abuts a scree slope. Dash some of these rocks together to smell their sweet smoky scent. The gate further ahead is a beautiful example of a lever arm latch; use of the suspended "bat" to lever the slip over the posts can be undertaken without threat of being gashed by barbed wire.

23.0 From the head of the meadow below the gate, the trail crosses the springfed creek and wraps around the old cabin to switchback up through the oaks for a 0.2 of a mile portage. (Avoid the road that leaves the meadow back towards its mouth.) The trail crests the hill at a dark, shaly slump and continues north toward another strip of aspens. There are many cow trails, but one trail is most prominent.

23.8 A cairn and cairned post mark the divide before your descent across Dorry Canyon.

24.7 Just after passing the cairned post, turn 90° left to take the fall line. Branches arranged on the ground have been used to show the way in years past.

26.0 Trailhead/-tail

(clockwise from top left) sacred datura
cottonwood
claret cup cactus
columbine

SHEEPHERDERS' HEAVEN A

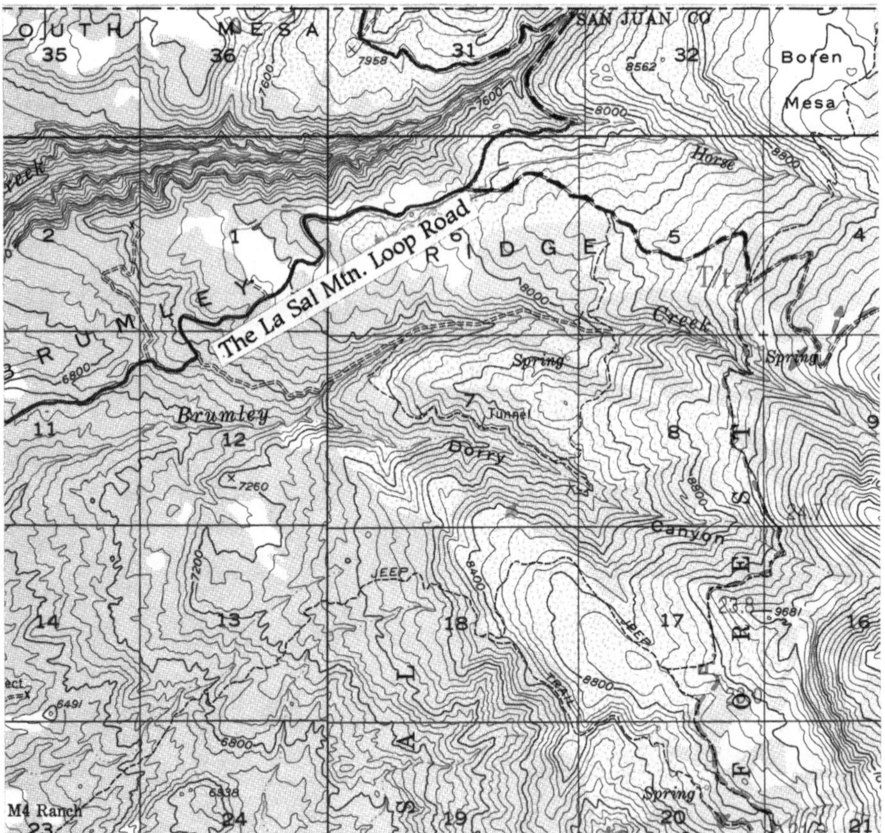

SHEEPHERDERS' HEAVEN B

Mike Campbell on the Trans La Sal

LA SAL PASS

Type: Figure "8" Loop
Length: 21.2 miles
Difficulty: Physically gonzo-abusive / Technically difficult
Best Season: Mid-June through October
Elevation: Trailhead/-tail—6,400 ft., High—10,280 ft., Low—6,040 ft.
Land Agency: USFS
Route Summary: This ride starts by climbing the rugged La Sal Pass Road from near the Pack Creek Picnic Area all the way to the pass. A spur from the pass goes to a watershed control terracing project, where a singletrack traverses the ridgeline which defines the upper Pack Creek drainage. The track zigzags through a magnificent piece of forest, bypassing two potential connecting roads to the Pass Road before finally intersecting it by means of a singletrack. A 1.3 mile descent on the La Sal Pass Road is the recrossed ground in the "8." A rough-and-tumble 4 mile descent on a shifty old roadbed finds you at the boundary of a private ranch, where with care taken not to disturb any horseback riders, you can ride the horse trail that parallels Pack Creek up to near its Picnic Area.
Options: Besides the option of being able to turn around at any point on the Pass Road, you can make a longer loop of it by extending the rough-and-tumble descent to cross Dorry Canyon for Brumley Creek, where a route intersects the Loop Road.
Attractions: This ride offers the most exciting singletrack riding in the La Sals. It taxes endurance, finesse and brute strength. And it affords peeps of Hell Canyon that'll make you want to assign it a "project number" on your list of places to explore. (Yes, this approach to exploring makes you a "project-ile.") The views of Canyonlands are, as always, a good excuse to rest.
Riding Surface: Both hardpacked and loose, rock-studded sediments and loam on a one-laned jeep trail and singletrack
Notes: In the future, the South Mountain singletrack will probably be cleared to allow for a mostly singletrack loop of the mountain from La Sal Pass counterclockwise back to itself. The descent portion of the Figure "8" ride could then be tacked on to this loop to make a "career" ride.
Logistics: No permit or shuttle is necessary.
Trailhead Access: From Main x Center St.'s in Moab, head south on Highway 191 for about 7.9 miles to take the Loop Road spur towards the "Picnick" area, which "T's" in a half mile. Go right to climb towards the mountain on Spanish Valley Drive, taking the spur right in another 4.9 miles for a final 2.8 mile drive to a point just beyond the Picnic Area. After avoiding the dead end road **(R)**, the (unposted) parking area and trailhead is on the left a turn away.

Mileage Log and Route Description:
0.0 The Pass is an arduous 9 miles and 4,000 feet before you. Unlike the

Geyser Pass Road, the La Sal Pass Road would require a four-wheel drive vehicle to surmount.

4.1 (L) This obtuse spur road is part of the suggested return route.

5.4 (R) A discreet singletrack intersects the road—the very one you'll be emerging from later.

9.7 At this "fat man's fence," carry through the labyrinth to the terracing, immediately dropping down two benches for easy contouring. As you near a green stake fence, a gate through it is a couple hundred feet down slope, but it's as easy to step over it and continue. All braids of the track come together to parallel an orange stake fence. Watch out for errant pieces of barbed wire as you bypass deadfall close to the fenceline.

10.6 In this grassy clearing, you'll want to bear right 90° from the half-55 gallon drum which is used to keep the livestock's salt out of the soil.

11.4 The trail crosses a (usually) dry creekbed as it comes into view of the first of two dark ponds. Although the route zigs (obtuse left) from here, you may not notice until you find yourself on a doubletrack heading back towards the Pass Road.

12.0 After passing the cattle trough and entering a thin forest, a primitive blockade of tree limbs means to guide your imminent zag (obtuse right). If you miss it, the trail peters out at a ridgeline overlook of Canyonlands that ought to be seen anyway.

12.4 Just before crossing a creeklet, take the track that continues downhill to the left. The trail swings right again as you descend into a clearing, quickly going left, then right again to mount a climb out of the clearing. (From this clearing, the Hell Canyon Trail continues down to Pack Creek, where the name becomes more and more suitable. A route for determined trials riders.)

13.6 (Previously mile 5.4) Take a left on the La Sal Pass Road.

14.9 (Previously mile 4.1) Take the acute spur onto the final descent.

16.7 By continuing straight past this spur left, you could cross Dorry Canyon to get to Brumley Creek and the Loop Road, but the recommended route goes left on this spur. The "chained" area of uprooted trees was probably done to increase graze for livestock, even though no viable grass seems to grow here. Chaining is also executed to provide winter forage for game species. The Forest Service has formal protocols guiding chaining proposals and public input to them. Environmental organizations keep abreast of these changes, and can help you "cast your vote" by telling you whom and when to write regarding land use policy.

17.5 The road drops left off this ridge where a few pinyon pines still stand. Take a right on the next possible spur (to avoid the washed out road around the corner). You are approaching a ranch which offers trail rides by horseback that commonly use this area. Be alert for them, ready to stop and dismount if encountered.

19.7 As the track approaches a fenceline, then a gate through it, take the obtuse left singletrack down the hill, going left at the "T" and staying left to parallel Pack Creek back towards the Picnic Area. When the track becomes overgrown, look for the chute to the creek with the track up the other side to the pavement.

21.2 Trailhead/-tail

Other Roads / Rides in the La Sals

Two scenic out-and-backs from the Castleton-Gateway Road access Adobe and Fisher Mesas, which provide views of Castle Rock, the Priest and Nuns, Fisher Towers, the Colorado River, and various other redrock canyons. The upper Sand Flats Road is pretty ponderosa country, and the short Kokopelli Trail connector from it to the Loop Road is recommended riding. Spurs off the Geyser Pass Road to Boren Mesa and three others to Brumley Creek are nice. The uppermost of the three accesses Gold Basin, a popular three-pin area. The middle-elevation one terminates beneath the cliffline that graced the cover of <u>Outside</u> Magazine's Little Known Places issue of 1990. The lowest one, near the Loop Road, provides a fun alternate route back to the Loop Road lower down the mountain. The loop up the Lackey Basin road and down via Pole or Doe Canyons could make a sound, short loop. The road up Beaver Basin is quite nice, especially in the fall, but Beaver Pass is a better hike than bike ride. The John Brown Canyon descent 3,500 feet to Gateway, Colorado on a gravel road can set you up for the climb up opposing Ute Canyon onto the Uncompahgre Plateau, the high road to Telluride. And lastly, the forest service has Carsonite-posted the South Mountain Loop, a thirty-mile route from the Pack Creek Picnic Area up Pack Creek, across Carpenter Basin, past Coyote Spring and up and over La Sal Pass.

Some roads to stay away from due to their general teeth-gritting, kidney-jarring orneriness include the Entrada Bluffs Road, from Fisher Valley to Dewey (although a few miles up from Dewey, slickrock routefinding can take you to a nice Dolores River Overlook), the Pinhook Draw "road" between the Pinhook Battleground and Castleton, and most of the redundant, rocky roads in the pinyon/juniper zone to the west and south of the La Sals.

LA SAL PASS A

SAN JUAN CO   SAN JUAN

LA SAL PASS B

8562 32   Boren 33   34   Haystack Mtn 35   10800 36
Mesa   1642

Horse   9800   Geyser Pass   Spring
E   5   4   Creek   3   2   1
9970   10800

Creek   Spring   10000

8   9   10   11   12
Mt Mellanthin   11302
2646

Canyon   Gold
Basin   Horse

17   9681   16   15   14   13
Dark
12207
12050   1230

Spring
20   21   Mt Tukuhnikivatz   23   Mt Peale 24
Canyon   22   12488   VABM 13721
1260

Spring
28   27   26   25
10400

La Sal Pass   Medicine Lake

32   33   34   35   36
1253

South
Mtn   1798
1022   1535

Spring

5   9200   10800
1142

Elk Ridge dreaming

The Abajos Area

The Abajo (aka Blue) Mountains are a range of "island mountains" near the town of Monticello. They are forested in lodgepole pine, Douglas fir and aspen, and have two small manmade lakes on their northern skirt. The summit is called Abajo Peak, in Spanish—"Lower" peak, because at 11,360 feet, it is lower than Mt. Peale (12,721) in the La Sals to the north. The suggested rides leave from trailheads on the North Creek Road, a pavement and gravel connector between Monticello and Blanding, a town further south. As these trailheads occur high in the two communities' culinary watersheds, you are forbidden to camp here. However, there are many beautiful undeveloped campsites further down the mountain in meadows and glades.

Outtake #5   Trees in a treeless land

High desert groundcover shades only 5-15% of the sandy soil from the sun. Lower elevation plants are scaly, spiky and scrappy, reflecting in their appearance the tenacity of survival in a harsh environment. Between 5,000 and 7,500 feet the pinyon pine and juniper "pygmy" forest dominates the land, a blanket of dark green rent here and there by a canyon. The juniper tree seems molded by the desert, twisted by wind and stunted by drought. Its scale-like leaves and compact size help it minimize evaporation loss. And its classic partly-dead silhouette is indicative of another water-conserving trait: in particularly dry times, the tree will cut off the sap flow to selected limbs, thereby insuring life to its remaining growth.

Cottonwood trees are always found at water sources, and as such are the shade tree of the American southwest. Yet the cottonwood/willow plant community is the rarest of this nation's 104 such communities. One finds cottonwoods in potholes on the Slickrock Trail, in stock ponds on the White Rim, and near springs at unexpected points along many a sandy road. But mostly, they grace riversides and old homesteads along the canyon floors, as they live to be a hundred years old or more.

The aspen trees are the climax community, or most mature species, in forests between 8,000 and 10,000 feet. A beautiful white-barked deciduous tree, the aspen produces four times more food and cover than pine, fir and other evergreens, thereby supporting a greater diversity of plant and animal life. An individual aspen reproduces by cloning itself with small interconnecting shoots from its root system, a system which doubles as a filter, effectively yielding a cleaner quality of water than that found in other forest types.

Like the cottonwood, the aspen turns a vibrant gold in the fall, a color which somehow draws forth a nostalgia, an understanding for and appreciation of the mortality of things.

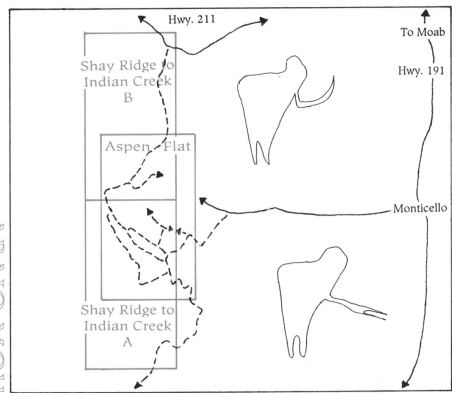

Hwy. 211

Shay Ridge to
Indian Creek
B

Aspen Flat

Shay Ridge to
Indian Creek
A

To Moab

Hwy. 191

Monticello

The Abajos as seen from the Needles' Horse Canyon

ASPEN FLAT

Type: Loop
Length: 8.4 miles
Difficulty: Physically difficult / Technically difficult
Best Seasons: Mid-May through October
Elevation: High—9,540 ft., Low—8,320 ft., Trailhead/-tail—9,275 ft.
Land Agency: USFS
Route Summary: From one of the culinary canals, the singletrack climbs up to Bear Creek on the flank of Shay Ridge to work its way across to Aspen Flat, a grassy clearing reigned over by a single aspen. The route doubles back from here on the Red Ledges Trail, dipping across Indian Creek before exacting a 0.35 of a mile portage to a short access trail which loops back to the trailhead/-tail via the North Creek Road.
Options: From the Aspen Flat Trail's intersection with the short access trail, a turn away from the North Creek Road offers a very rugged hike-a-bike beneath the Red Ledges proper which can take you to Robertson Pasture, a picturesque piece of mountainside that offers two more trail options. The Aspen Flat part of the route can be tacked onto the Shay Ridge Trail to provide a nice loop as well.
Attractions: A short loop through a beautiful forest
Riding Surface: Hardpacked singletrack and a mile of gravel road
Geology: The "laccolithic" origins of all of southern Utah's island mountains means they are would-be volcanoes that never vented to the surface. Only erosion could bare the remains of the cooled, solidified magma to the surface, and its erosional resilience is made obvious by the mountains' height over the surrounding country.
Logistics: No permit or shuttle is necessary.
Trailhead Access: The town of Monticello is 55 miles south of Moab on Highway 191. From 200 (or 2nd) South and Hwy. 191, turn toward the mountains and climb the Blue Mountain Road about 5 miles before turning left onto the signed North Creek Road (or F.S. Rd. 79). This gravel road winds up North Canyon to crest a pass and descend across upper Indian Creek, and about 8.5 miles from the Blue Mtn. Rd., a spur to the right may be denoted by a brown, Carsonite "grape stake" with "TRAIL 018" on it, the Aspen Flat Trail. Descend the spur a short ways to a trailhead parking area near the culinary canal.

Mileage Log and Route Description:

0.0 Start off west on the doubletrack, almost immediately crossing the canal to its right side embankment.
0.3 Upon coming back up to the canal, look for the trail marker directly across the canal in the woods. Get your granny for the grunt ahead and keep her engaged through the false summits.

0.6 Look 30° left from the two central aspens in this second glade for a rock cairn and trail "tunnel through the trees."

2.0 Short, stiff portage at Bear Creek

2.5 After leaving Bear Creek's south fork, look for the cairned post **(L)** to turn upslope 45°, thereby avoiding the vague trail which continues ahead on a fall line.

3.9 After you weave through the forest on many split trails, this large clearing is Aspen Flat. Before you leave the treeline for the clearing, look sharply to your right, where you'll see the Red Ledges Trail, the route back to the trailhead/-tail. (If you've enjoyed this trail so far, consider continuing down past the intersection with the Shay Ridge road and going left at the "T" beyond for the stupendous view of the Needles country from Shay Saddle. You could even hike-a-bike the road up to the top of Shay Mountain if so moved.)

4.7 Where the trail seems to end at the cow wallow in this steep glade, turn 90° right, up the hill to find the trail.

5.4 At the technical descent into Indian Creek, go downstream 100 feet to ride across just below the confluence of two creeklets. On crossing, angle upstream to improvise a trail across the shale until you spy it again next to the creek.

6.1 After this weaving, wiggling, jiving and juking, the trail abruptly climbs away from the creek. Upon shouldering your bike, switchback left, at your first opportunity.

6.5 Where two cairns or rockpiles sit at the top of the climb, stay right to contour the hillside. In 100 feet, another cairn or rockpile marks the junction with the short access trail back to the North Creek Road. (Be forewarned that going left to continue on the Red Ledges Trail requires a considerable tolerance for hike-a-biking and routefinding, though it accesses beautiful Robertson Pasture. From Robertson, you could either descend the furrowed singletrack to Spring (Foy) Lake, or climb back up to the North Creek Road.)

7.3 After passing through the gate, look for a headgate on the culinary canal down to your right, from where you can pedal up the short road to the North Creek road for the one mile ride back to the trailhead/-tail.

8.4 Trailhead/-tail

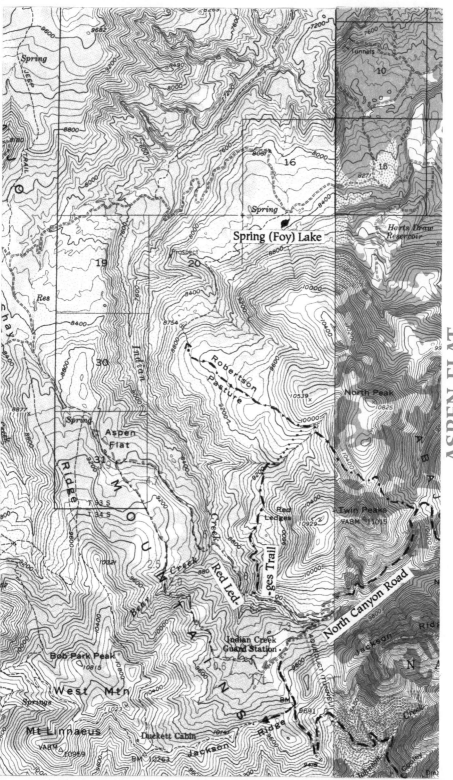

ASPEN FLAT

SHAY RIDGE TO INDIAN CREEK

Type: One-way
Length: 17.2 miles
Difficulty: Physically difficult / Technically difficult
Best Seasons: Mid-June through October
Elevation: Trailhead—9,685 ft., High—10,850 ft., Trailtail/Low—6,100 ft.
Land Agency: USFS
Route Summary: 2.5 miles of climbing up Jackson Ridge and around Bob Park Peak raise the singletrack to the crest of Shay Ridge, where views across Canyonlands rival the views clear to New Mexico as seen from Jackson Ridge. The singletrack descent gets exceedingly steep before it intersects a doubletrack and the junction of the Shay Mountain Road on Shay Saddle. Before crossing Indian Creek, an inconspicuously narrow roadcut marks the lower leg of this ride, a challenging singletrack to Highway 211 near Newspaper Rock State Park.
Options: The Shay Ridge leg of this ride can connect to the Aspen Flat trail to make a fine loop.
Attractions: The diversity of foliage one can see includes spruce, fir, aspen, ponderosa, pinyon, juniper, oakbrush, cottonwood, sage, and any number of wildflowers (depending upon which elevation is enjoying "spring"), like desert mallow, iris, wild rose and columbine. Views from this ride are equally outstanding, and they include Shiprock, Monument Valley, Comb Ridge, Cathedral Butte, Land's End, and the Henry Mountains. It descends 4,750 hedonistic feet, so make sure you carry an extra brake cable. There is something very stilling about being on top of the world with a bicycle, nothing but a skinny track to keep you tethered to REALITY.
Riding Surface: Hardpacked to sandy singletrack and doubletrack on gravel and hardpacked jeep trails and two-laned dirt roads
Geology: (Refer to the Aspen Flat "Geology" summary.)
Notes: Pack a long sleeved shirt and a pair of Levi's along to ward off possible overgrown rose bushes on the Indian Creek singletrack.
Logistics: The shuttle involves leaving a vehicle at or near Newspaper Rock State Park, which is accessed by going about 15 miles on Highway 211 from its junction with Highway 191 (42 miles south of Moab).
Trailhead Access: The town of Monticello is 55 miles south of Moab on Highway 191. From 200 (or 2nd) South and Hwy. 191, turn toward the mountains and climb the Blue Mountain Road about 5 miles before turning left onto the signed North Creek Road (or F.S. Rd. 79). This gravel road winds up North Canyon to crest a pass and descend across upper Indian Creek, and about 9 miles after leaving the Blue Mtn. Rd., the trailhead **(R)** at the road up Jackson Ridge may be denoted by a brown Carsonite "grape stake" with "TRAIL 115" on it, the Shay Ridge Trail. The North Creek Road plummets down to Blanding beyond Jackson Ridge.

Mileage Log and Route Description:

0.0 Surprisingly different views are allowed with each break in the trees as you climb up Jackson Ridge.

1.6 (L) "TRAIL 015," the skinny sidehill to Allen Canyon is ridable, and makes an okay ride to the Causeway.

1.8 After passing the wooden sign **(L)**, turn right, off the doubletrack at a lone boulder just before the road forks. An inobvious singletrack threads through the timber and climbs around the east side of Bob Park Peak. There is usually snow here until mid-June.

4.1 (L) This trail to Blue Creek (014) is a steep descent which continues over to the white sandstone cliffs of Tuerto Canyon.

6.9 (L) After passing the Tuerto Canyon Trail (011), you come to the Aspen Flat trail **(R)**, number 018. You could take this back on the Aspen Flat Trail to the trailhead at Jackson Ridge, a quality ride of over six more miles to close a loop.

7.8 (L) "TRAIL 022," the Hop Creek trail to Cottonwood Canyon appears to be completely and irretrievably overgrown. Before continuing right, from the junction of the Shay Mountain Road, take a quick trip over to the edge of Shay Saddle for a fine view of the upper Cottonwood Canyon and Needles areas.

> Above six thousand feet, the pinyon-juniper woodlands
> spread as far as the eye can see, uphill, across valleys, and
> over mountaintops, looking like huge blue-black blankets torn
> where cliffs and canyons break the surface.

Weldon Heald, <u>Sky Island</u>, 1967

9.9 Don't miss this narrow spur to the left as you speedball along. It is reduced to an ATV track, then a singletrack, as it parallels Indian Creek out to Highway 211. Low branches, sand and washout bypasses make this an exciting route. There is but one stream crossing, and it occurs on the home stretch.

17.1 Watch out for the barbed wire gate on the blind corner just before reaching the highway. Take a left on the pavement to reach Newspaper Rock.

17.2 Trailtail

SHAY RIDGE TO INDIAN CREEK A

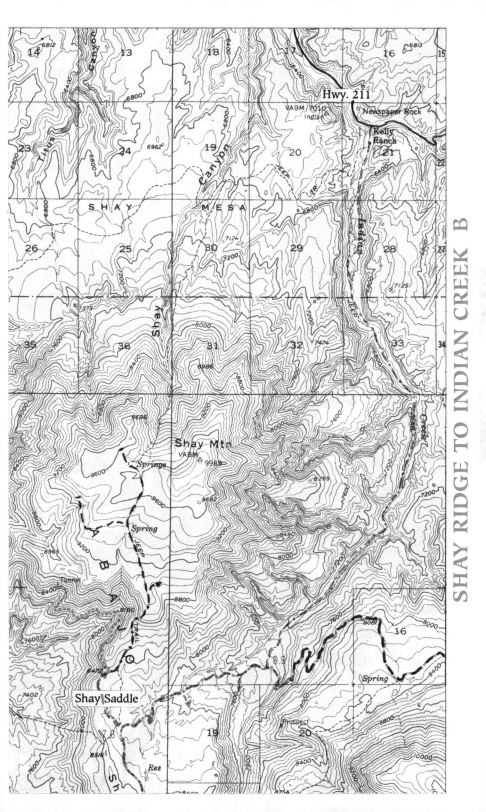

SHAY RIDGE TO INDIAN CREEK   B

Other Roads / Rides in the Abajos

Although the Abajos' fine trail system has abundant and intricately connected trails, they require a persistent, patient and strong mountain biker to be enjoyed. In other words, most of them keep you off the bike as much as you're on it. Those that might appeal to a rider profile like this include the many trails mentioned which intersect the two rides detailed, as well as the Shay Mountain Trail from the mountain's top to either Cottonwood Canyon or Indian Creek, the latter of these the "better." The crown jewel of abusiveness is the route from North Creek Pass up a ridiculously steep mud-slope portage to Cooley Pass and the Gold Queen Basin Road near Abajo Peak's radio towers for the paintshaking-machine ride down to Monticello.

Abajo Mountain scenes

The Elk Ridge Area

Elk Ridge is an 8,000-foot alpine ridge over twenty miles long that roughly parallels the Abajo Mountain range to the east. It is unique in that you can pedal out any of its limbed spurs through aspen and ponderosa forests to views of dramatic, slickrock-hemmed canyons. The Ridge functions as a divide of sorts, for canyons draining its west and north flanks augment the Colorado River, and canyons draining the east and south flow to the San Juan River. With a Wilderness and Primitive Area on its west, a National Park to its north, a National Monument to its south, and a National Forest east of it, the Ridge dominates one of the west's more hallowed geographies.

ELK RIDGE

Type: One way multi-day trip (usually 2-3 days)
Length: 55.5 miles
Difficulty: Physically easy / Technically easy
Best Seasons: Mid-April through October, but avoid when wet due to clay soils
Elevation: Trailhead—6,880 ft., High—8,760 ft., Low, Trailtail—5,320 ft.
Land Agencies: USFS and BLM
Route Summary: After the six mile climb from the trailhead to the two matching outcrops called the Bears Ears, this route is more or less level and downhill. Dozens of spurs lead to great viewpoints and camp spots as you traverse the Ridge on two-wheel drive roads, and ultimately it drops off the Ridge proper to Salt Creek Mesa, where views of the Needles area's complex canyons are astounding. The route then descends into Cottonwood Canyon, first traveling the rim above its inner gorge, and later, splashing across its creek several times before reaching its end at Dugout Ranch and Highway 211.
Options: Popular alternatives include spurs to Blanding via the Causeway and (especially) to the Needles by way of Beef Basin.
Attractions: Beside its extraordinary beauty, Elk Ridge offers explorers the chance to collate the canyons below for routes into them. During wet years, certain glades on the Ridge fill deep enough to be swimmable. Deer are abundant, as are signs of bear and cat. One can auto tour Natural Bridges National Monument before the ride in just a 25 mile round trip, and visit the Needles District of Canyonlands National Park after the ride.
Riding Surface: Packed sediments, rock-studded sediments and clay on two-laned dirt roads.
Geology: Most of Elk Ridge proper travels across the Wingate formation, the layer of massive burnt orange cliffs that so prevalently define the Canyonlands

basin. However, this fact is obscured by vegetation, until you reach an overlook, that is, and can identify formations by their standing with regard to one another. The Bears Ears (mile 6.0) show orange Wingate through a heavily patinated surface, but this is the only obvious evidence of the Ridge's geologic makeup for the next thirty miles.

The many overlooks to which you can pedal reveal the canyons below to be in the Cedar Mesa sandstone, a massive white layer that erodes into curvilinear slickrock shelves. As you gain your first views north to the Needles area (mile 34.2), you'll notice the red and white banded appearance of its rock. This striping is the result of the interfingering of two distinct sediment types. As this area was the site of an ancient seashore, a "tide" of its advances and retreats some 250 million years ago is recorded in the rock, which erosion has brought to surface for our viewing pleasure. Thus, the rock's red-colored aspect, called the Cutler sandstone, represents the freshwater deposits that were washed off the mountains and laid down as the sea receded, and the white rock is the Cedar Mesa, a sediment brought in with any of the (at least 29 distinct) advancing marine environments.

The road surface at mile 34.2 is in the Chinle formation, its resilient Mossback member the layer which defines and protects Salt Creek Mesa. The road surface may exhibit the fossilized tire ruts that testify to the high clay content of Chinle. The (Wingate) Boundary and Cathedral Buttes are visible shortly after this point, but like the Bears Ears and Horse Mountain, their geologic identities are not nearly as vivid as the rows of Wingate cliffs that soar clear of Elk Ridge to define Cottonwood Canyon. The Chinle soils at mile 43.0 span a range of colors that are caused by oxidized minerals, fairly representing a typical slope of this formation in southern Utah's canyonlands.

Logistics: A lengthy shuttle is the sticking point with this ride, which, beside the need for a rugged sag wagon, is why many people do it with tour outfitters. Companies and individuals out of Moab can provide anything from shuttle service to full support, and a comprehensive list of them can be gotten by contacting the **Grand County Travel Council at 805 N. Main St., Moab, Utah 84532; ph. (801) 259-8825.** No permit is necessary.

Trailhead Access: Go 78 miles south on Highway 191 through Monticello and Blanding to turn west on Highway 95. In about 32 miles, turn onto Highway 275 (towards Natural Bridges) and proceed for 0.7 of a mile to an unposted gravel road on the right—the trailhead. (Another road on the right just beyond this goes to Deer Flat.) If you leave a vehicle at the trailhead, park it in one of the nearby turnouts adjacent to Highway 275.

To leave a shuttle vehicle at ride's end, take Highway 211 towards the Needles District from Hwy. 191, about 42 miles south of Moab. In another 19 miles, take the left turn onto a gravel road where you see buildings (of Dugout Ranch). You might ask the owner to allow you to park somewhere on the ranch property, but without permission, make sure to leave your vehicle on public property beyond the cattleguard/gate that is just past the buildings.

Descending towards Salt Creek's banded slickrock canyons on the Elk Ridge Trail

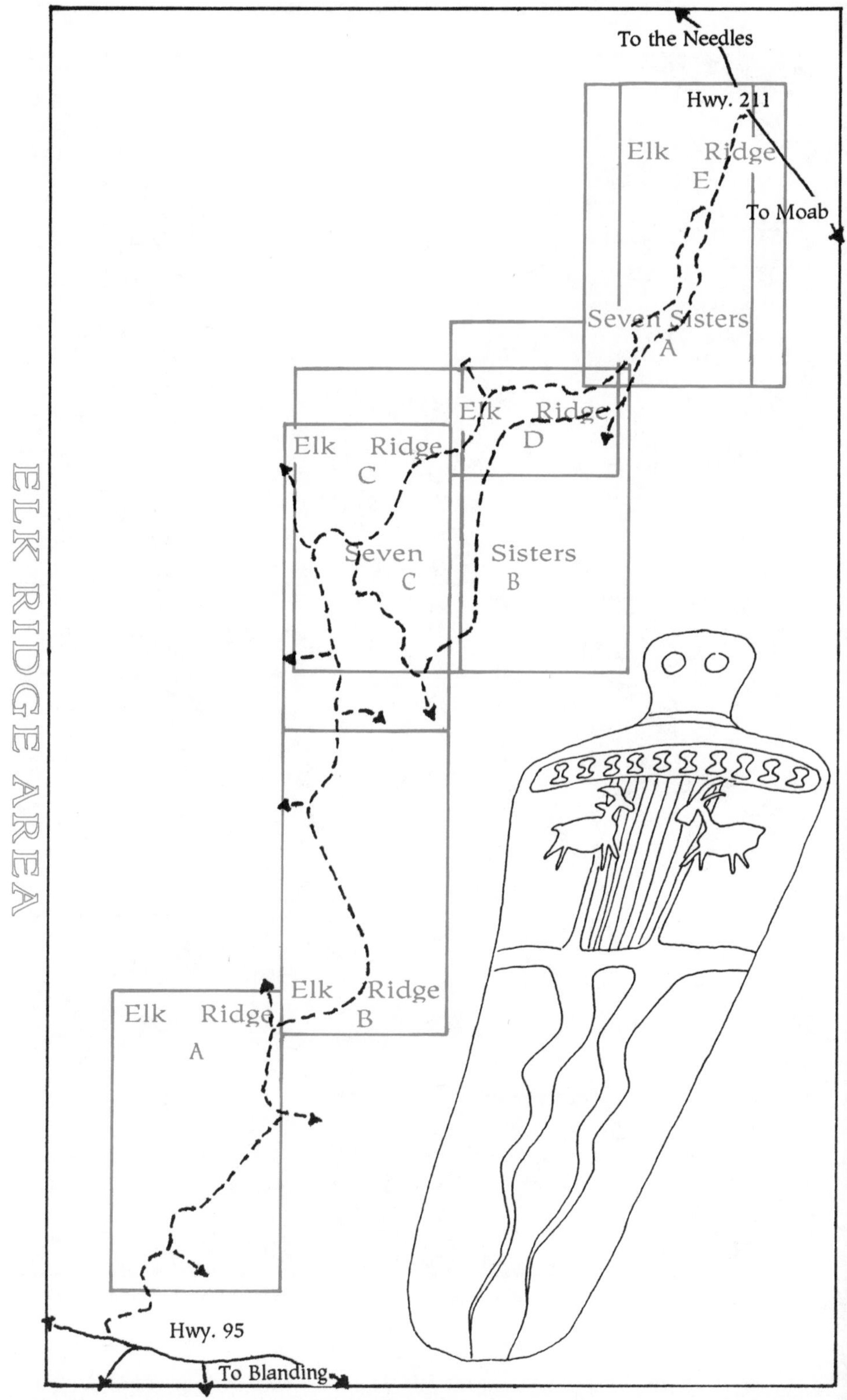

ELK RIDGE AREA
To the Needles
Hwy. 211
Elk Ridge E
To Moab
Seven Sisters A
Elk Ridge D
Elk Ridge C
Seven C
Sisters B
Elk Ridge B
Elk Ridge A
Hwy. 95
To Blanding

ELK RIDGE A

ELK RIDGE B

To Beef Basin

To the Causeway

ELK RIDGE C

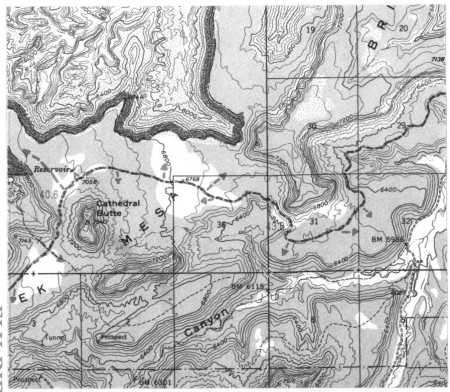

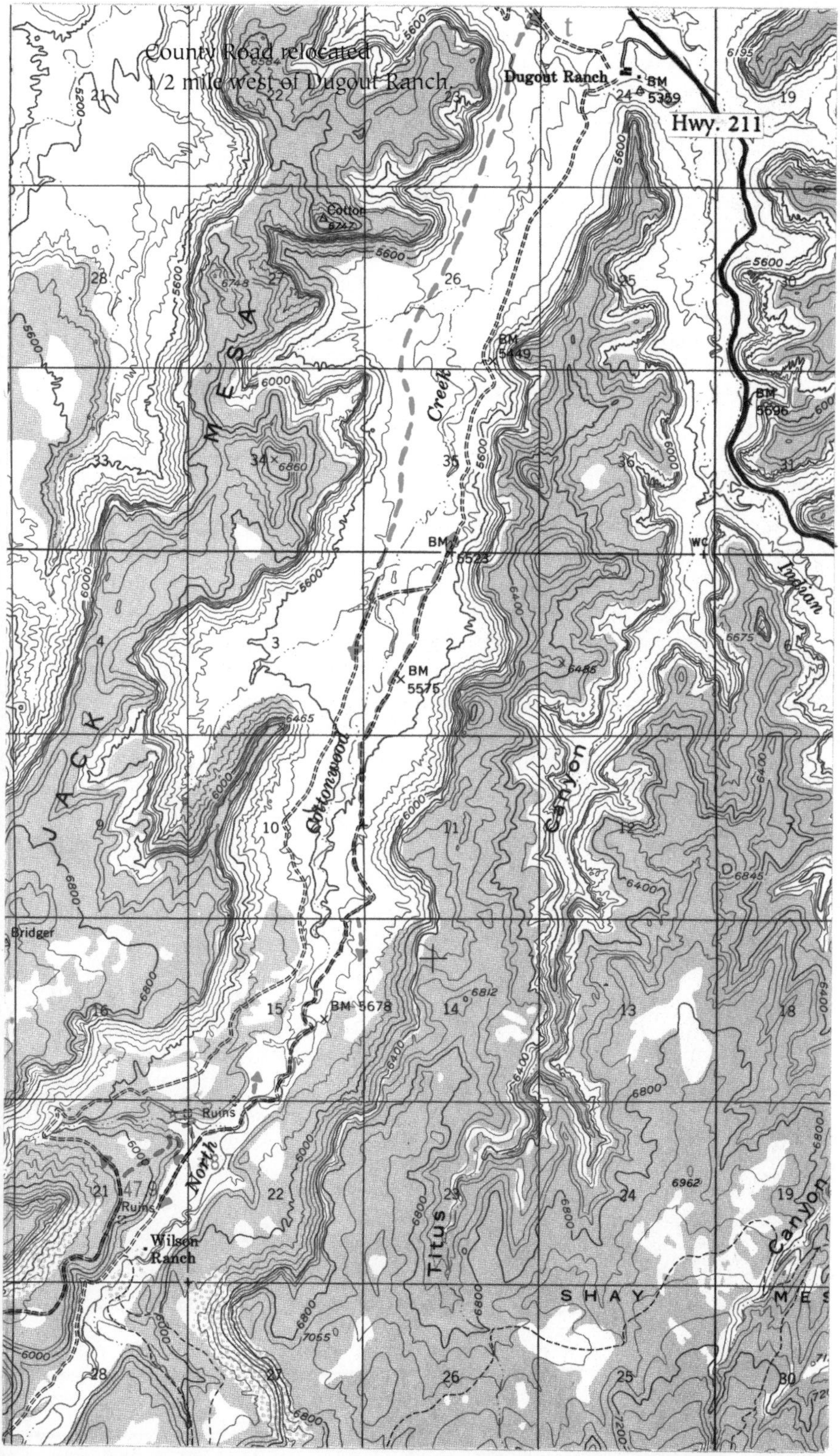

County Road relocated
1/2 mile west of Dugout Ranch

Dugout Ranch

BM
5389

Hwy. 211

Cotto...

BM
5449

BM
5696

M E S A

6000

BM
5523

BM
5575

J A C K

Creek

Cottonwood

Canyon

Indian

BM 5678

Bridger

Ruins

North

Ruins

Wilson
Ranch

Titus

Canyon

S H A Y

M E S

WC

5465

5468

6812

6845

6962

7055

6660

Mileage Log and Route Description:
0.0 Begin the six mile climb up through the pinyon-juniper forest to the Bears Ears. (Note: the trailhead is not quite on the Elk Ridge A map)
6.0 Bears Ears pass
11.6 (L) This is the critical intersection of the route. Take the obtuse left spur towards "Big Notch" and "Gooseberry Guard Station" on North Elk Ridge
19.2 The Notch is one of those classic places with "duelling views": something like "Channel Change Gap" on the Lockhart Basin ride; "The Causeway" on the Elk Ridge-Blanding connecting road by the same name; and "The Neck," near Land's End. Chippean Ridge and the Abajo Mountains backdrop Notch Canyon to the east, and the Dark Canyon Wilderness recedes to the west.
20.7 (L) North Notch Spring is a sight worth "drinking in."
25.3 (R) Gooseberry Guard Station is a quaint place where water can be hand pumped into your bottle.
26.6 Another critical intersection at which to turn left. A right goes to Blanding via the Causeway Road (F.S. Rd. 95).
28.5 (R) This acute doubletrack offers some alternative ways to Dugout Ranch. (Consult the Seven Sisters C map for ideas.)
34.2 (R) Possible spur connector from mile 28.5.
40.6 (L) Rough 2.8 mile spur to Cathedral Point—a truly glorious sight...

> Save a piece of country like that intact, and it does not matter in the slightest that only a few people every year will go into it. That is precisely its value...
>
> But those who haven't the strength or youth to go into it and live with it can still drive up...and simply sit and look.
>
> And if they can't even get to the places...where the present roads will carry them, they can simply contemplate the idea, take pleasure in the fact that such a timeless and uncontrolled part of the earth is still there.

Wallace Stegner, <u>The Wilderness Idea</u>, 1961

43.0 (L) The end of Bridger Jack Mesa looms above you. Bridger Jack was one of San Juan County's earliest residents, a man considered by settlers to be the "handsome-est, friendliest, and smartest" Ute Indian around. Jack was shot dead by his "best friend" in a showdown resulting from a poker dispute.
47.9 Take the acute right turn here if you don't mind getting your bike wet. If you continue straight, the two routes will intersect in 5.0 miles.
48.7 (L) This box canyon has some well preserved native American ruins. Please don't lean or walk on the structures.
55.5 Trailtail at Highway 211.

The view of Arch Canyon from Point Disgusting

High desert lightning over Canyonlands National Park

THE SEVEN SISTERS BUTTES

Type: Loop
Length: 43.4 miles
Difficulty: Physically moderate to difficult / Technically moderate
Best Seasons: Spring and fall, but avoid when wet due to clay soils
Elevation: Trailhead/-tail, Low—5,500 ft., High—8,140 ft.

Land Agencies: BLM and USFS

Route Summary: This route starts with a long, consistent, in-the-saddle climb up Cottonwood Canyon's "high road" that gains 2,600 feet in 18.6 miles. It climbs along Salt Creek Mesa, then pitches into the oak brush on a washed out jeep road that contours around Horse Mountain. At almost exactly the halfway point in the ride, gravity starts to assist aching muscles as the trail perimeters the Seven Sisters on its way down Stevens Canyon to Cottonwood Canyon, where it uses the "low road" to loop back to the trailhead. If there is advantage to pedalling the route counterclockwise (the way it is written up), it is 1) the climb's surface is smoother than the descent's or 2) your bike's chain won't get wetted by stream water until the last few miles of the ride.

Attractions: Native American ruins and great views amidst a sub-alpine environment

Riding Surface: Hardpacked and loose sediments on two-laned dirt roads and jeep trails

Geology: (Refer to the Elk Ridge "Geology" summary)

Logistics: No shuttle or permit is necessary.

Trailhead Access: From Moab, go south on Highway 191 about 42 miles to the Needles entrance road, Highway 211. In almost 20 miles, shortly after passing the gravel turnoff to Dugout Ranch, take the following left onto a dirt road which sets a wide and straight path up Cottonwood Canyon. In just over three miles, a conspicuous cottonwood tree grove reachable by a quick detour across the creek is the saddling-up point.

Mileage Log and Route Description:

0.0 From a discreet parking area in the vicinity of the cottonwood grove, begin the long gradual climb up to Salt Creek Mesa.

18.6 Take this discreet-looking spur left, which pushes up through the oaks and bends out of sight. After passing through the gate atop the hill, skirt along this "e-road" to switchback down across the drainage to your right.

20.4 Where the road splits into two singletracks, take either up to a clearing where several vague roads intersect. Continue on the prominent, red dirt one.

21.0 Take the acute spur that descends to the left, and in less than a mile, you'll see the southernmost of the Seven Sisters Buttes, which this ride completely encircles.

25.2 Bear right, at the spur towards "Mormon Pasture."

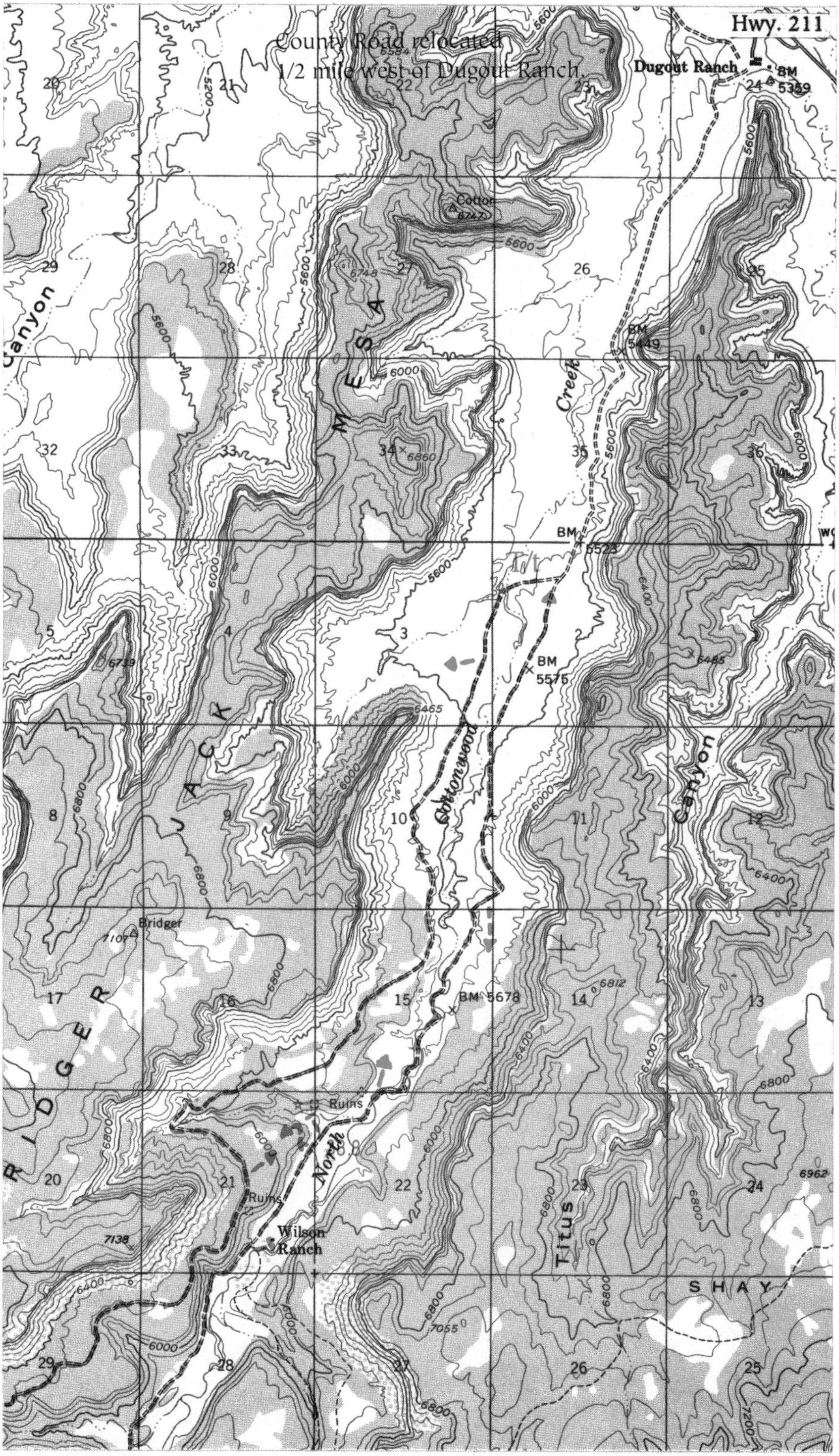

County Road relocated
1/2 mile west of Dugout Ranch.

Hwy. 211

Dugout Ranch

BM 5389

Cotton 6242

BM 5449

BM 5522

BM 5575

BM 5465

BM 5678

BM 5678 6812

Bridger

Ruins

North

Ruins

Wilson Ranch

7138

7055

6962

MESA

JACK

RIDGER

Canyon

Creek

Cottonwood

Canyon

Titus

SHAY

SEVEN SISTERS A

6719

6748

6744

6445

6860

SEVEN SISTERS C

SEVEN SISTERS B

26.1 Bear left at this unposted but prominent spur to angle north down the colorful, butte-lined valley.

38.8 (L) Spur up this box canyon accesses some native American ruins. Nine hundred years ago, this would have been a super farming area with a broad, meandering creek, not the cut-banked run that you see now. Intensive farming is the skill that set the Anasazi apart from other cultures. Continue downstream for seven stream fordings. If it is cold or if you want to avoid the water for some reason, the road that switchbacks up near the mouth of the box canyon provides access back to the "high road," which you can descend with only one ford.

43.4 Trailhead/-tail

Other Roads / Rides in the Elk Ridge Area

From mile 26.6 on the Elk Ridge road, the Causeway Road provides a scenic 30 mile connector to Blanding. At mile 32.3, the spur to Beef Basin connects to the Elephant Hill trailhead in the Needles, also in 30 miles. Although it can be prohibitively sandy for unaggressive riders, it passes through beautiful, archeologically-rich country. The many dead-end spurs from Elk Ridge are worth exploring, without exception. Two ultra-rugged routes to avoid are the trail from Crystal Spring on North Long Point to Beef Basin and the Vega Creek trail from the Causeway to Cottonwood Canyon.

The point of Mormon Mountain

Ruins, Cottonwood Canyon

In a lonely redrock canyon, up on a wall varnished dark by mineral oxides, the etching of a broad-shouldered warrior stands immutable. Although his "purpose" is debatable, archeologists can give us a pretty good idea which group of canyon dwellers created him by associating carbon dated organic remnants like corn pollen and yucca fibre with artifact styles found in the same soil strata on site.

Most petroglyph (pecked) or pictograph (painted) panels appear to be a mishmash of elements, many identifiable. There are theorists who treat each panel as a singular "story," or chapter of an ongoing saga, reading not only events but maps or dreams into the panel. A large panel was recently discovered atop Comb Ridge that shows persistent scratching on strategic points of a glyphed buck deer, as if it had been used to bless projectile points for hunting success. An overtly functional use of petroglyphs involved the observation of shadows cast upon "sun spirals" to determine summer or winter solstices. And large, ghostly "humanoids" painted high on alcove walls suggest the tracing of figures standing around a ceremonial fire.

It's edifying to spend time in the backcountry with a trained archeologist. (S)he may do the oddest, almost intuitive things, like drift over to an area dominated by a specific type of vegetation and pick up a potsherd. Or pull off a chunk of pack rat's nest and smell it to see how old it is, examining it for evidence of a nearby archeological site, like smoke-stained bone splinters. Or even date the rusty tins at an abandoned prospector's shelter by noting their metal type and construction. By knowing when he was around, it can be better determined how the environment has changed or resisted change, a theme central to understanding the context of artifacts, and thus, civilizations. Most amazing of all is when (s)he leans over and pulls an arrowhead out of a sandy-floored alcove where hundreds of mountain bikers every year stop to seek shade.

Just as we travel the path of least resistance, so did the ancient ones. This is why we can so easily drive or bike to remarkable petroglyph panels flanking the Colorado River or the Moab Valley. Although the area around Moab has long been known to be a kind of overlapping boundary between the contemporary cultures of the Fremont and Anasazi, it has been discovered to be the hunting and gathering grounds of the Desert Archaic people, too (from about 9,000 to 2,000 years ago). In about 500 B.C., the first definitive Anasazi took up a sedentary lifestyle centered around farming corn and squash, supplemented as always by hunting and gathering and the tending of plants such as prickly pear cactus and ricegrass, to fortify the diet. In contrast, the Fremonts were almost strictly hunters, and according to some theories, hunted themselves into extinction. Anyhow, by about 1300 A.D., both cultures had vanished from the Four Corners area entirely. The Anasazi seem to have faded soon after reaching a cultural zenith, represented by a retreat from open ground pueblos to cliff palaces. Whether this retreat stemmed from intertribal splintering, paranoia of marauding tribes or a resource grab hedged against a drought-stricken environment, no one can know, but all of us can speculate.

As you admire the warrior's likeness on the sandstone wall, it is hard to escape the misty, atavistic sense of wonder his presence evokes.

> They scratched farms out of the valley floor; built their aeries of riprap and mud; incised their gods and dreams on the cliffs; hunted deer, rabbit, desert bighorn; made baskets and pottery, lots of it, decorated with cord relief and colors of a smoldering barbaric beauty.

Rob Schultheis, <u>The Hidden West</u>, 1978

> They tried its deepest secrets. Now they have vanished, extinct as the tapir and coryphodon. But the undeciphered message that they left us remains, written on the walls. A message preserved not in mere words and numbers but in the durable images of line on stone. WE WERE HERE.

Edward Abbey, <u>Down the River</u>, 1978

Canyonlands National Park's Needles Area

Two of the three rides here are extremely difficult, the trail surface commonly changing from ledgy rock to deep sand (or vice versa) with no transition. Thus it is hard to both ride and enjoy the intricate scenery. But if you rejoice at the prospect of technical riding, you'll love the Needles. And when you stop, you'll love the view. The Colorado River overlooks provide the shortest routes to the rim of the Park's inner gorge, and they are phenomenal.

Please recall that Park lands are managed with an emphasis on preserving the resource, with an attendant score of regulations that you should know and practice. Bikes must stay on the road bed at all times, etc. (Refer to the section on Land Use.) The frontcountry campground at Squaw Flat provides dozens of sites on a first-come, first-served basis, but backcountry campsites at Salt Creek, Devil's Kitchen and Horsehoof Arch can be reserved in advance at the visitor center in the Needles. Gasoline and food are unavailable, and drinking water is seasonally available at Squaw Flat, but it is nearly unpalatable, for it is trucked in and sits in a tank for long periods of time. (An outpost just outside the Park boundary sells food, gas, showers, camping spaces, scenic flights, and that elusive milkshake.)

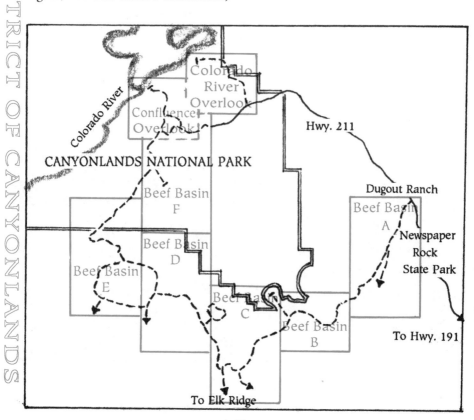

Angel Arch and Molar Rock under moonlight

BEEF BASIN

Type: One way multi-day trip (usually 2-3 days)
Length: 54 miles
Difficulty: Physically difficult / Technically difficult to gonzo-abusive
Best Seasons: Spring and fall, and long enough after rainfall for clay roads to be navigable, but sand roads to be firm (which is one or two days after a rain, all things being equal)

The Needles (clockwise from top left)
Chesler Park
Chesler Park
Chinle soil and Cathedral Butte
Cyclone Canyon

Elevation: High—8,250 ft., Low/Trailtail—5,050 ft., Trailhead—5,320 ft.

Land Agencies: BLM, USFS, and NPS

Route Summary: This route climbs 2,800 feet out of Cottonwood Canyon to Horse Mountain in 24 miles, where it turns north towards the distant skyline of the Needles. It descends to the Beef Basin area, going through House Park and Ruin Park before dropping into the first of several "grabens," long grassy parks confined by rock cliffs. The road enters Canyonlands and shifts from graben to sandy graben before turning to penetrate the challenging home stretch through rows of spires. Elephant Hill mandates the "technical feel-how" a mountain biker must exude to solve route-cleaning problems in the Needles, but unfortunately, the Hill is periodically trussed and primped with asphalt fill. It isn't enough, however, to keep zealous jeepers from burning rubber, smashing fenders, and gouging out tail lights on its many angular walls and ledges.

This route would be a more difficult ride from Elephant Hill to Dugout Ranch because much of the climb through the Beef Basin area would be in deep sand.

Options: This route is easily made a loop if you don't mind pedalling 19 miles further on pavement back to the trailhead. A short cut from Salt Creek Mesa can save you 850 feet of climbing and 3.1 miles of riding at the expense of a 0.2 mile portage on a rarely used 5.4 mile-long connector. Another option provides an alternative, longer way from House Park to Ruin Park over little-used back roads that pass within yards of freestanding native American ruins. The Joint Trail, a popular short dayhike amidst the Needles proper, starts a half mile down a sandy, dead end spur. Also, this ride can be hooked up to the Confluence Overlook ride, for they cover some common ground.

Attractions: This is a very rich archeological area, as it was central to the Anasazi's seasonal migration route between the Colorado River and the Abajo Mountains. Initial views of the Needles are like a distant city skyline, which looms larger with each mile pedalled. When you finally pedal through them, the road uses unlikely narrow, rock alleys that are bisected by joints and fractures. Walking and climbing through some of these passages can be almost as claustrophobia-inducing as spelunking. The Joint Trail is a popular hike that wriggles through this subterranean world, and as you emerge out of the fissure, squinting, your eyes feast on one of the prettier sights in Canyonlands, a place that no amount of appearances on scenic wall calendars can trivialize.

Riding Surface: Hardpacked sediments and clays give way to frustratingly deep sand, and at the last, ledgy bedrock, on jeep trails and two-laned dirt roads.

Geology: The long climb up Cottonwood Canyon will give you adequate time to study the burnt orange cliffs of the Wingate sandstone. This formation, and the colorful clay-laden soils which emerge from beneath its accompanying talus slope (the Chinle formation), are ubiquitous throughout canyon country.

The red and white banded aspect of the Needles represents a vivid and graphic "facies change," a geologic term describing the interfingering transition of two sediment types in age-equivalent or laterally continuous depositional beds. (Huh?) Basically, to the north and east of here, a red sandstone ("undivided" Cutler) dominates this strata, and to the west and south, a white sandstone predominates (Cedar Mesa). The two types interfinger here, at the place where an ancient seashore fluctuated back and forth, leaving sediments from nearby mountains bedded alternately with sediments from a coastal sand dune- and marine environment. (Just a one foot rise in sea level can increase the reach of a shoreline for miles inland, especially if the landform is relatively flat, as the Needles area was 275 million years ago, when the earth had but one giant land mass called Pangaea.) A view from Salt Creek Mesa north across the Needles (mile 12.8) verifies this banding coloration in the rock, but by the time you reach the BLM boundary (mile 26.7), views to the distant west show buttes of solid white Cedar Mesa that were not interfingered.

At mile 40, you receive your first view of a "graben," or sunken salt valley. Due to the instability caused by a brittle overburden of rock on top of a putty-like mass of salt (the leftover evaporites from the receding ocean), a 100 square-mile part of the Needles area is sloughing off towards the Colorado River, faulting in long, parallel fractures called grabens. In many cases, this fracturing is happening so rapidly (in a geologic time scale) that erosion cannot even establish drainage patterns out of these grabens. At mile 39.7, a spur accesses a sinkhole (called Bobby's Hole) developed by water that found a way down since it couldn't effectively drain out of this valley. The river runs ten times steeper through nearby Cataract Canyon than above the Confluence, the force of a narrower channel and increased gradient being the river's only way to keep the rapidly collapsing canyon walls from completely damming it.

Logistics: Since this ride can require the use of a shuttle, you'll need to park a vehicle at Elephant Hill before backtracking to Dugout Ranch. (If you want to make a loop of it by pedalling the extra 19 paved miles, then no shuttle is required. The gracious owners and operators of a small general store, gas station and campground near the Park boundary on Highway 211 may let you park your vehicle overnight on their property, although they cannot take responsibility for it.)

Because of the ruggedness of the trail from about mile 39 on, laden support vehicles usually backtrack from this point to meet the party at the base of Elephant Hill. The abruptness of many of the hills and turns on the Needles' backcountry roads requires a short wheelbase vehicle for unhindered passage. Licensed mountain bike outfitters in Moab provide shuttles and/or catered support for this route. A list of these companies can be gotten by writing the **Grand County Travel Council, 805 N. Main St., Moab, Utah 84532, ph.(801) 259-8825.**

Trailhead Access: From Moab, go south on Highway 191 about 42 miles to the Needles entrance road, Highway 211. In almost 20 miles, shortly after passing Dugout Ranch, take the following left onto the Cottonwood Canyon dirt road. This intersection marks the trailhead for the Beef Basin loop. The road is broad enough that you should be able to park at its edge, rather than pull off of it and further impact the fragile plant life.

Mileage Log and Route Description:

0.0 Continue up the Cottonwood Canyon road astride your preferred vehicle.

3.5 (L) Last chance to wet your shirt before the long pull up the canyon.

14.9 (R) Recommended rough 2.8 mile spur to Cathedral Point (a.k.a. Big Pocket Overlook)

18.5 This inconspicuous doubletrack right, into a chained area, marks the start of a shortcut over to the Beef Basin through-road that is 3.1 miles shorter and saves 850 feet of elevation gain. However, it is rockier, and a rough 0.2 of a mile hike-a-bike cannot be avoided.

  0.0 (previously 18.5) Continue into the chained area. This pinyon-juniper area was "chained" in the 60's to create an open feeding area for cows that could be seeded with non-native grass. Chaining is the knocking down of all large growth by an anchor chain suspended between bulldozers as they churn across the ground. It is presently done (along with the "rollerchopping" of smaller growth) to create or sustain wildlife habitat and to stabilize areas from "sheet" erosion. Heather Muscelow, a Forest Service wildlife officer, explains that chaining is used to "knock plant succession back," in order to create a mosaic of feeding and shelter zones for elk and deer, in an effort to simulate a natural, pre fire-suppression pattern.

  There are voices which question the efficacy of chaining, though. Utah State professor of Forest Resources Ronald Lanner has stated that "BLM-financed research in the 1970's found that chained areas did not have lower sediment losses than forested areas," thus diminishing the argument for chaining based on watershed control. Furthermore, firefighters are known to have difficulty in actually getting pinyon-juniper to ignite while trying controlled fires or back-burns. And one can't help but feel that so much dead wood lying in bulldozed clumps actually does increase the fire hazard over that of a living forest. The question as to whether providing habitat for livestock and wildlife is a necessary or desirable duty of our government, and justifies the wholesale destruction of old growth pinyon-juniper, is answered differently by different people. Let your opinion be known in matters like these, because after all, it's your land. If you support environmental organizations, request that they monitor issues important to you.

  Write: District Ranger, Manti-La Sal National Forest, 125 W. 200 So. Moab, Utah 84532

When a man despoils a work of art we call him a vandal,
when he despoils a work of nature we call him a developer.

Joseph Wood Krutch, <u>The Desert Year</u>, 1952

BEEF BASIN A

County Road relocated
1/2 mile west of Dugout Ranch

Dugout Ranch

BM
5389

Hwy. 211

21   23   24   19

MESA

Cotton
5745

28   27   26   Creek   25   30

5748   5600

BM
5489

6000

33   34   35   36   31
×
6860

BM
5698

Cottonwood

BM
3.5   5528

W

Canyon

Creek

4   3   2   1   5675

6485

BM
5575

BRIDGER

North

Titus

9   10   11   12   5845

6400

Bridger
5407   16   15   14   13   18

16   15   BM 5678   14   6812   13   18

6800

Ruins

Titus Canyon

21   22   23   24   6962   19
Ruins
Wilson Ranch   Canyon

SHAY   MES

7055   SHAY

28   27   26   25   30

Montezuma

The view of Lavender Canyon from Cathedral Point

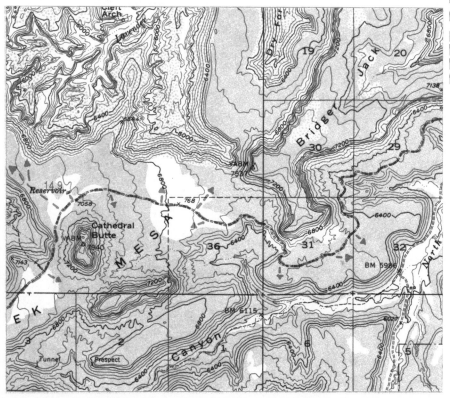

BEEF BASIN C

Cathedral Point

Wedding Ring Arch

7180

Spring

6355

6400

6400

6000

6400

6800

7200

TRAIL

ANGEL

BRIGHT

Fork

Creek

(optional shortcut)

S A L T

(A4)

CREE

Canyon

Boundary Butte

7200

7853

7200

Prospect

18

7996

17

16

Butte

8765

8000

To Elk Ridge

9065

MANTI - LA SAL

Horse

Mtn

Davis Pocket

TRAIL

Davis

Sisters

Mormon

Seven

Point

8400

9400

30

29

28

24.1

6800

6962

7355

7210

8800

8200

22.3

BEEF BASIN D

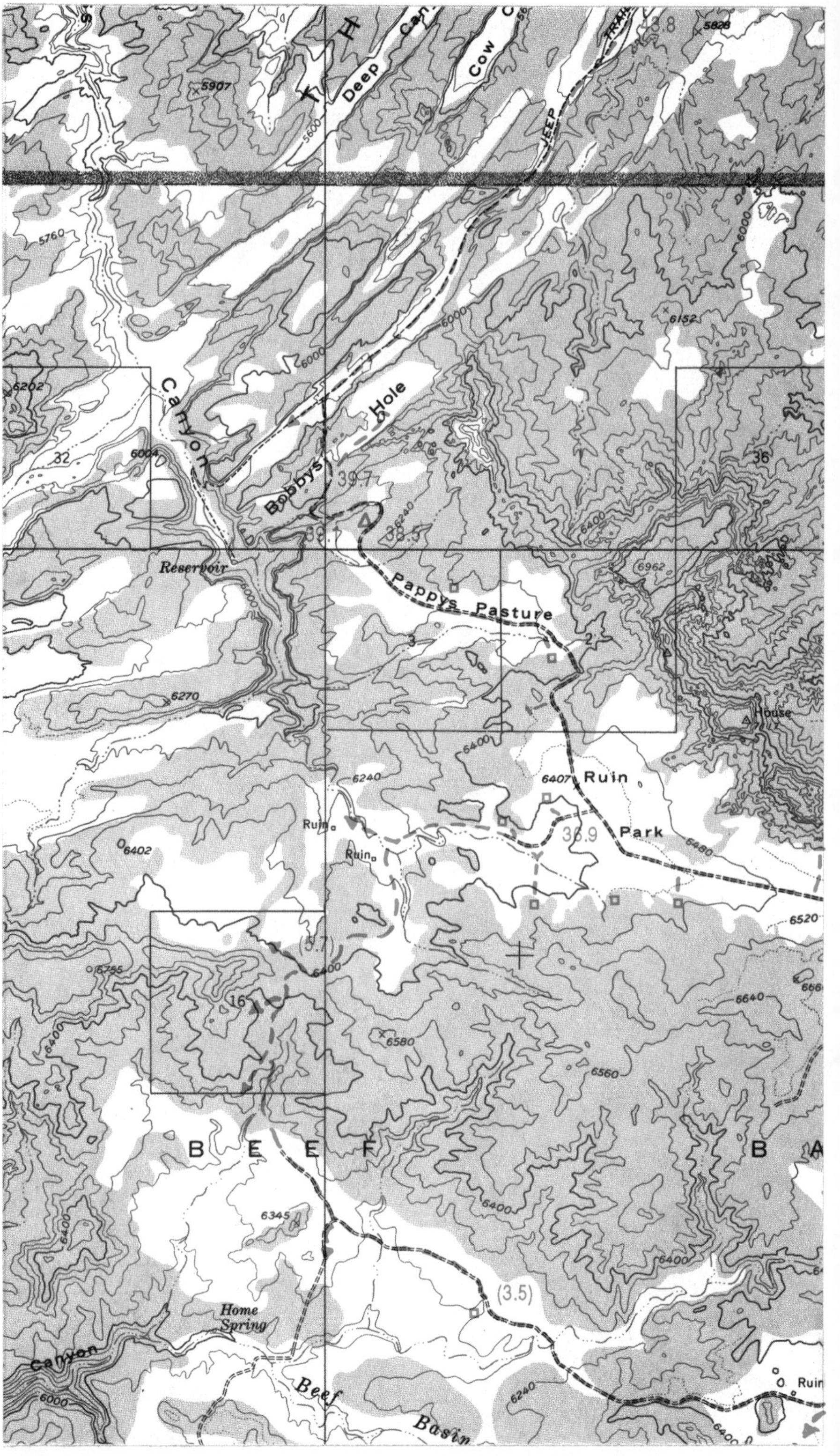
Deep
Cow
JEEP
TRAIL
5907
5828
5760
6152
6202
Canyon
Bobbys
Hole
39.7
38.3
32
6004
36
Reservoir
Pappys
Pasture
6962
3
2
6270
House
6400
6240
6407
Ruin
Park
Ruin
Ruin
6402
36.9
6480
6520
(3.7)
6755
16
6580
6640
6560
B E E F
B A
6345
(3.5)
Home
Spring
Canyon
6000
Beef
Basin
6240
Ruin

BEEF BASIN F

0.4 At the edge of the mesa, take the dugway that descends past a spring-fed trough.

4.3 After the rough, switchbacking descent, the road ends in this creekbed. Cross it directly to pick up the trudgesome hike-a-bike up a narrow gully between the trees.

5.4 Beef Basin road

18.5 Continue along Salt Creek Mesa towards Horse Mountain.

24.1 After turning right onto the Beef Basin road, be careful of the ruts which magically appear when vehicles slop through here after a rain, as you (otherwise) enjoy the downhill.

27.3 (R) Shortcut route reconnects **(indented previous mile 5.4)**

30.6 Watch out for this hard-to-see gate across the descent.

33.2 From this intersection with the BLM register box, there is an alternate route to nearby Ruin Park which is both six miles longer and more difficult than the regular way right, but passes some substantial native American ruins before connecting back to it.

> **0.0** (previously 33.2) Bear left at the register box. (But why did it stay here?)
>
> **3.5** Notice all the prickly pear cactus hereabouts. The Anasazi are known to have cultivated the plant, as both the fruit and the leaf are edible.
>
> **5.7** Take the right turn at the top of this hill, where the road "T's" onto an obscurer route still.
>
> **9.8** "T" at the Beef Basin road

33.2 Continue right, from the register box.

36.9 (L) Spur to Farm House Ruin, where the alternate spur connects to the Beef Basin road **(indented previous mile 9.8)**.

38.5 (L) These two (unposted) campsites mark the place where most motor vehicles should not pass.

39.1 (L) "4-WD Vehicles Only" sign at the "Little Drop," country cousin to Cataract Canyon's Big Drops.

39.7 (R) Spur to Bobby's Hole, a salt sink (watch your step) just before cresting the hill for Little Drop Two, another ugly descent that drops into the first obvious graben on the route. "Graben" is German for grave.

43.8 (R) Roadside stakes denote another salt sink (spring 1990) whose presence may alter (if not erode away) the course of the road in the future.

46.2 (R) This 0.5 of a mile spur accesses the trailhead for a must-do hike to Chesler Park, the heart of the Needles.

49.3 (R) Spur 0.6 of a mile to Devil's Kitchen camp, where the trail becomes a one-way affair that denies further progress.

50.4 The route is somewhat befuddling after you break through the redrock pass and descend the "Silver Stairs." In less than 0.2 of a mile, you'll take the signed one-way spur right most of the 3.4 miles back to Elephant Hill.

54.0 Trailtail at Elephant Hill

The effects of chaining

Farm House Ruin

CONFLUENCE OVERLOOK

Type: Loop
Length: 14.6 miles
Difficulty: Physically difficult / Technically difficult to gonzo-abusive
Best Seasons: Spring and fall after rains
Elevation: High—5,200 ft., Low—4,880 ft., Trailhead/-tail—5,050 ft.
Land Agency: NPS
Route Summary: From the infamous Elephant Hill, a highly technical jeep trail evolves into a sandy bugger at Devil's Lane. It stays in sandy "grabens" the rest of the way to the Confluence, and in some smooth downhill places the road is invitingly cambered.
Options: One can opt to turn on Devil's Lane towards Chesler Park and Beef Basin. The dead end doubletrack up Cyclone Canyon near the Confluence is usually too sandy to venture.
Attractions: The Green River is the largest tributary to the Colorado that still flows freely to its confluence, and indeed, it flows from a canyon every bit as deep and wide. The ambitious can bound the 800 feet down to the Confluence from near the overlook to see firsthand the eddying and gradual mixing of the two different colored sediment loads.
Riding Surface: Ledgy bedrock and persistent sand all on jeep trails
Geology: (Refer to the Beef Basin section on "Geology" for background.) One pattern you will notice is that the white strata of the Cedar Mesa sandstone is more likely to form toadstool shapes and the red strata tend to create spires and domes. Since the two colors of sandstone are from two different parent sources, they exhibit different resistances to erosion. In this case, the white rock is harder, the red beneath it already eroding sufficiently to create caps in the white. The spires that are red-capped taper to blunt points, a sign that erosion is occurring as fast from the top down as it is diminishing in girth, and in some of the squat, domey features, even faster.
Notes: An entrance fee is charged at the visitor center. If you're camping at Squaw Flat (either before or after your ride), consider using the three easy dirt miles between it and Elephant Hill for a warmup ride. Also, much of the route to and from Devil's Lane is one-way, counterclockwise.
Logistics: No permits are needed for day use, and a shuttle is optional.
Trailhead Access: Elephant Hill is essentially the end of Highway 211, some 40 miles from its junction with Highway 191. Travel south on Highway 191 about 42 miles out of Moab to turn at this junction.

Mileage Log and Route Description:
0.0 Find your lucky gear for the "stairway to heavin'," the purge, the "interval straining" over Elephant Hill, the threshold to the Needles backcountry.
5.2 (R) This is where you'll pick up the one-way return to Elephant Hill after backtracking from the Confluence Overlook.

8.2 From the end of the road, it's less than a half mile walk to the overlook. "Too thick to drink, too thin to plow," the Colorado can carry a sediment load dense enough to make a gallon of its water over 70% heavier than a gallon of tap water. During spring runoff, its rapids have flipped thirty-foot rubber boats, yet in the late summer, one can sometimes wade across the river. The two rivers below are such formidable barriers to travel that it would take twelve hours of driving and walking from here to get to the point overlooking the Confluence in the Island District, a rim just a half mile away. Access to the Maze District's overlook would take twice as long, but you 'd be disappointed to discover that you can't get far enough out the "finger" to substantiate the effort.

> Dominating land and man, it is the greatest single fact within an area of nearly a quarter million square miles. Bigger than its statistics, it is one of the great rivers of the world...
>
> And this at last seems the ultimate task to which the Colorado is appointed... to move bodily, sand by sand and peak by peak, through the measureless milleniums man calls eternity, the whole great Colorado Pyramid out into the sea.

Frank Waters, <u>The Colorado</u>, 1946

14.6 Elephant Hill Trailhead/-tail

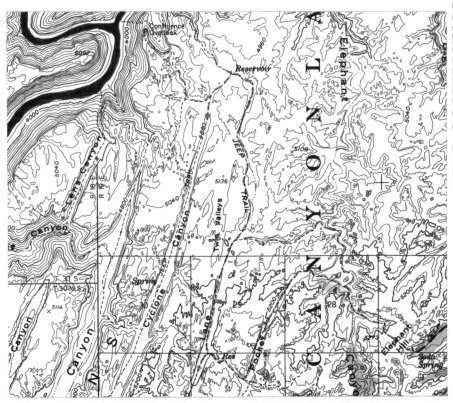

Runaway Bike Ramp, the Needles

176

Needles area riding (clockwise from top left)
near Chesler Canyon
overlooking Salt Creek
near Devil's Kitchen
Devil's Lane

Elephant Rock, the Needles

COLORADO RIVER OVERLOOK

Type: Out-and-back
Length: 14.4 miles
Difficulty: Physically moderate / Technically moderate
Best Seasons: Spring and fall
Elevation: Trailhead/-tail/High—4,900 ft., Low—4,740 ft.
Land Agency: NPS and BLM
Route Summary: This straightforward route starts at the Needles Visitor Center, skirts the Jump at lower Salt Creek and contours around the canyon established by the Jump to end upstream of its mouth at the Colorado.
Attractions: A lofty view of both Salt Creek Canyon and the Colorado river gorge
Riding Surface: Hardpacked, rock-studded sediments and bedrock on a jeep trail
Geology: The cavernous Jump of Lower Salt Creek marks the surfacing of the Elephant Canyon formation, a chalky gray limestone that is studded with fossilized clams, snails, and plant-like animals called crinoids. Although this formation, at 1500 feet thick, dominates the river gorge downstream, it is less than 1,000 feet thick here, and somewhere upstream before Moab, it tapers out to nothing. Again, this is the nature of a seashore, to have marine-deposited formations merge into or interfinger with coastal-deposited ones. That fossilized sea life is so abundant indicates that Canyonlands was once a quiet, shallow sea, just ten to twenty feet deep, which provided sunlight to the algae blooms upon which all sea lifeforms were dependent.
Notes: An entrance fee is collected at the visitor center.
Logistics: No permit is necessary for day use.
Trailhead Access: About 34 miles on Highway 211 in from its junction with Highway 191 (which is 42 miles south of Moab), park at the Needles visitor center.

Mileage Log and Route Description:
0.0 Shortly after the visitor center, stay left at the fork.
2.6 (L) Before crossing Salt Creek, it is suggested that you walk down to the Lower Jump.
4.5 Junction Butte dominates the skyline before you after you re-enter the Park. The sea of equally spaced shrubs around you consists of blackbrush, Indian ricegrass and Mormon tea.
7.2 The Colorado River usually runs red, as its name implies, but one hundred years ago, it normally "ran clear as a mountain stream" (except during spring runoff), according to pioneer Frank Silvey. It seems that southern Utah is in a period of accelerated erosion within an era of accelerated erosion. Last century's wagon train routes are impossible to follow in places where cut bank arroyos have gashed them, and they usually traversed the mildest possible landform.

Potholes in the Needles

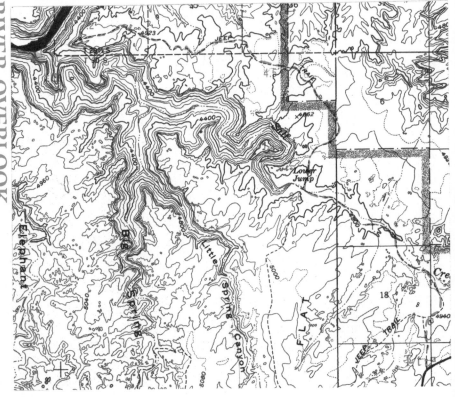

As you enjoy the view, savor the irony in this quote, which was penned by a man who stood at the end of his regiment's long journey but a few miles from here.

> The region last explored is of course, altogether valueless. It can be approached only from the south, and after entering it there is nothing to do but leave. Ours has been the first, and will doubtless be the last, party of whites to visit this profitless locality.

> Lt. Joseph C. Ives, <u>Report to the U.S.Government</u>, 1861

14.4 Trailhead/-tail

Other Roads / Rides in the Needles Area

Unfortunately, most explorations in the Needles area are too hindered by sand to be very ridable. However, if the sand is wet or frozen it can be firm enough to support a wheel. Upper Salt Creek, Lavender and Davis Canyons have jeep trails that might be appealing under the right circumstances. (The nearby ride through Lockhart Basin, the alter ego to the White Rim Trail, is listed under the Canyon Rims Area rides.)

Upper Cottonwood Canyon

Microbiotic Crust–the building block of the desert

Outtake #7   The Desert's Cornerstone

Cryptogamic soil, that "hidden marriage" of non-vascular plants that keeps the desert from blowing away, has been renamed "microbiotic crust." Besides moss, lichen and algae, the crust's major organism is cyanobacteria, which has been reclassified into its own kingdom, neither plant nor animal.

"The name 'microbiotic crust' was chosen because it is easy to remember and carries no taxonomic implications," says Jayne Belknap, a biologist for Canyonlands National Park. This dark crust is essentially the desert's topsoil, as it stabilizes sand against erosion while fixing nitrogen and other nutrients critical to establishing soil fertility. It grows about one millimeter per year, which translates to a hundred year recovery rate for heavily impacted areas, like on or near the Slickrock Bike Trail.

The destruction of microbiotic crust is like "cutting down the tropical rainforest on a miniature scale," such is its organic diversity. It is sensitive enough to be used as a living air quality monitor, but mostly it reflects the carelessness of human traffic in its sensitivity to the effects of tire tracks. The crust can withstand some compression and even pockets of pulverization (such as cows might inflict), but the continuous tracks of bikes and motorcycles groove, displace and cover it. With its network of fibrous sheaths crushed, and with a newly created groove for water and wind to inflict further erosion, it becomes unable to photosynthesize.

Errant tracks are "Bad Form", Hidden Canyon Rim Trail

Author's Editorial:

You know, given the rapidly eroding nature of canyonlands, it's safe to say but hard to admit, that errant tracks do more lasting damage to our ideals of natural beauty than they in actuality do to its beauty. "Beauty" is subjective, and finding It is, I think, critical to the psyche.

The land doesn't know it's pretty; it's indifferent to all but function (which is another type of beauty, certainly). What I'm getting at is that, despite evidence to the contrary, it's nice to feel as if we're one of few who've gazed upon a certain wild vista. Makes the view more impressive and the journey to get there that much more eventful. This valid sentiment could be called the Pioneer Instinct, and isn't just the seeking of beauty in isolation, but beauty in the guarantee of such.

Microbiotic crust reveals tracks so plainly that, beyond the biological impact, a perhaps worse, more volatile psychological impact occurs. Especially to those of us who live here, who see the continual degradation (tracking), who can read signs of the masses on the ground before us.

While to riders this book ought to be a service which can help make limited time here more enjoyable, to others, the information provided only serves to make the Pioneer Instinct type of beauty that much rarer.

To those critics I can only say, please try to be more accepting of others (because "they" are "you"). Venture off the roads and trails if you expect solitude, and, for real adventure, forego ALL maps—street, topo or verbal. A journey into the unknown may not be convenient, but it's certain to be memorable.

The Canyon Rims Recreation Area

The Canyon Rims Recreation Area is a high plateau isolated on three sides by the Colorado River and Kane Springs Canyon. Its northernmost point is called the Anticline Overlook, which presides over Hurrah Pass, making it the closest part of the Recreation Area to Moab yet the furthest away by road. The massive, pleated, burnt orange Wingate cliffs—"the Canyonlands coaming"—are the barriers to direct travel, as usual. One of the suggested rides is confined to the mesa top, and the other wanders the broad benchland below, an alter ego to the White Rim Trail across the river. Three primitive campsites and several designated overlooks attract some visitation here, but basically it is an unheralded gem (which makes those heralded gems like Dead Horse Point and Island in the Sky sparkle that much more—with the glare of sun on windshields).

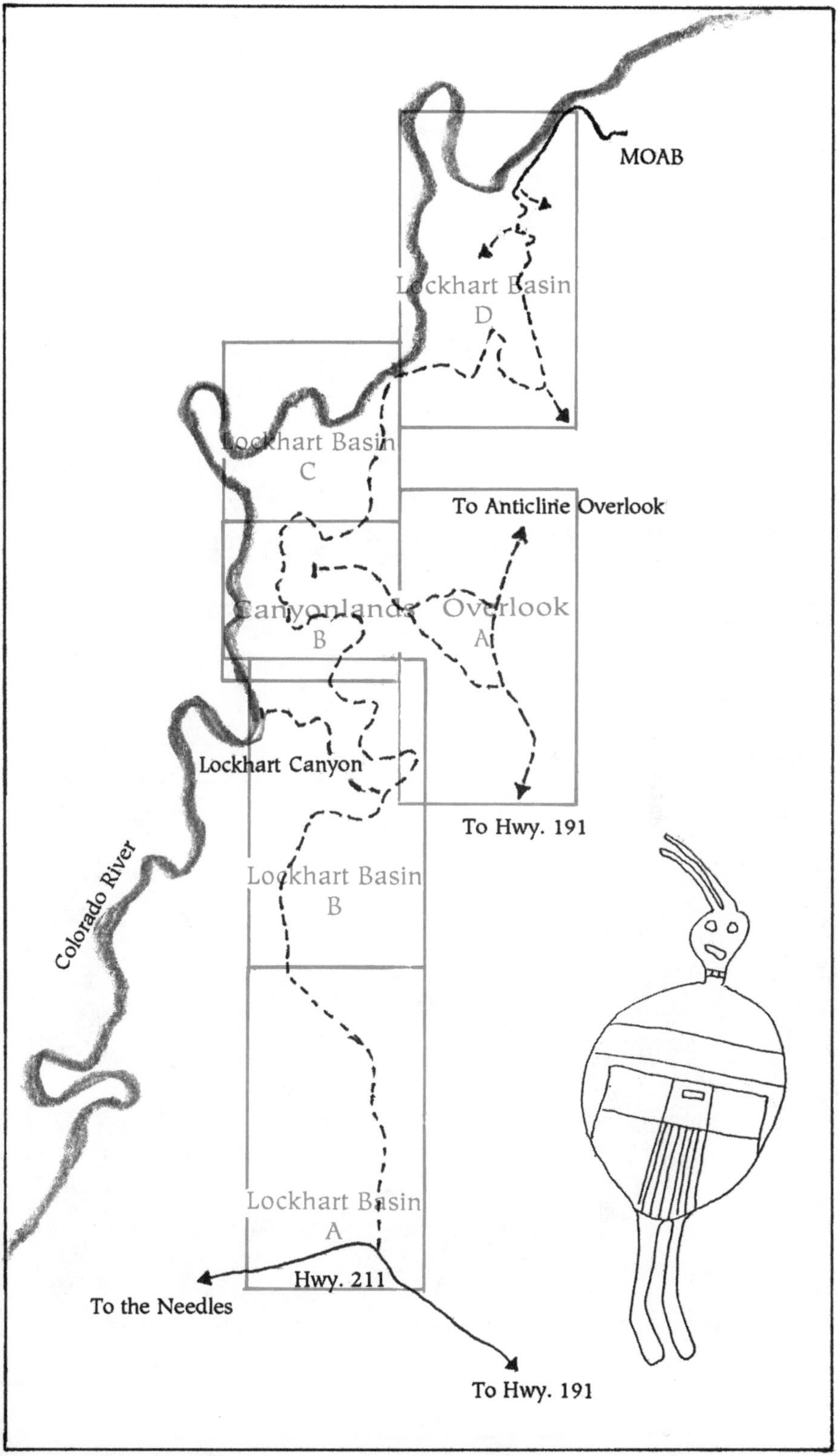

MOAB

Lockhart Basin
D

To Anticline Overlook

Lockhart Basin
C

Canyonlands Overlook
B   A

To Hwy. 191

Lockhart Canyon

Colorado River

Lockhart Basin
B

Lockhart Basin
A

Hwy. 211

To the Needles

To Hwy. 191

CANYON RIMS RECREATION AREA

Anvil Rock, Canyon Rims Area

CANYONLANDS OVERLOOK

Type: Loop
Length: 15.2 miles
Difficulty: Physically moderate / Technically moderate
Best Seasons: Spring and Fall, including during or after rainfall
Elevation: Trailhead/-tail/Low—5,820 ft., High—5,925 ft.

Land Agency: BLM

Route Summary: From its trailhead on the road to the Anticline Overlook, this route utilizes some of the sandy seismologic exploration roads that lace the area to access a protruding point with 270° views of the Canyonlands Basin. After backtracking from the point, a previously bypassed spur goes past the head of Dripping Springs Canyon for a look-see into it before connecting back to the Anticline Overlook road.

Attractions: You may see pronghorn antelope, for they are active in the daytime, unlike deer, elk or bighorn. Simply "being" on open plateaus is their best defense, as they are capable of running almost 60 mph over predictable terrain. Rim walking is a nice way to discover erosions such as arches, fractures and balanced rocks. "Tonsils" arch is a wonder in stone anatomy, as are the "sensurreal" views that arrest, frisk and handcuff your attention.

Riding Surface: Hardpacked sediments, rock-studded sediments and drift sand on jeep trails and two-laned dirt roads

Geology: Only a few whale-backed domes of pale Navajo sandstone remain to indicate that the plateau's resilient surface rock is the Kayenta formation. Except for the actual rim, the Kayenta is pretty well buried under sand and coarser sediments. A quarter of a mile northeast of mile 5.0, a rare occurrence has taken place. The ledgy, light-toned Kayenta is stripped off the Wingate, but the Wingate didn't collapse with its usual columnal spalls. It resisted weathering to establish a slickrock surface, and a large one at that. Views into Meander Canyon on the Colorado show maroon Cutler sandstone on the bench that the Lockhart Basin Trail traverses and Elephant Canyon formation lining the innermost gorge. Our beloved White Rim formation is clearly visible across the river, but in its eastward thinning couldn't span the gulf to this side of the river.

Notes: Since this ride starts near the far end of the plateau, you might want to visit the Needles Overlook on the way out here, and the Anticline Overlook a little further down the road.

Logistics: No permit or shuttle is required.

Trailhead Access: About 32 miles south of Moab, a large wooden sign near Highway 191 announces the paved spur to Canyon Rims Recreation Area. In 14 miles, take the gravel fork right, towards the Anticline Overlook for another 8 miles to the (unposted) trailhead, where a dirt spur left leads to a white building. There may be a sign, "Primitive Road—Travel at Your Own Risk." Park in a suitable place off the road.

Mileage Log and Route Description:
0.0 From the trailhead, head rimward, bearing right at the fork. Be sure to follow the posts with machine-routed arrows, as they will direct you to Canyonlands Overlook.
1.0 Near the dam constructed of blasted rock, or "fill material," gravitate to the rock's righthand edge to pick up the jeep trail before it crests the hill.
3.3 (R) The doubletrack spur from this four-way intersection is your way back to the Anticline Overlook road after having "looked over" or "looked out for" Canyonlands.
6.9 All power spots should have vaulted thrones such as this!

> At first it seems like geologic chaos, but there is method at work here, method of a fanatic order and perseverance: each groove in the rock leads to a natural channel of some kind, every channel to a ditch and gulch and ravine, each larger waterway to a canyon bottom or broad wash leading in turn to the Colorado River and the sea.

> Edward Abbey, <u>Desert Solitaire</u>, 1968

10.5 (previously 3.3) Take this doubletrack towards the head of Dripping Springs Canyon, from where you can see Tonsils Arch on the rim across the canyon.
12.5 At the last, biggest wash crossing, the road out of it is very unused looking, because jeepers can bypass this move by continuing downstream.
13.0 After the old roadbed rises into the open, look for a cow track 90° right that leaves from the rusty barrel to connect to the Anticline Overlook Road.
15.2 Continue past Hatch Point Campground to the trailhead/-tail.

Kathy Aldous exploring a slickrock outcrop near Canyon Rims

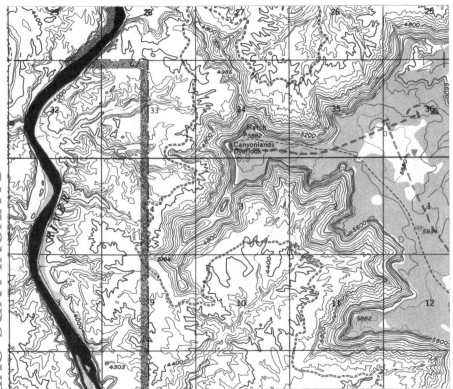

The view towards Moab from Canyonlands Overlook

CANYONLANDS OVERLOOK A

Dripping Spring
19
20
21
22
5705
Flatiron
5880
4400
5200
30
29
28
27
5600
4800
Trough Springs
5643
31
5607
32
33
34
To Anticline Overlook
5600
5817
12.5
13.0
5600
3.3
HATCH
Grain Tank
Hatch Point Campground
5840
JEEP TRAIL
5840
15.2
16
T/t
1.0
5920
Trough
6068
6039
5600
6000
6000
5792
4675
4800
6111
6110

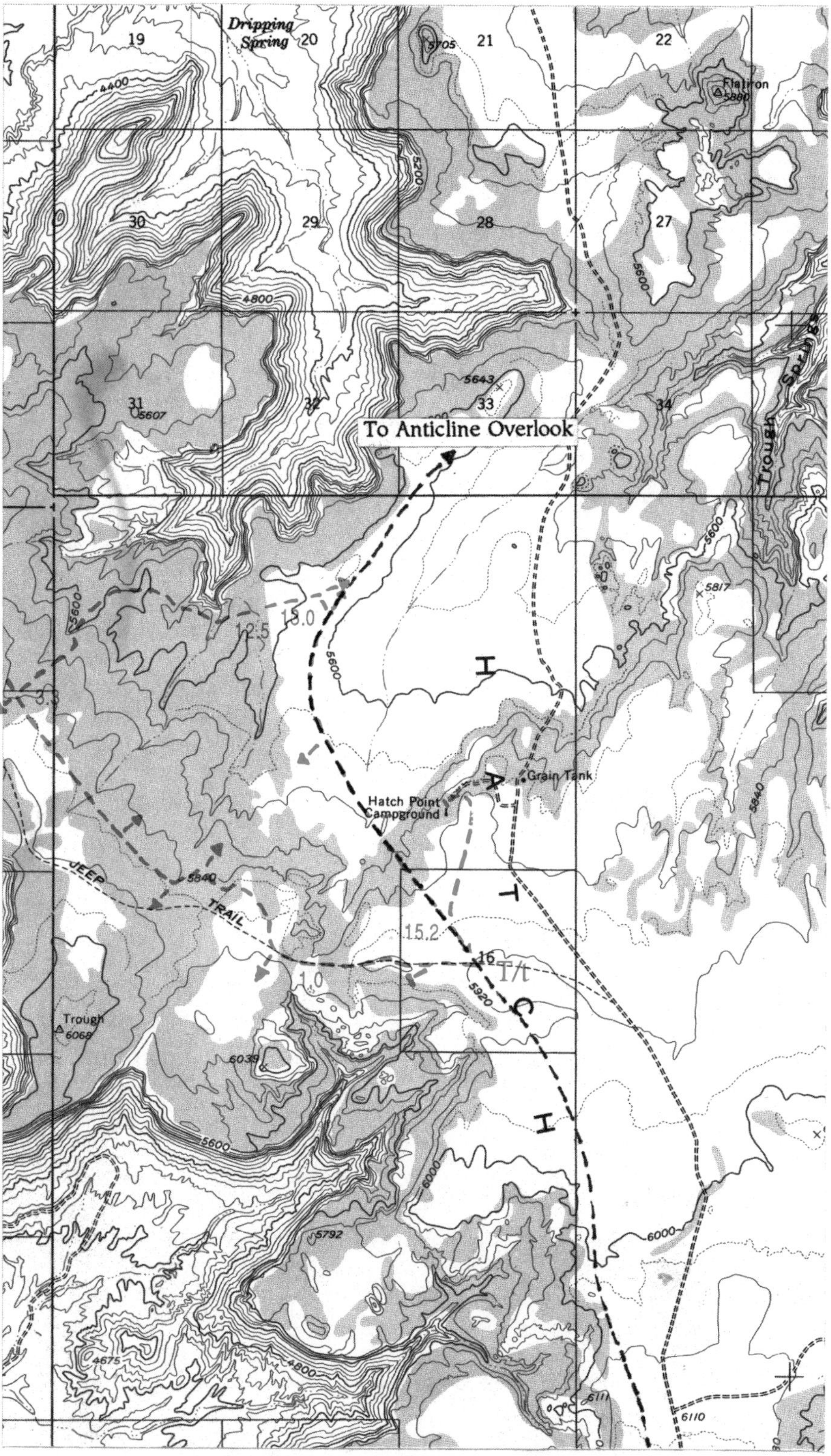

LOCKHART BASIN

Type: One-way (either a long day or multi-day ride)
Length: 55.4 miles, including 4.8 on pavement
Difficulty: Physically difficult / Technically moderate to difficult
Best Seasons: Spring and fall, but not after rain
Elevation: Trailhead/High—4,930 ft., Low—3,960 ft., Trailtail—4,025 ft.
Land Agency: BLM
Route Summary: From its trailhead on Highway 211 near the Needles, this easily followed ride crosses the archeologically-rich Indian Creek to traverse a broad benchland, much like the White Rim Trail. But since the Lockhart Basin Trail is further removed from the river, it hasn't the gaping canyons cut to its very edge like the White Rim. Instead, it weaves through a wonderland of goblin rocks and shrieking effigies carved into the convoluted Cutler sandstone. These sometime appear as totem poles or balanced rocks, but mostly they are strange, transmogrified profiles, prominently splayed with white flecks or sulking in deep shades of purple, chocolate or rust. After Channel Change Gap, the trail begins its tortuous descent to the Colorado river in a drainage that may force a support vehicle to turn back. Long views of the Colorado from a riverside limestone ledge must be forsaken for the climb up to Hurrah Pass on a bulge in the topography called the Cane Creek Anticline. The descent into Kane Springs Canyon continues out to its mouth at the Colorado for the cruise back to Moab.

For unsupported riders, there is no "disadvantage" to starting the ride from Moab, except more elevation gain.
Options: Spurs off of this route include the out-and-backs to the river via Lockhart Canyon, and the Chicken Corners spur out to the Gooseneck area beneath Dead Horse Point. Several other rides intersect this route, too, such as the three variations on Amasa Back, Pritchett (Hunters) and, of course, Hurrah Pass, which is merely a segment of the Lockhart Basin ride.
Attractions: Lockhart Basin is a vast, austere, and possibly fearsome place. It is not over-managed by any agency, because it is a "poor man's Canyonlands." It is also no place to suffer an emergency, for even if you were to hike to the rim (possible in Lockhart Basin proper), there would be little if any traffic on the nearest dirt road. There are no obvious potholes to store rain water, although some stands of gauzy tamarisk shrubs have a tight affiliation with a couple of stock ponds. The ultra-sandy ride down Lockhart Canyon (Lathrop east) enters the National Park near the river and accesses a nice beach during low water flows.
Riding Surface: Hardpacked sediments, rock-studded sediments and sand on jeep trails and two-laned roads
Geology: The Cutler sandstone predominates throughout the ride, although you intersect the contacts with the Chinle above and the Elephant Canyon's limestone below. The towering Wingate walls that escort you for most of the

194

way diminish as Kane Springs Canyon narrows to its mouth, where strawberry blonde fins of Navajo sandstone usher you upriver to Moab.

Notes: Since the trailhead is on the way to a popular hiking area (the Needles), it makes sense to catch a ride with people headed that way rather than drive the circuitous shuttle. Be sure to have all your bottles filled before the drop-off, because there's nothing at the trailhead.

Logistics: As mentioned, support vehicles can have a difficult time negotiating some parts of the route (specifically, mile 33.1. Even commercial outfitters can be reluctant to support this trip, and they'll likely insist on travelling it from the Needles to Moab, as it's written here). Support vehicles on multi-day trips should carry the usual selection of shovels, sledges, boards, jacks, pry bars, come-alongs, etc. A shuttle is optional and no permit is required, unless you camp at the mouth of Lockhart Canyon within Canyonlands National Park.

Trailhead Access: The spur to Highway 211 is 42 miles south of Moab on Highway 191. In another 29 miles, an (unposted) gravel spur right, recognizable by a cattleguard at its outset, is the trailhead. The trailhead is 2.7 miles before entering the Park.

Mileage Log and Route Description:

0.0 There is no formal parking area at the trailhead, but in the next three miles before the Indian Creek fording, there are many suitable, maybe even shady, places. (Don't keep someone from using a nice campsite, though, just to park your car.)

2.6 (R) Indian Creek campsite, with toilet. There are numerous native American ruins in the rock nearby.

2.9 The downstream of the two fords is usually shallowest, even though it's closer to the falls. The falls are in Elephant Canyon limestone. Its erosional resistance has contributed to the creation of this falls, as have the spuming floods of "tomato soup" that regularly flood this far reaching canyon. (When the creekbed is dry, or nearly so, it offers some challenging riding down its course.) Take the roundhouse road up around the dune to reach the pass ahead.

15.4 (L) This graded but sandy spur goes 5.3 miles down Lockhart Canyon to the Colorado River. Stay right when encountering spurs.

20.1 As you round this point, you can see the broken monoliths of Wingate sandstone below Canyonlands Overlook. They look like a mitten and a pyramid.

29.4 Channel Change Gap, the first unimpeded view upriver to the rock highlands near Moab. Goodbye, Needles. This is smack dab cross-hairs-on-the-map in the middle of Nowhere.

> The canyon country does not always inspire love. To many it appears barren, hostile, repellent—a fearsome, mostly waterless land of rock and heat, sand dunes and quicksand, cactus, thornbush, scorpion, rattlesnake, and agoraphobic distances. To those who see our land in that manner, the best

Erosions, Lockhart Basin Trail

reply is, yes, you are right. It is a dangerous and terrible place. Enter at your own risk. Carry water. Avoid the noonday sun. Try to ignore the vultures. Pray frequently.

Edward Abbey, The Journey Home, 1977

33.1 To a person behind the wheel, all other rough descents were warmups to this. Sometimes there are just inches to work with, so scout the run with a discerning eye.

33.9 Turn sharply right near the base of the drainage to stay in it, avoiding the errant spur that crosses and dissipates on the hillside beyond. The drainage will intersect a larger, sandy wash, where you should continue right.

34.1 (L) Spur to Chicken Corners, a popular campsite with a nearby arch overlooking the river gorge. An exceedingly narrow cow trail edges around the Corners to access the Gooseneck peninsula.

37.0 After the spur **(R)** to Dripping Springs Canyon, keep an eye peeled for the road that splits left in this sandflats and river cobble area. The cobbles' presence here is a reminder that the Colorado ran wide and free just ten million years ago. With the subsequent uplifting of the Colorado Plateau, wide meanders became deep notches, leaving cobble stranded high and dry. This same uplifting is what has allowed the river to cut across strongly defined geographic features like Moab Valley with seeming impunity.

37.6 Where the road abuts the rim, you are again on the Elephant Canyon limestone. It is a thin bed here, as you are near the edge of extent in its interfingering, or "facies change," with the Cutler. The gray, fine-grained, stratigraphied appearance of the marine deposited limestone contrasts with the sweeping red, coarse-grained, deposits of the river-deposited Cutler sandstone. On a large scale, this lateral transition (or facies change) from coarse to fine is exactly what you'd expect to find at a river estuary, for as a river nears the sea, its suspended sediments drop out in a predictable way. The "dovetail effect" is the observation that large particles settle out first, then finer and finer particles drop out the farther off shore the fresh water advances. Since this effect occurred in a relatively still, shallow sea, its solidified record is pronounced. The only fact that confuses this is that the seashore advanced (and retreated) twenty-nine times while these sediments were settling, the "tide" that created the interfingering effect seen here. Note the fossilized clams in the rock at your feet.

38.3 (R) Where the road split rejoins, continue left out the low-walled wash.

38.5 (L) Spur to Jackson Hole which allows a portage up to Amasa Back. The continuing road uses a convenient ledge to climb the bulging anticline or upfold in the strata to Hurrah Pass. It is another 14.4 miles from the Pass to Moab on a prominent road. Consult the Hurrah Pass ride for its description.

55.4 Main St. x Center Sts., Moab.

Jeff Brody "splitting the rocks"

LOCKHART BASIN A

LOCKHART BASIN B

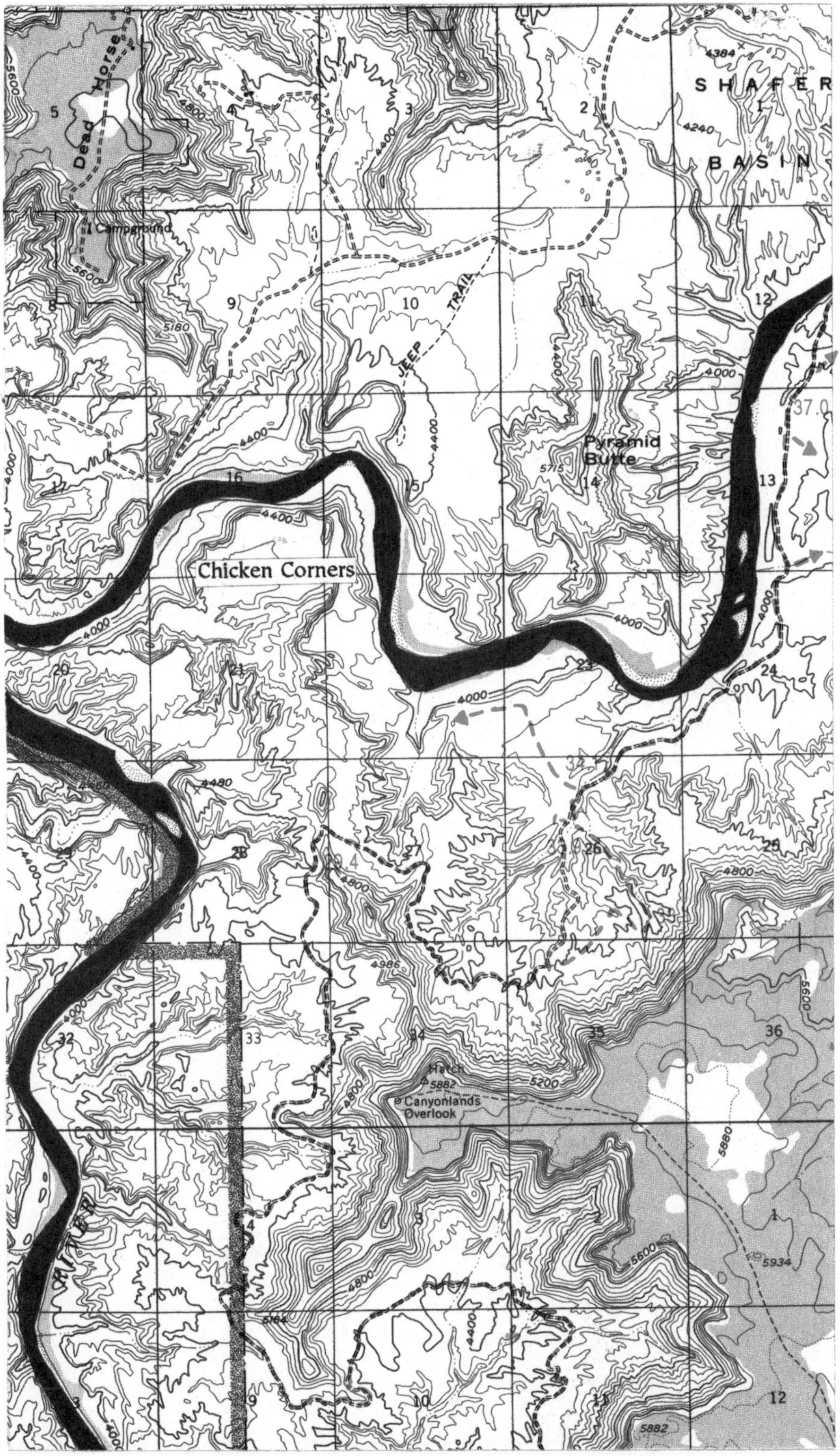

LOCKHART BASIN C

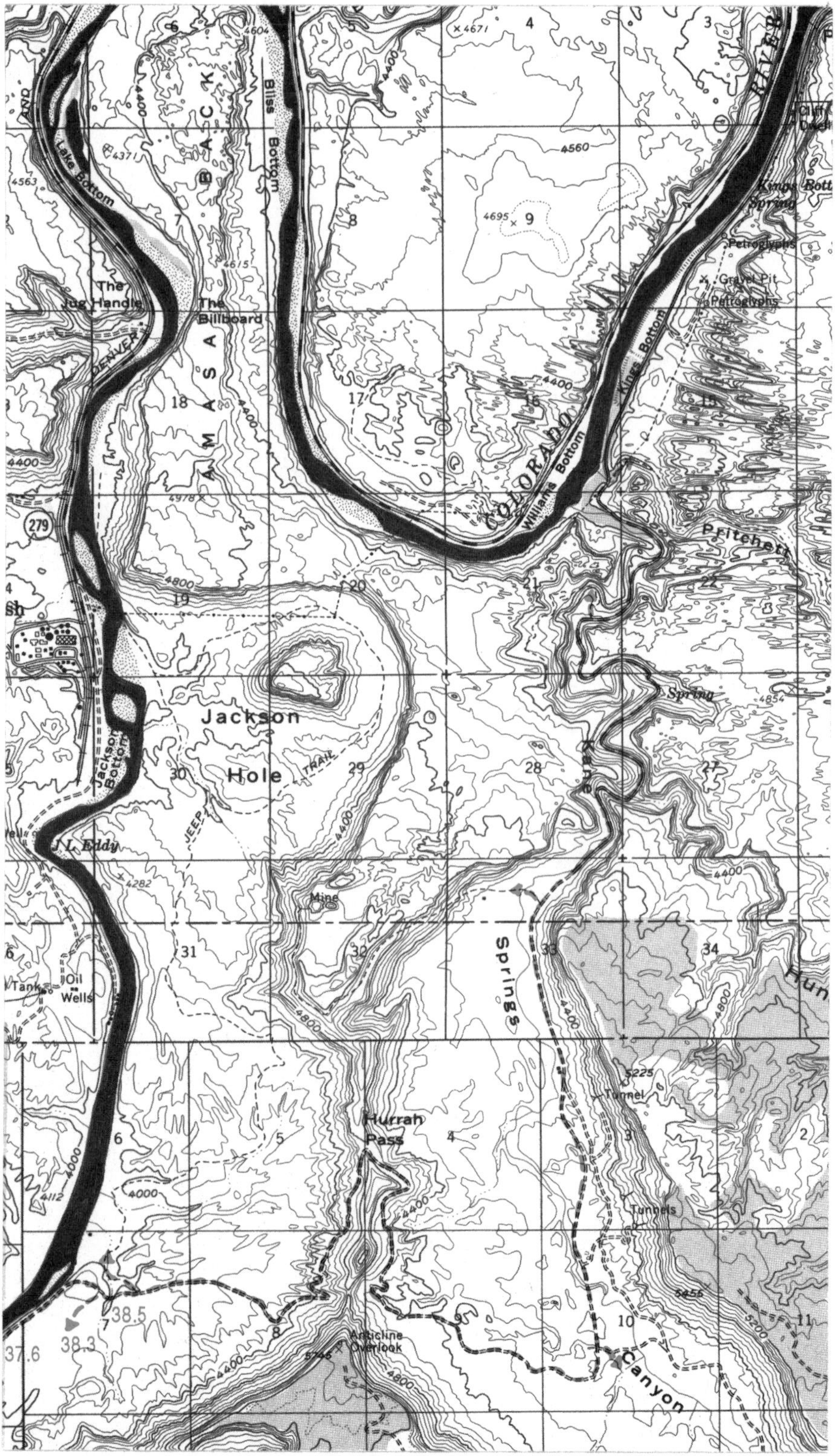

LOCKHART BASIN D

Other Roads / Rides in the Canyon Rims Recreation Area

Dozens of jeep trails and several graded roads crisscross the Canyon Rims plateau. One graded road connects Highway 211 west of Photograph Gap to the Anticline Overlook road near Wind Whistle campground, but the wrong turn can take you into some sandy circumstances. An "inside" road parallels the Overlook road from Highway 191 near Looking Glass Rock across an area of odd, isolated Entrada Slickrock outcrops, connecting to the Anticline Overlook road where the paved spur to Needles Overlook deviates from it. Finally, an enterprising routefinder would enjoy the rough singletrack down Trough Springs Canyon to Kane Springs Canyon, where a sandy jeep trail continues out to Moab.

Lockhart Basin Trail scenes (clockwise from top left) clay soils
wooden cattleguard at park entrance in Lockhart Canyon
Cutler sandstone erosions   Lockhart Butte

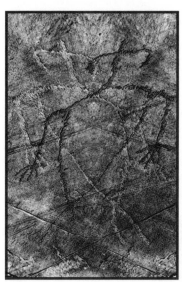

Brothers of One Heart

Boy and Bird over Canyonlands

Kokopellis

The Owl

The Gemini Bridges Area

Between Arches and Canyonlands National Parks, the Gemini Bridges area is a mesa bowed in its middle, incised by intricate canyons and tilted just enough to drain into the Colorado River. It is rimrocked on three sides, and all of these rims sustain popular bike routes—Seven Mile to Little Canyon Rims, Gold Bar Rim and Poison Spider Mesa (to the Portal Trail). But central to the mesa are the Gemini Bridges. They were named by rockhound extraordinaire Lin Ottinger, who located them around 1961 on a tip from an understated cowboy. A decade went by before Lin could find them again, such were the uncertainties of backcountry travel in that day. Now, it isn't uncommon to hear of people playing hacky sack on them or wheelying across them. (Natural selection has its own special way of dealing with folks so inclined.) Before guidebooks were published and signs were erected, the Bridges were easily overlooked. One can nearly stand on top of them without appreciating the gravity (or potential for gravity) of the situation.

The principal cause for the many roads which weave through this area is, of course, minerals exploration. Many drill sites are capped with large poles (and we jokingly herald each one the authentic, the final "West Pole"), but others are hidden under rocks or aluminum dishes. Many hours of amusement can be frittered away in dropping rocks down these drill holes, especially when there is the "ker-sploosh" of water at the bottom. Echoes, too, are a great source of amusement. The "jump" or dry waterfall at Bull Canyon is probably still ringing from the salvos emitted there, for there's a kind of fulfillment in letting your voice go where your feet can't.

Behind the Rocks WSA

Wingate cliffs

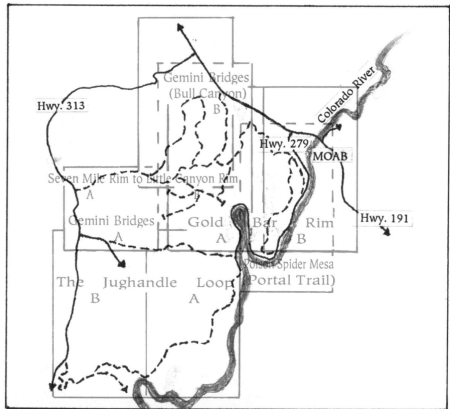

Hwy. 313

Gemini Bridges
(Bull Canyon)
B

Colorado River

Hwy. 279

MOAB

Seven Mile Rim to Little Canyon Rim
A

Gemini Bridges
A

Gold
A

Bar

Rim
B

Hwy. 191

Poison Spider Mesa
(Portal Trail)

The   Jughandle   Loop
B   A

Rider, ruin, Indian Creek vicinity

THE JUGHANDLE LOOP

Type: Loop
Length: 36.3 miles, including 9.2 miles of pavement
Difficulty: Physically difficult / Technically moderate
Best Seasons: Spring and fall
Elevation: Trailhead/-tail/Low—3,960 ft., High—6,180 ft.
Land Agencies: BLM and NPS
Route Summary: From near the Potash Plant, this route parallels the Colorado River downstream on an easily followed road, staying on a slightly rising bench as the river cuts deeply through the strata. Upon intersecting the White Rim Trail, the formidable 1,450 foot ascent of the Shafer Trail's switchbacks looms ahead. From the pavement atop Canyonland's Island in the Sky, the route skirts Dead Horse Point to reach the Wingate cliffs at Pucker Pass, the top of a 1,900 foot descent through Long Canyon back to the trailhead/-tail.

The only reason to take this loop counterclockwise would be to achieve the climb up Long Canyon before the sun is too high. If you get a later start, the shade at the upper reaches of the Shafer Trail makes a pleasant lunch stop.

Attractions: This ride offers splendid views both into from above and out of from within the upper Canyonlands basin, roughly defined by the burnt orange Wingate sandstone cliffs—"the Canyonlands coaming"—of Island in the Sky, Dead Horse Point and the Canyon Rims. Classic overlooks of the Gooseneck of the Colorado fortify its camera-worthiness even further.

Riding Surface: Cobble- and rock-studded sediments and pavement on two-laned jeep trails and highway

Geology: The first nine miles of this route occur in the undivided Cutler sandstone, a brick red rock that erodes into bulbous shapes, like melted wax or dripped sandcastles. The Cutler reveals its interfingering with a hard, gray, fossil-ridden limestone of the Elephant Canyon formation at mile 10.1. This layering or interfingering of two separate rock types is the effect of an ancient shoreline that would leave limestone deposits as the sea advanced and sandstone deposits when it receded. After passing the Shafer Canyon campsite (mile 14.8), you climb through the modest layer of blocky, White Rim sandstone. The ascent up the Shafer Trail passes through here rather amorphous Moenkopi and Chinle formations to bust through the sheer Wingate cliffline at the canyon's head. The descent of Long Canyon reverses the sequence of this geologic stackup, except two formations are missing. The White Rim deposit simply didn't occur this far east, and the Cutler is out of sight, underground. From Pucker Pass (mile 32), you'll notice that all of Long Canyon slopes convexly to the river. The Wingate is no thicker at the mouth of the canyon than it is here at the head. You are near the elongate, sloping crest of the Cane Creek Anticline, an "anticline" defined as none other than an upfolding warp in the strata. Since upwarps need downwarps to equalize the pressures that caused them, the adjacent Gemini Bridges area became the "syncline", or dipped strata.

Notes: The first miles of this ride have been called the "Moab Roubaix" in response to the hammering effect of its packed cobble surface. The route abuts the evaporation ponds integral to the "solution mining" of potash, an ingredient in commercial fertilizers. Water is forced far underground to dissolve soluble minerals, then pumped to the surface so that potash can be recovered upon its evaporation.

Logistics: No permit or shuttle is required.

Trailhead Access: Highway 279 spurs off of Highway 191 about 4 miles north of Moab. Take it another 13.6 miles to an (unposted) trailhead where the dirt road right, past Jughandle Arch, continues up Long Canyon.

Mileage Log and Route Description:
0.0 Continue down the pavement towards the Potash Plant.

3.2 (L) A short climb begins directly after this spur to the Potash Boat Launch, a put-in for float trips through Cataract Canyon to Lake Powell's Hite Marina. Jet boats also put-in here, and they serve the double function of retrieving canoeists who've paddled down the Green River to the Confluence and beyond to Spanish Bottom.

5.8 (R) Before the climb tops out at the evaporation ponds, you may notice the fist-sized catacombs in the slickrock. Various theories attempt to explain these "solution pockets." Helmut Dolling, the State Geologist, believes they might be "petrified air pockets" that were deposited in wet sand and were unable to rise to the surface. Others have concluded, less plausibly, that the pockets once held ironstone orbs that have eroded out. The author's opinion, in never underestimating the potential of genetic "per-mutations," is that the Rockpecker, a missing link between dinosaurs and modern birds, created the pockets. With neither thumbs to create legible petroglyphs, nor the correct mud flats to leave tracks for fossilizing, this sentient creature drilled its message in rock for our reckoning... Really.

10.1 (L) The gray limestone at the head of this canyon cut is this route's first encounter with the Elephant Canyon formation, the dominant rock in the inner gorge of Canyonlands.

12.5 An unforgiving drop off the edge of the road at this bend demands caution.

13.1 (L) The views of the "Goosehead"? from this spur are not to be missed.

14.1 From this "jump" of Shafer Canyon, a walk along the south rim will reveal a simple downclimb to the river. It may be too thin to plow and too thick to drink, but it ain't too wet to swim.

14.8 (R) Shafer Canyon campsite requires a   Park Service permit for use.

15.9 From the kiosk at the White Rim Trail, keep an eye peeled for the desert bighorn that roam the talus in the Shafer basin as you climb your way through sixty million years of sandstone.

21.3 (L) The Island's Visitor Center is a mile down the road. It has audio-visual

displays, with books, maps and film for sale, toilets and a drinking fountain.
32.0 (R) This is another spur to a must-see viewpoint: Long Canyon frames Behind the Rocks and the La Sal Mountains.

> Many of us carried cameras in our saddle bags, and they were often used, but images on paper or projected on a screen have a missing dimension… Being a purely mechanical device it cannot plumb the emotional response to the exquisite beauty of a cactus blossom shrouded in thorns, the call of a canyon wren echoing from the walls of a silent gorge, the tinkle of a tiny cascade in a land where water is more precious than gold, the camaraderie around an evening campfire among friends who have shared a hard day in the saddle.

> Randall Henderson, <u>On Desert Trails</u>, 1961

36.3 Enjoy your well-earned descent through Pucker Pass (you tell me) down to the trailhead/-tail.

Upper Canyonlands basin

JUGHANDLE LOOP B

The Knoll
⊗6313

7

8

6000

Landing Strip

Little Valley

6120

6174

×6000

18

17

6046

Oil Wells

B I G

F L A T

△6

6195

6000

19

20

6000

6040

Res

Big Flat Res

30

29

Hwy. 313

5920

DEAD

HORSE

Gravel Pit

5920

6000

5920

36

STATE

31

32

6012△

CANYONLANDS NATIONAL PARK

5906

2

6

5

Middle

Fork

East

Sea
lat

×5895

21.3

4800

5600

Campground

Shafer Canyon

Fork

South

WHITE RIM

Dead Horse Pt.

5000

5449

158

4800

4800

4400

4800

4400

Goose

TRAIL

18

4808

le Neck

5950

5924

Spring

Neck

JUGHANDLE LOOP A

GEMINI BRIDGES (BULL CANYON)

Type: One-way (with an optional "partial loop" through Bull Canyon)
Length: 13.7 miles
Difficulty: Physically easy / Technically moderate
Best Season: Spring and fall
Elevation: Trailhead/High—5,940 ft., Trailtail/Low—4,575 ft.
Land Agency: BLM
Route Summary: The basic Gemini Bridges route follows well marked roads on its descent across Arth's Pasture to Little Canyon, a "hanging valley," whose uppermost reaches look like they ought to drain towards Highway 191, but don't. A steep descent out of Little Canyon reaches the trailtail at Highway 191, with the option to coast back to Moab.
Options: Bull Canyon provides an optional detour to the box canyon "under-looking" the Bridges. You can also continue to Bull's spilloff into Day Canyon, and a short backtrack accesses a partial loop past Two Tortoise and Monticello Rocks to the basic Gemini Bridges route. Various dead end spurs up Four Arch, Dry Fork of Bull Canyon, and Porthole Arch Canyon are possible options, too.
Attractions: This ride can tour most of the canyons central to the Gemini Bridges area, canyons walled by slickrock fins and tapered facades. Debate still occurs as to whether the twin Gemini Bridges truly span a watercourse, for it's the rare person who has seen it flow. Even if they are "merely" arches, they are a sight to behold.
Riding Surface: Rock-studded sediments, packed drift sand and washbottom sand on jeep trails and two-laned dirt roads
Geology: The curious thing about the Gemini Bridges area is that it is one of the few places where Wingate sandstone has eroded into slickrock fins and domes. Where it becomes "un-capped" by the Kayenta formation, it usually spalls away in columnal fractures clear to its base. The Bridges are at the contact between the two layers and are representative of the back- and under-cutting effects of erosion on a harder, overlying layer. The Kayenta formation is light to white, sometimes chalky purple-brown, and it composes the entire Gold Bar Rim nearby, as well as most of Arth's Pasture, where it is covered by soil and vegetation. The handful of rocks that rise conspicuously above the area are remnants of the Navajo sandstone that has been mostly scoured away. This area is reflecting the stress of two forces—the synclinal sinking adjacent to the Cane Creek Anticline (see Jughandle Loop or Hurrah Pass "Geology" summaries) and the radical uplifting of the fault block along the western wall of Moab Valley—stresses that have bowed the Gemini Bridges area from its rims inward. With this tilt, four canyons cut drainages that intersect the river all within the space of a mile, across from the tip of Amasa Back.

Logistics: Although use of a shuttle from the trailtail back to the trailhead is common, it might be easier and less time-consuming to hire a "taxi" to the trailhead for a drop-off.

Trailhead Access: The (posted) trailtail occurs on the way to the trailhead from Moab, a dirt spur to the left off of Highway 191 11.2 miles from Main x Center St.'s. The (posted) trailhead is another 1.3 miles to Highway 313, then up it for 12.8 miles to a dirt spur (left, between mile marks 10 and 9).

Mileage Log and Route Description:

0.0 Begin by descending on the Boulevard, the prominent throughway across Arth's Pasture.

4.0 A (signed) acute spur to the right leaves the Boulevard for Gemini Bridges near the "West Pole."

4.7 At the "T," a right turn can take you 2.9 miles up the sandy Four Arch Canyon, a box canyon with a pastoral feel and at least four arches near its head.

5.6 A sign with an arrow machine-routed on it marks the right turn to Gemini Bridges from a vague, four-way intersection. Stay right at the first fork (mile 5.7), then, bearing left, let gravity sift you down through the myriad routes to the Bridges, which are on Bull Canyon's very rim. Upon leaving the Bridges, stay right, at previous mile 5.7, to continue your odyssey.

6.3 (L) At the obtuse spur, bear right again to head east on this slickrock and sandflats road which re-intersects the Boulevard in little over a mile.

8.4 At this huge intersection, you have the option of touring the Bull Canyon drainage by taking the obtuse spur to the right, onto the "Trigger" road. (The description of this option will be indented.) The basic route reconnects with this option in 0.6 of a mile by continuing straight, bypassing the spurs to the right, and descending a hill of fill material into Little Canyon at mile 9.0.

> **0.0 (previously 8.4)** Descend into the Bull Canyon drainage via the Trigger road.
>
> **1.3 (L)** This spur climbs to Two Tortoise Rock and beyond to close the loop with the basic Gemini Bridges ride. However, there are some places ahead you might care to check out before taking this turn.
>
> **1.7 (R)** A (signed) spur to Bull Canyon ends beneath the Gemini Bridges in another 2.1 miles by avoiding all spurs to the left.
>
> **1.8 (R)** This spur goes another 3.4 miles up the Dry Fork of Bull, where there's a (sometimes dry) springfed cattle trough, a potential "ride-thru" arch, a cross-sectioned, collapsed fin and several old mineworks to explore.
>
> **2.1** At the sand dune, you are near the 400 foot "jump" of Bull Canyon close to its junction with Day Canyon, the turnaround spot at the end of the Trigger. (The route description will be twice indented for its continuation from previous mile 1.3, the spur to Two Tortoise Rock.)
>
> > **1.3** After a quick switchback, stay right, at the road split.
> >
> > **1.8** Bear left onto the first of two spurs on this ridgetop, unless you want to take the dead end to Two Tortoise for the walk to the river overlook beyond.

213

2.8 From this sandy crossing of lower Little Canyon, you could make an emergency escape down Little Canyon, portaging across a blasted ledge and out to Highway 279.

4.0 Turn left as you skirt Monticello Rock in order to avoid the route up to Gold Bar Rim.

5.1 After flailing through the sand, this is the rendezvous with the basic Gemini Bridges route (mile 9.0).

9.7 (R) Dead end spur 0.7 of a mile up Porthole Arch Canyon.

11.4 (R) You can see how Little Canyon is "hanging" on the rim overlooking Highway 191, but drains back towards the river. Despite appearances, it never would have drained towards the highway, as the erosion which revealed it occurred 150 million years after bulging salt lifted this rim-to-be along its fault block.

The spurs just passed all climb through a light-blue, clay-rich formation called Chinle. This is indicative of mining roads throughout the region, which, because of the carbonized organic remains in Chinle that attract seeping uranium, became popular places to push roads. And since this layer is easy to bulldoze, is not solid rock, and has a friendlier angle of repose than cliffy formations, many of the area's roads end up crossing the Chinle. Travelers should beware that Chinle road cuts are slippery when wet. The gumming and clogging of your bike's components can impair and even shear them off.

13.7 Trailhead/-tail

Bighorn ram skull

Never purchase before taking a test drive

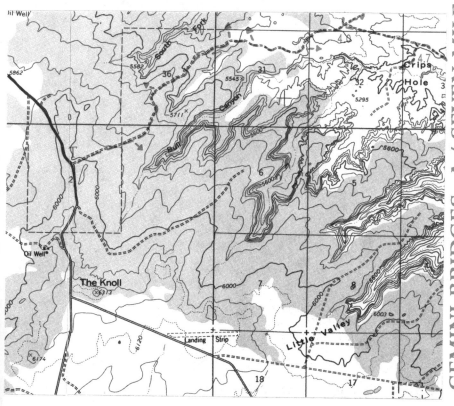

GEMINI BRIDGES (BULL CANYON) B

Canyon
BM 4484
BM 4405
4800
4400
3
2
1
Wash
4604
Hwy. 191
4610
4800
BM 4583
6
PIPELINE
Tunnel
11
Pit
12
7
4800
Tunnel
Court
VABM 5701
BM 4568
4808
5200
16
15
14
13
11.4
18
Oil
4800
16
15
14
4800
Moab
BM
21
22
23
5067
19
5200
5045
Little
5025
Gold Bar
5192
27
26
25
30
4800
4800
4942
The Boulevard
4823
18.4
4.0
Monticello Rock
5200
Canyon
Trigger Road
Canyon
Bull
5.6
5162
34
35
36
31
ERN
13
28
Canyon
4823
GRANDE
Two Tortoise Rock
Canyon
4800
Pin
Canyon
Bull
Fork
3
4651
Dry
4604
TRAIL
Bar
4371
4563
4800
Bliss Bottom

SEVEN MILE CANYON RIM TO LITTLE CANYON RIM

Type: One-way
Length: 21.7 miles
Difficulty: Physically moderate / Technically difficult
Best Season: Spring and fall
Elevation: Trailhead/High—5,940 ft., Trailtail/Low—4,575 ft.
Land Agency: BLM
Route Summary: Like the Gemini Bridges route, this trail descends the Boulevard to the "West Pole," but flares north instead of south. It takes some unlikely turns on its way to the rim of Seven Mile Canyon's South Fork. (Highway 313 follows its North Fork for a ways.) It proceeds to leave the rim and climb a spine separating the Seven Mile and Little Canyon drainages, culminating in some wild, 360° views of the warped, trenched, hoisted, cleaved, and punched-through rock that makes so much of this rugged area *de facto* wilderness. From this dramatic point near the head of Little Canyon, the route stairsteps down Mirror Gulch and becomes somewhat obscure, as the plane of Kayenta defies tracking. Even after it reaches soil roadbeds, numerous spurs compromise decisive travel. The route crosses an arm of Little Canyon just above a pouroff, then swings southward to rejoin the Boulevard for the ride out Little Canyon to Highway 191.
Attractions: This ride is the natural complement to the Gemini Bridges ride, as it has the same trailhead and trailtail, and promotes a literal "overview" of this complicated area. The terrain is as diverse as the difference between slickrock and drift sand, with potential for excellent slickrock routefinding and outright off-trail playing on Wingate sandstone, an opportunity afforded by a rare geologic serendipity.
Riding Surface: Rock-studded sediments, slickrock and wash sand on jeep trails and two-laned dirt roads
Geology: (Refer to the Gemini Bridges "Geology" briefing.)
Logistics: Although use of a shuttle from the trailtail back to the trailhead is common, it might be easier and less time-consuming to hire a "taxi" to the trailhead for a drop-off.
Trailhead Access: The trailtail occurs on the way to the trailhead from Moab, a dirt spur to the left off of Highway 191 11.2 miles from Main x Center St.'s. The (posted) trailhead (to "Gemini Bridges") is another 1.3 miles to Highway 313, then up it for 12.8 miles to a dirt spur (left, between mile marks 10 and 9).

Mileage Log and Route Description:
0.0 Begin by descending on the Boulevard, the prominent throughway across Arth's Pasture.
4.0 Just before the turn to Gemini Bridges, take the doubletrack left.

217

4.4 Take a right at this vague four way intersection obscured by a juniper **(R)**
7.6 (L) Avoid this spur after negotiating the two ledge drops. It's hard to say whether these jeep routes are harder on the rock or the trees nearby, whose convenient, branch-shorn presence makes great winch anchorpoints.
10.8 From this perch, you'll notice that the rock beneath you has no counterpart eastward, in Arches. While this rim was thrust upwards by bulging salt, the mass across the way dipped down, providing vertical displacement of a mile either side of the Moab Fault. As you leave the rim you'll be greeted by the other 180° of the world, a revelation that makes one want to name this place something inspiring, like "Cow Point."

The next couple of miles are quite challenging, as you descend through Mirror Gulch (named after its habit of separating jeep from side-view mirror) and generally parallel Little Canyon's rim. Although use of the trail finding techniques mentioned earlier in this book can help, an absolutely foolproof means of routefinding is to doggedly trace out each likely spur until it dead ends or intersects a meaningful trail.
11.5 (L) Ignore the audacious, double-humped ascent to find the contour-able route lower on the slickrock. When you come to the rim of Little Canyon, consider striking out on foot to explore some intricate fingers of Wingate. After continuing the slickrock descent for half a mile, the route angles away from the rim-paralleling route about 15° to pick up a roadcut in the thin pinyon-juniper.
12.9 Take this acute spur right.
13.7 (L) The cottonwood trees advertise a swimming hole.
14.5 Take this acute spur (left, onto the slickrock roadbed) that is shrouded by some trees. This turn leaves the conspicuous road for an inconspicuous one, but if you miss it, other roads ahead will get you where you need to go.
16.2 At the Boulevard, take a left to finish the ride along easy-to-follow roads.

The indefatigueable John Groo

218

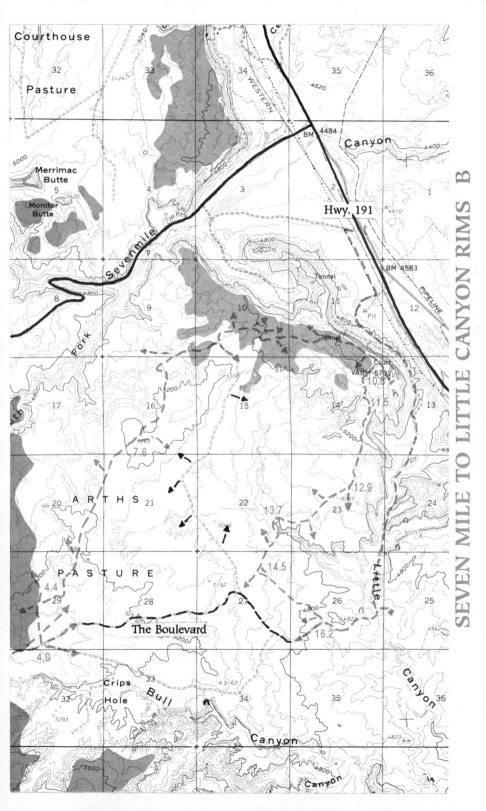

SEVEN MILE TO LITTLE CANYON RIMS B

View of Arches National Park from the "hanging" Little Canyon

Gold Bar Rim under heavy snow

GOLD BAR RIM

Type: One-way
Length: 15.9 miles
Difficulty: Physically difficult / Technically gonzo-abusive
Best Season: Spring and fall
Elevation: Trailhead—4,575 ft., High—5,500 ft., Low/Trailtail—3,965 ft.
Land Agency: BLM
Route Summary: From its trailhead on Highway 191, this route switchbacks up to the head of the "hanging" Little Canyon to traverse it for a couple of miles before turning to climb the massive shelf of rock that terminates at Gold Bar Rim, the cliff's edge some 1500 feet above the floor of Moab Canyon. The route becomes somewhat more difficult to follow as it traverses the Rim, but the generous use of cairns assists its finding. As it works southward along the Rim, thinning members of the ledgy Kayenta formation force a circuitous trail in places. Finally, at the top of the Portal Trail, an exposed singletrack pasted on a narrow ledge shimmies across to above the Portal, the place where the Colorado River leaves Moab Valley. The track then becomes extremely rugged in its fast drop to the trailtail on Highway 279.
Options: With as little as ten miles of pavement riding, you could make this a loop ride by starting from anywhere between the trailhead and trailtail.
Attractions: This trail is ideal for people who love trials riding. The Kayenta formation seems to erode piecemeal, a small boulder abutting a larger one, and so forth. The views are unimpeded, allowing a body to see from the Uncompahgre Plateau to the Book cliffs in Colorado and from the White Rim to Castle Rock in Utah, and most places in between. Although the route rarely goes to the very edge, you can often ride to it with no difficulty.
Riding Surface: Slickrock, rock-studded sediments and wash sand on jeep trails, two-laned dirt roads and singletrack
Geology: (Refer to the Gemini Bridges "Geology.") The Portal Trail descends the Kayenta formation all the way. The ledges were tilted by a salt mass's upward intrusion along the fault block that edges the Moab Valley.
Notes: The Portal Trail is so exposed to vertical edges that in places it is hardly safe enough to walk beside your bike. The subtleties of reading trail across bedrock makes navigation difficult on Gold Bar Rim. Preferably, ride with a buddy who's ridden this trail before.
Logistics: If you were to make a loop of this ride, probably the best place to leave a vehicle would be somewhere along Highway 279 near its junction with Highway 191 north of Moab.
Trailhead Access: The trailtail is roughly 4 miles down Highway 279 from its start at Highway 191, which is also roughly 4 miles from Moab. There are several turnouts near it, and it is denoted by a small brown sign with the profile of a hiker stenciled on it. If you pass the first campsite (the Lion's

Park) on the right, you've gone too far (although the Portal Trail does connect to this cottonwood shrouded pull-in).

The trailhead is at a dirt spur left from Highway 191 10 miles north of Moab (Main x Center St.'s) where a sign denotes access to Gemini Bridges.

Mileage Log and Route Description:
0.0 The road turns to parallel the highway before making the big climb.
4.8 Where a right turn climbs the hill of fill material towards Gemini Bridges, take a left into the wash.
6.4 This is a critical turn to make a left on after passing Monticello Rock. The route (straight) dead ends in just over a mile.
7.3 (L) Spur one mile to overlook "The Bride" in Pothole Arch Canyon.
8.8 As you near the rim, a short spur (L) to the edge provides a fine viewpoint. The route then follows "golden spikes" painted on bedrock across Gold Bar Rim. There is one deviation from this jeep trail, a fun singletrack which closely parallels the rim instead of descending several hundred feet. Not a minute's ride from the spur to the rim, this deviation wiggles left through some knee-high boulders just after the first ledge dropoff.
9.5 The jeep trail connects from the right. Take another trip to the rim to see up close the rockfall that happened in early 1989.
10.4 Just before a high outcrop of rimrock causes the route to descend off the rim, you can climb into and through a five-foot arch that sits out on the edge. Routefinding for the next few miles is complicated by multiple trails. After reaching the dry wash that drains into Bootlegger Canyon, stay left, climbing continuously on bedrock, then on the dirt road for a mile up to the rim.
13.6 Where the road again reaches the rim, look for the large cairn that denotes the singletrack start of the Portal Trail.

14.7 Well, you've completed the exposed part. Across the river is the Moab Rim Trail, the Portal Trail's alter ego. Check your brakes, your headset, your forks and frame for hairline fractures, your helmet strap and your life insurance policy for this gonzo-abusive gust of gravity.

15.9 BLM Trail Register. Let them know who you is and how you be. A fork goes either to the pavement or continues right, for another 0.4 of a mile to the Lion's Park campsite.

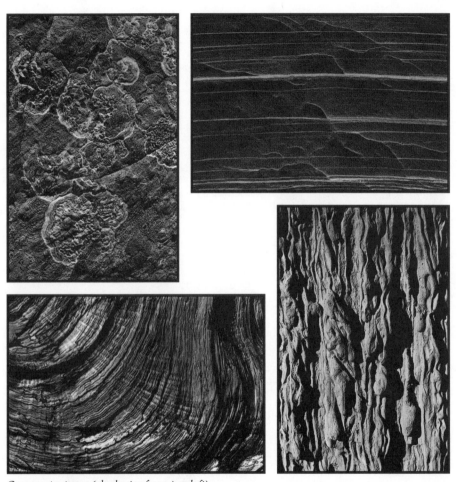

Canyon textures (clockwise from top left)
lichen
striated rock
dried sand drippings
juniper tree

223

GOLD BAR RIM A

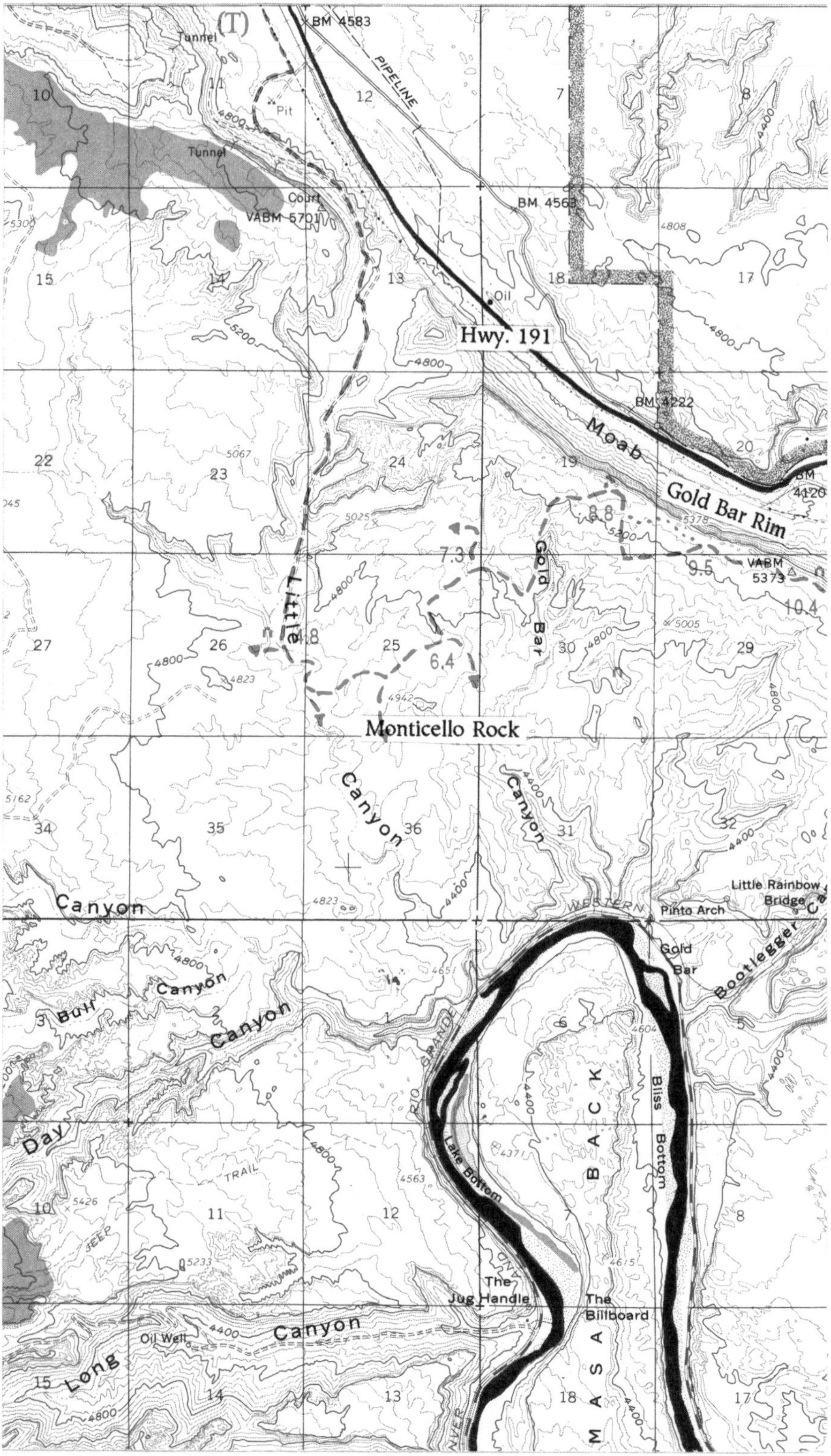

Courthouse

Sheep Rock Tower of Babel

Courthouse Towers

Three Gossips The Organ

Park Avenue

LaSal Mtn Viewpoint

Wash

Monument Hdqrs
Water

Canyon

BM 4021

Substation

279

Ore Reduction Plant

Matrimony Spring

128

COLORADO

Reservoir

Water Tank
BM 3985

Elk Mtn Mission Historical Mon

M O A B

Sewage Disposal

Moab
(BM 4026)

Mill

The Portal Trail

R I V E R

Sewage Disposal

TraiNer Parks

The Portal

Cliff Dwellings

Kings Bottom Spring

Petroglyphs

Petroglyphs

Kings Bottom

High Sch.

Pack

Jackson Res.

Water Tank

Drive-In Theatre

PIPELINE

The view of Behind the Rocks from Poison Spider Mesa

POISON SPIDER MESA (PORTAL TRAIL)

Type: Out-and-back (with the option of closing a loop via the Portal Trail)
Length: 11.4 miles (or 12.0, including at least 1.4 miles on pavement)
Difficulty: Physically moderate to difficult / Technically difficult (to gonzo-abusive)
Best Season: Spring and fall
Elevation: Trailhead/-tail/Low—3,965 ft., High—5,040 ft.
Land Agency: BLM
Route Summary: From the Colorado River, this trail switchbacks up cobble roads, creases blasted slickrock passes and struggles across deep sand to emerge atop the alluvium of Poison Spider Mesa. Multiple-trailing can confuse the way over a field of slickrock humps breaching in an ocean of sand, but line-of-sight orienteering will guide you to the high dome concealing Little Window, an arch that frames the river far below.
Options: For the "hard corps" an intermittent sand and rock struggle through a maze of multiple trails up to the Gold Bar Rim can set you up for a descent of the infamous Portal Trail, a gonzo-abusive trail if only for to walk a bike. The Navajo sandstone supplies freeform routes to anywhere on the Mesa.
Attractions: Poison Spider combines purist slickrock skills with blast-and-blow surfaces like cobble, sand and ledgy rock. Its view of Behind the Rocks Wilderness Study Area, crowned by the La Sals, is one of the prettiest sights anywhere, especially after having been earned by the strenuous climb.
Riding Surface: Cobble- and rock-studded sediments, drift sand and slickrock on jeep trails, singletrack and overland routes across slickrock
Geology: The Navajo sandstone, made famous by the Slickrock Trail, is the dominant formation on Poison Spider Mesa. Close scrutiny will reveal it as the compressed and cemented remains of windblown sand dunes. Striated and tilted "bedding planes" sweep upwards to terminate abruptly across the grain of others, their dome-like shapes merely enhancing a dizzying curvaceousness. (Refer to the Gold Bar Rim "Geology" summary.)
Logistics: No permit or shuttle is necessary.
Trailhead Access: From its junction with Highway 191 about 4 miles north of Moab, take Highway 279 5.8 miles to the "Dinosaur Tracks" sign, where a spur ascends a rocky ledge to the Mesa. There are turnouts nearby for trailhead parking. Be forewarned that laden tractor-trailers barrel around the downstream bend fast enough to take you unaware, so keep your booty off the road!

Mileage Log and Route Description:

0.0 The varnished rock tilted near the rim 100 feet above the gate has all sorts of tracks left by prehistoric lizards as they roamed the coastal swamps and freshwater mudflats near an ancient seashore. It is unusual to find their tracks in the Kayenta formation, for they're usually seen in the Morrison or Moab Tongue of the Entrada. "These animals generally left tracks where there was water only temporarily. Moab was like the Sahara Desert, pretty dry like now, but sandy, not rocky," according to Dr. Martin Lockley, a University of Colorado geologist.

2.3 As you encounter the first sand trap, be mindful to let the bike steer itself. Try to stay laterally balanced on it, with your weight as much as possible on the rear wheel. After turfing and plowing, the trail climbs some blasted "stairs," then takes an immediate right, through another blasted pass for more "bean pumpers." The next two blast zones are easily bypassed on the left.

3.1 Once you've reached the alluvium terrace, **the painted stencil of a jeep on the bedrock** will become a familiar trail guide.

4.8 (R) Spur on slickrock to a river overlook. The vegetation here includes blackbrush and Mormon tea or ephedra, a plant with medicinal values as a mild stimulant, decongestant, and pain reliever for joints.

5.1 Upon descending the hill, most of the next mile is an exercise in routefinding. The Navajo sandstone dome almost due east, with a blunt left side but long, inclining right is your target. Anything from a bee-line to a riverside meander can chart you there, and following the ubiquitous jeep stencil is sure to get you close.

5.7 Duck in alongside the shady side of the dome, sidehilling between the junipers and its face to skitter down the ramp dividing the bowl right, and the juniper garden left. The "viewing deck" to the arch and the Portal below is the turnaround spot for those not continuing on the Portal Trail, and the way back means simply retracing your tracks.

One last sobering thought. A mountain biker fell to his death from the Portal Trail. If you are not a solid bike handler, if you suffer from vertigo or if you don't recognize your own limits, you're going to hate the WALK down, for it's harder than the ride.

Once we reached the level of the most promising ledge, we could see only a section of it. The rest was out of sight around the bend, and we had no way of knowing whether it pinched out to nothing. The shelf where we stood was close to nothing—just a narrow strip, wide enough for one man, with a slanting shoulder that dipped steeply downward for a few yards from the shelf and then dropped off sheer.

Pure COWARDICE (*author's emphasis*) got me onto that ledge: the fear of what the others would think if I did not dare follow them.

Jerome Doolittle, <u>Canyons and Mesas</u>, 1974

To continue from the viewing deck, work directly away from the river to pick up the white stencils on a nearby dome.

6.2 The route drops onto a sinfully sandy jeep trail, spurring left, then avoiding two spurs to the left before meeting a "T." Turn right at this intersection to approach Gold Bar Rim.

7.9 From this viewpoint overlooking Moab Valley, the Gold Bar Rim Trail intersects from the north, and the Portal Trail singletracks across the ledge to the south. Wile E. Coyote, eat your heart out.

9.0 Well, you've completed the exposed part. Across the river is the Moab Rim Trail, the Portal Trail's alter ego. Check your brakes, your headset, your forks and frame for hairline fractures, your helmet strap and your life insurance policy for this gonzo-abusive gust of gravity.

10.2 BLM Trail Register. Let them know who you is and how you be. A fork goes either to the pavement or continues (right) for another 0.4 of a mile to the Lion's Park campsite. On the highway, your warmdown passes Wall St., a cliff popular amongst climbers that was made famous by local "rock jock" Kyle Copeland, another of Moab's resolutely flawed characters.

Routefinding near the river gorge, Poison Spider Mesa

Poison Spider Mesa as seen from the Kane Creek Road

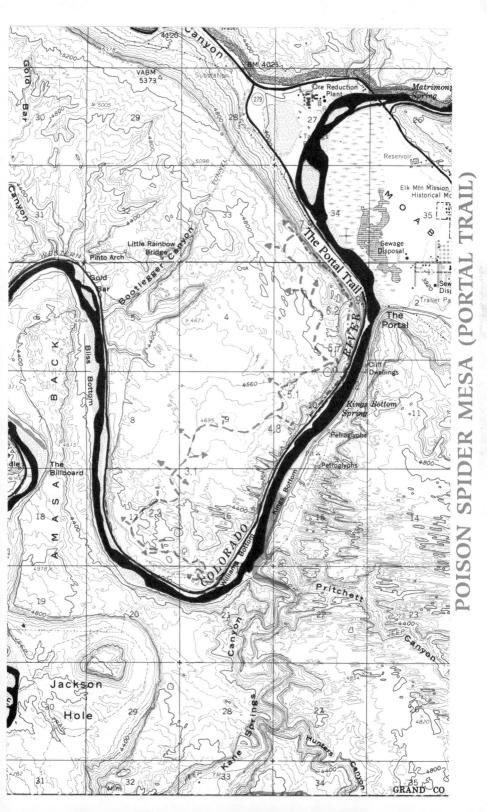

POISON SPIDER MESA (PORTAL TRAIL)

Other Roads / Rides in the Gemini Bridges Area

Stemming from Highway 313 and its connector to Pucker Pass, there are countless sandy roads to points overlooking each of the canyons in the Gemini Bridges Area. The most ridable of these is the spur to a river overlook on the point between Long and Day Canyons. Many of the sandy roads end near intriguing downclimbs through splits in the Wingate, and one side canyon even allows jeep traffic through a rocky passage. Suffice to say, one could portage a bike down into Bull, Day or the broad amphitheater-shaped canyon due west of Potash to pick up sandy road exits below. Seven Mile Canyon is traced by several roads that intersect the Boulevard, but where they get interesting, they too are prohibitively sandy.

Natural Selection Viewpoint on the Slickrock Trail

In life, it seems, we seldom have genuine callings. Our careers are incidental, almost by definition, to what truly blisses us out. Mostly, we do what others can't, or don't. Thus, our proclivity towards mountain biking.

A rare combination of backcountry abilities separate us from hikers, equestrians or ORV users. Not only are we mechanically self-sufficient, but we can travel far in a day with little compromise ceded to weight, manueverability or access, because when the going gets rough, the rough carry their bikes. We can portage or hike-a-bike around obstacles which discourage others. We can ford creeks and climb walls, scale talus and skirt falls only because our machine is small and light and uses a renewable energy source—us.

This fortuitous little dance has its drawbacks, though. Shoulders go arthritic in just twenty minutes of portaging. Water bottle cages get tweaked. Saddles get scored by branches, and chain oil leaves "novice marks" on sleeves and cuffs. But worse, the bike is always bumping into something just as you are in between strides. On exposed climbs, the effect is daunting. You are off balance, and attempts to recover it have you ramming the bike even harder against that solid something that threw you off balance in the first place.

Therefore, it is necessary to extend your personal space to include your bike when you're carrying it, and if possible, even when you're not. There is a synergistic effect, an overall riding health which is dictated by the relationship between carrier and carried, person and bike being interchangeable. Fear for your bike's safety. And be happy to carry it, after all the places it's carried you.

The Moab Area

It is surprising how swiftly one can forsake the plastic and pavement for the privacy of the backcountry. To most people, Moab MEANS the Slickrock Bike Trail, that rumpled bedspread of stone that cloaks the valley. And while there are many worthwhile rides around, none is as notorious or as popular as the Bike Trail. When your slickrock learning curve falters, take a day off to explore Hurrah Pass, Back of Behind or Flat Pass to see the scenery behind the scenery. You'll be drawn out on the subtleties that are compressed to extremes on the Bike Trail, where only rock and sand predominate. You'll see (other types of rock and other types of sand!) creeks, canyon bottoms, petroglyphs, springs, and even "real" trees.

THE MOAB SLICKROCK BIKE TRAIL

The Slickrock Bike Trail, the world's own "designer bike path," needs no introduction. It is a good place to explore—to practice getting lost—for sooner or later you'd come to a rim of its mesa for a look across valley or canyon that's either teeming with people or conspicuously absent them. It's been said that anything you can conceive of can exist. On the Slickrock, this notion is a palpable fact, where concepts such as "will" and "savvy" measure as large as "brute strength," which more often hinders than enhances good judgement.

It would be presumptuous to cast restrictions on the Trail: Type, Length, Difficulty, and so forth, because despite the 12.7 miles (on Main Trail) painted lines that suggest routes, the mesa in its entirety offers a free and unrestricted approach to mountain biking that can be staggering when finally grasped. Complaints of the Trail's overcrowding are spoken by lemming-like minds. The Slickrock Trail is, and ought to remain, a place to "enlighten your load."

> ... if you survive, if you make it, you learn to despise not the Canyon but your own fear and foolishness, in being unprepared, and return again and again, ready to risk everything for one more intimate encounter with the most sublime place on the planet. Who could ask for a finer place than our Canyon in which to taste life deeply by risking life? By hanging it over the edge?
>
> Edward Abbey, <u>Down the River</u>, 1982

(A fine map of the Slickrock Trail that sandwiches an aerial photo with satellite-pinpointed trail detail, overlaid by specific route names and difficulty ratings, has been published by Latitude 40° Inc.)

Family Fun

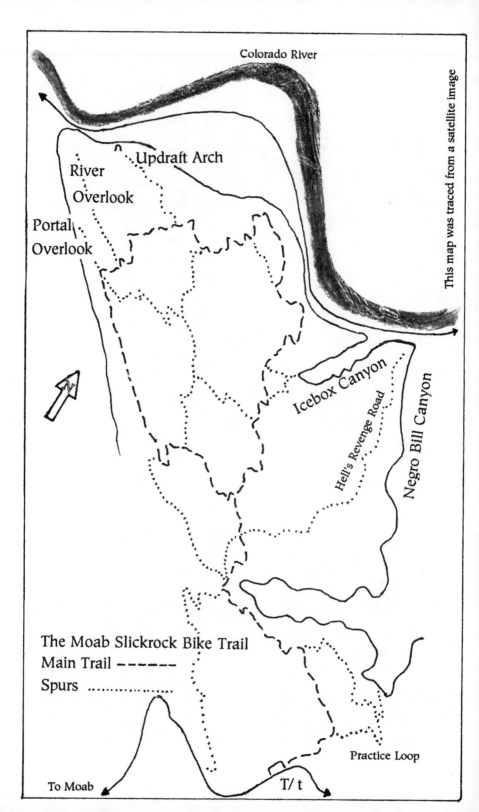

Colorado River

This map was traced from a satellite image

Updraft Arch

River
Overlook

Portal
Overlook

N

Icebox Canyon

Hell's Revenge Road

Negro Bill Canyon

The Moab Slickrock Bike Trail
Main Trail − − − − −
Spurs ....

Practice Loop

T/ t

To Moab

Slickrock: the most fun you can have with your clothes on

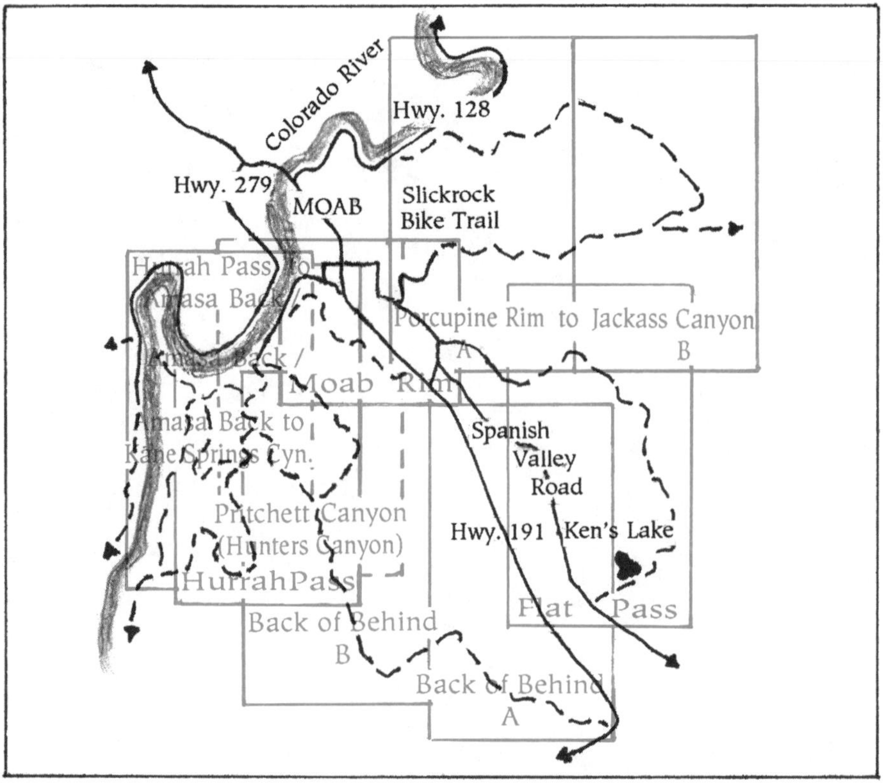

Colorado River
Hwy. 128
Hwy. 279
MOAB
Slickrock
Bike Trail
Hurrah Pass to
Amasa Back /
Porcupine Rim to Jackass Canyon
A
B
Amasa Back /
Moab Rim
Amasa Back to
Kane Springs Cyn.
Spanish
Valley
Road
Pritchett Canyon
(Hunters Canyon)
Hwy. 191
Ken's Lake
HurrahPass
Flat Pass
Back of Behind
B
Back of Behind
A

Typical terrain near Sand Flats Road

PORCUPINE RIM TO JACKASS CANYON

Type: One-way
Length: 20.8 miles, including 6.4 miles on pavement
Difficulty: Physically difficult / Technically difficult
Best Season: Spring and fall
Elevation: Trailhead—5,900 ft., High—6,810 ft., Low/Trailtail—3,970 ft.
Land Agency: BLM
Route Summary: From some stock tanks on the Sand Flats Road, this always confusing route climbs about four miles to Porcupine Rim, the cliff high above the community of Castle Valley. After lingering near the Rim, the route picks up an old seismograph road that more or less bee-lines down towards a prominent knob of Navajo sandstone called Coffee Pot Rock. At the last possible chance, a right turn from one of the many skewed four-way intersections keeps you atop the ridge above Coffee Pot Rock in order to bypass it. From here, the even faster and rockier descent threads the ridge between Drinks and Jackass Canyons to later dip across Jackass and connect with an ingenious singletrack that follows a single, angling ledge for nearly 4 miles of duking and dodging down to the Colorado. A 6.4 mile warmdown on the pavement back to Moab rounds out the ride.
Options: A 10.4 mile climb of nearly 2,000 feet up the Sand Flats Road from Moab can precede the route as described to make a loop.
Attractions: Because of its potential for high speed, plus a great singletrack, this ride has become one of the area's most popular. Enormous views of Castle Rock, the Priest and Nuns, the Colorado River gorge and Arches National Park make this a scenic ride, but the inevitable jarring might damage a camera.
Riding Surface: Rock-studded sediments, drift sand and pavement on jeep trail, singletrack and highway
Geology: As you climb to the trailhead from Moab, the Navajo sandstone cannot quite "keep up" with the ever-steepening tilt of the land. Coffee Pot Rock and three or four other outcrops are isolated beacons of Navajo in a ledgy, Kayenta-dominated pinyon/juniper forest. Porcupine Rim is virtually identical to Gold Bar Rim in its creation, except it's 1,300 feet higher. Like Moab Valley, Castle Valley is a salt valley or salt-intruded anticline. And like Moab Valley, the fault block is located under the valley's western border. The inexorable subsurface pressure of 15,000 feet of bulging salt lifted, bulged and ultimately cracked the brittle rock above, trenching the long gash that was to become Castle Valley. Porcupine Rim is "fast" collapsing into this widening gulf, as illustrated by the long talus slopes at its base. The singletrack descent to Highway 128 utilizes a tilted shelf that resulted from this massive upheaval, just as the Portal and Moab Rim Trails do.
Logistics: The most common way to do this shuttle is to take one vehicle to

the trailhead and leave another in Moab. Various taxi services and bike outfitters in Moab provide drop-offs for a nominal fee.

Trailhead Access: From Moab, head towards the Slickrock Trail but keep going. Two metal stock tanks by the (left) side of the Sand Flats Road at mile 10.4 from Moab signify the (unposted) trailhead.

Mileage Log and Route Description:

0.0 You may want to top your water bottles off at the springfed tanks. Please leave the gate as you found it, that is, open or closed.

5.2 After several views from the Rim, the road begins to set its sights on Coffee Pot Rock. Go right at this spur to AVOID the mile-long straight-shot to see what's brewing. If you by some chance get "sucked" down to the rock, a spur connects it back up to the throughway by means of a short climb.

10.4 The route descends the ridge towards the three prominent outcrops, crosses some bedrock, then veers left here where a road continues straight to an unbelievably abrupt view of the river at Big Bend. Some tight turns on loose rock preface the quick dip across Jackass' wash.

11.2 After the first pitch up the sandy hill, the singletrack spur is clearly marked by cairns. The nearby view into Jackass Canyon is a shocker, the kind that makes you distrust your own body. The best piece of advice for the upcoming singletrack, at least at the time this book was written, is to stay right whenever you're faced with a split in the track.

14.4 After heading the final drainage, beware of traffic on Highway 128.

20.8 Main x Center St.'s

The collared lizard, the canyon's most brazen of critters

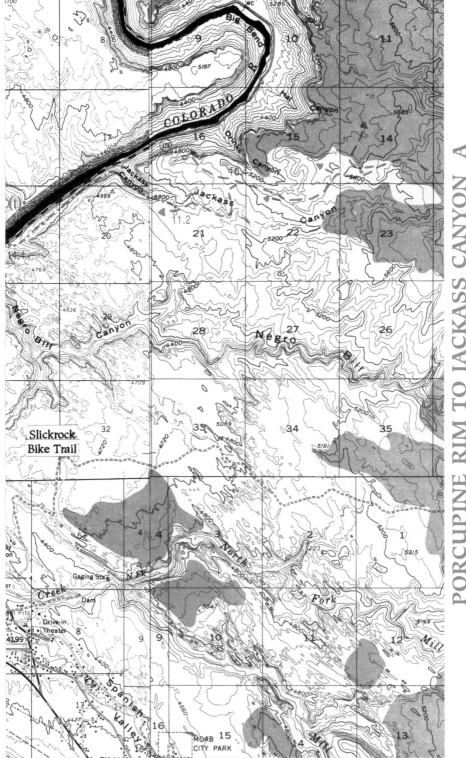

PORCUPINE RIM TO JACKASS CANYON B

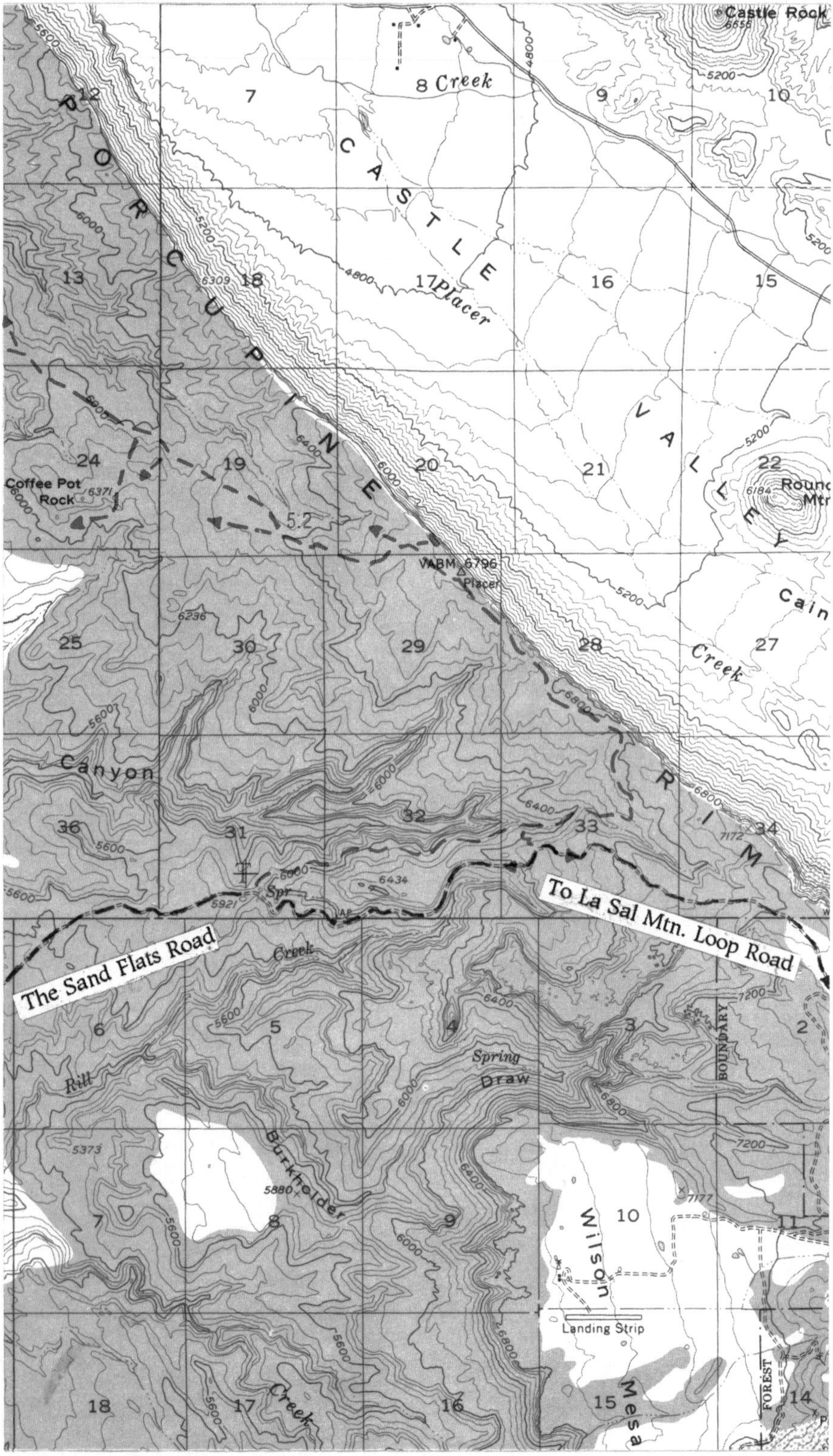

The "Canyonlands Coaming," aka Wingate cliffs

243

FLAT PASS

Type: Loop
Length: 17.9 miles, including 6.2 miles on pavement
Difficulty: Physically difficult / Technically difficult
Best Season: Spring and fall
Elevation: Trailhead/-tail/Low—4,500 ft., High—5,960 ft.
Land Agency: BLM and private easement
Route Summary: From its four-way stop intersection with Spanish Trail Road, this route takes the paved Spanish Valley Drive up to and past Ken's Lake, a diversion reservoir from Mill Creek's south fork, a.k.a. "Righthand." A steep gravel road crests Flat Pass to parallel Righthand upstream a ways before crossing it and continuing the climb towards the base of South Mesa. Several demanding technical moves keep this rocky route interesting (carry a headset wrench!) as it peaks near the base of the mesa, then winds through rolling country over to Mill Creek again. Righthand is forded three times in a picturesque slickrock canyon before reaching the spur that takes you up and out of its canyon over to Moab.
Attractions: Upper Righthand is a little-visited area with much to offer those willing to hike for a couple of hours. It is canyon country with mountain influences, and there is the attraction of perennial water, a blessing not lost on the native Americans who left their mark here.
Riding Surface: Rock-studded sediments, sand, stream cobble, gravel and pavement on jeep trail and two-laned roads
Geology: Flat Pass proper is a notch atop the long wall of Navajo sandstone that borders Spanish Valley, the continuation of Moab Valley. The wall is fairly narrow, and may some day be undercut and punched through by Mill Creek, but for now the creek runs along the "grain" of the Navajo fins to its confluence with Lefthand. The rock buttressing South Mesa is the Entrada sandstone, but it is a thin, somewhat broken representative of such. The force of the rising magma that became the La Sal Mountains compressed, cracked and hastened the erosion of overlying layers like this Entrada.
Logistics: No permit or shuttle is necessary.
Trailhead Access: From Main x Center St.'s, head east on Center Street, going right on 400 East and left on Mill Creek Drive, as if going to the Slickrock Trail. Continue on Mill Creek past the Sand Flats Road for another mile, passing the acute spur left to Murphy Lane but taking the next acute left onto Spanish Valley Drive. Another 2.2 miles brings you to the four-way stop (Spanish Valley x Spanish Trail Rd.'s), where the route description begins.

Mileage Log and Route Description:
0.0 Continue south on Spanish Valley Drive
5.4 Take the left turn to Ken's Lake, but continue past, up the gravel road.

6.8 (L) The diversion gates can turn half of Righthand's water towards Ken's Lake. The reservoir impounds water that's gravity fed to Spanish Valley. Just prior to the pass, petroglyph figures watch over the proceedings.

7.3 Take the obtuse spur left, across the creek, to begin the "assault with a lively weapon" climb towards South Mesa.

11.0 As you crest this little hill after the straight sandy stretch, the road splits. Stay left for the big dip across a dry creek bed. Shortly thereafter, the road split reconnects from the right, crosses, then continues up the hill to the left. Continue straight (right-ish) here, and if you find yourself on a sandy ridgetop, GO BACK. This ridge road dead-ends high above Mill Creek.

15.8 After negotiating the slick fords, you come adjacent to private land with orchards. The obtuse left turn takes you up and out of the canyon. Another left on Westwater Drive starts the descent along the golf course before a final left on Canyonlands Circle, the way back to the trailhead/-tail.

More canyon textures

245

Castle Rock

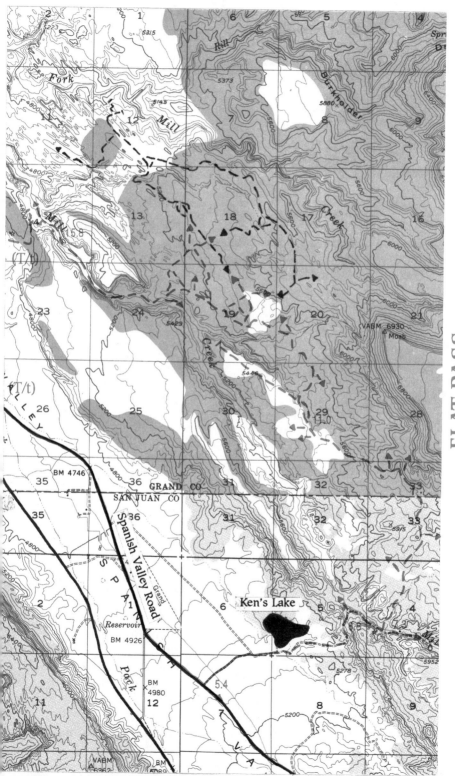

BACK OF BEHIND

Type: One-way
Length: 25.4 miles, including 4.8 miles on pavement
Difficulty: Physically moderate / Technically moderate to difficult
Best Season: Spring and fall and during or soon after rainfall
Elevation: Trailhead/High—5,510 ft., Low/Trailtail—3,965 ft.
Land Agency: BLM and private. At the mouth of Pritchett Canyon, by the Colorado River, the land's owner requires a fee of $1.00 per person to pass through.

Route Summary: From its trailhead on Highway 191, this route crosses a high pasture to near the sheer rim of Kane Springs Canyon. It then dips through the Hunter's Canyon drainage in an interim between its head, amongst the repetitive fins of Behind the Rocks, and its lower confines, a stream corridor cut through soaring sandstone walls. A unexpected pass brings you to the head of Pritchett Canyon, another beautiful defile whose stream bottom trail makes for an adventuresome descent to the Colorado River.

Options: Make a loop by starting with a 13 mile paved ride from Moab to the trailhead. Spurs lead to Kane Springs Canyon overlooks. This trail intersects the Hunters Canyon rim road to complete the bike-a-hike found in the Pritchett Canyon (Hunters Canyon) trail description. (P268)

Attractions: This route provides access to a half dozen arches, a cool seeping alcove, and great rimrock views, rounded out by antic-depicting petroglyph panels along the river.

Riding Surface: Rock- and cobble-studded sandy sediments and pavement on two-laned roads and jeep trail.

Geology: The trail starts out within sight of the fins and domes of Navajo sandstone that compose the Behind the Rocks Wilderness Study Area. After doing an end-around on some drift dunes, it meets Prostitute Butte (mile 3.0), a remnant Entrada Slickrock outcrop with two arches that give it a crude anatomical correctness. As seen in the Arches and Rainbow Rocks areas, chunks of a dense, fine-grained quartz called chert litter the ground. Chert can be flaked in a predictable way, a quality that made it useful for creating arrowheads and other bifaces like scrapers, drills and knives. A view from the rim of Kane Springs Canyon (about mile 10) will reveal the thin Kayenta formation capping pleated Wingate walls, with a Chinle talus slope below. Downcanyon, the Cane Creek Anticline begins its dirtywork, lifting the hem of Moenkopi mudstones near Hurrah Pass to reveal the Cutler sandstone in its redfaced contortions. Because of the salt structure which elevated the western rim of Moab Valley, and the lifting forces of the Cane Creek Anticline to the west, the Back of Behind strata reveals a bowed effect much like that of the Gemini Bridges area. The "promenade pedal" along the Colorado River (mile 20.6) is somewhat unlikely looking, as the northwest-southeast seams in the Navajo are bisected unassailably by the river gorge. Sheer walls down to river level are indicative of fast erosion. The Colorado Plateau has "risen through" its rivers in the last ten million years, leaving paradoxical patterns carved into the emerging rock.

Logistics: The shuttle requires that you leave one vehicle in Moab and one at the trailhead. Many outfits in Moab can provide taxi drop-offs to the trailhead.

Trailhead Access: About 13 miles south on Highway 191, just past mile marker 113, a (posted) dirt spur (right) marks the trailhead area.

Mileage Log and Route Description:

0.0 Generally, this route follows the most obvious dirt road, and at the occasional sign, heeds always towards "Pritchett Arch."

0.4 (R) The Behind the Rocks Trail is not recommended due to inconsistently ridable road surfaces and misleading spurs. However, it does abut the beautiful fin area ahead, and with tenacity, one of its numerous connectors to the Back of Behind Trail can see you through to Hunters Canyon.

3.0 (L) Don't get sidetracked on this prominent spur.

9.9 (L) After the hillclimb, this spur leads to a nice view of Kane Springs Canyon.

11.4 (L) Another recommended spur 2.5 miles to the edge of the canyon, a nice camp spot, and a scramble-down access to the valley floor.

14.5 (L) After you cross the wash bed of Hunters Canyon, pause to explore downstream to the sudden jump and pothole bridge. The plunge pool can be accessed by a talus slope out of sight on the canyon's southern wall.

Alcove forming is hastened by seeping water that penetrates porous sandstone and descends to a horizontal strata that is water-impervious. It is deflected outward, where opportunistic "hanging gardens" seed. Ferns, mosses, and flowering plants such as orchid, monkeyflower, primrose and camas produce mild acids which dissolve the host rock, reducing it to a sandy soil for a better foothold. Alternately freezing and thawing water further expands the fissures. When the weight of the growth exceeds the weakened support of the rock, a panel will spall off to further deepen the alcove. Over the course of a cold winter, an "aura" of sand will surround the base of each rock outcrop. Water is responsible for over 99% of the erosion that occurs in wild places (and mountain bikes account for the rest, according to some stories).

14.9 (L) A recommended detour, the climb to the lovely Pritchett Arch:

> A weird, lovely, fantastic object out of nature... has the curious ability to remind us—like rock and sunlight and wind and wilderness—that OUT THERE is a different world, older and greater and deeper by far than ours, a world which surrounds and sustains the little world of men as sea and sky surround and sustain a ship. The shock of the real. For a

little while we are again able to see, as the child sees, a world of marvels. For a few moments we discover that nothing can be taken for granted, for if this ring of stone is marvelous then all which shaped it is marvelous, and our journey here on earth, able to see and touch and hear in the midst of tangible and mysterious things-in-themselves, is the most strange and daring of all adventures.

Edward Abbey, <u>Desert Solitaire</u>, 1968

16.2 Past Pritchett Pass, the assault of White Knuckle Hill is an ever popular spectator sport during the annual Red Rock Four Wheelers' Easter Week Jeep Safari.
19.0 (L) Another potential walk, to Bighorn Canyon on the Kane Creek Road, past a dancing petroglyph and an arch.
19.3 (R) And a scrambling route to Teardrop Arch. (Make your elevation at the canyon's mouth.)
20.6 Turn right onto the paved Kane Creek Road.
25.4 Moab

Sand dune, Back of Behind Trail

BACK OF BEHIND A

BACK OF BEHIND B

View from the southern tip of Amasa Back

HURRAH PASS

Type: Out-and-back
Length: 28.8 miles, including 9.6 miles on pavement
Difficulty: Physically easy / Technically easy
Best Season: Spring and fall
Elevation: Trailhead/-tail/Low—3,965 ft., High—4,740 ft.
Land Agency: BLM
Route Summary: This easy-to-follow route leaves Moab to parallel the Colorado River through the Portal and down to a bend into Kane Springs Canyon, which accommodates it all the way to Hurrah Pass.
Options: Numerous rides stem off of the basic Hurrah Pass route, including Moab Rim, Pritchett Canyon, and Amasa Back's several variations.
Attractions: This ride is good for first-timers to the area, as it includes most of the elements common to all of the rides near Moab. It accompanies the Colorado River, rolling past prolific petroglyphs to a cottonwood-shrouded creek. A tasty, freshwater spring bubbles out of a wall along the trail before the canyon opens into a sheer-walled valley. Upon ascending a rock shelf to Hurrah Pass, you receive views of the Gothic architecture of upper Canyonlands basin to one side, and the slickrock fins surrounding Moab to the other.
Riding Surface: Gravel, rock-studded sediments, ledgy bedrock and pavement on two-laned roads and jeep trail
Geology: Just before leaving Moab Valley through the river portal (mile 1.5), hills to your left show dark hollows where the salt of the Paradox formation dissolved away as it was thrust into contact with the surface. A deep fault beneath this slope was penetrated by a salt mass with a consistency much like wet putty. This mass, a remnant of ancient evaporated seas, was pressurized and deformed by the weight of thousands of feet of sediments subsequently deposited on it and sought crustal weaknesses for "escape." The Moab Valley is a consequence of this activity. After the Portal, the strata dips away from the Moab Valley such that the contact between the Kayenta and the Navajo provides the ledge for the Moab Rim Trail (mile 2.8). By mile 5.5, however, the approaching hill marks the road's utilization of another Kayenta ledge as it climbs the flank of the Cane Creek Anticline, an elongate fold in the rock that peaks at Hurrah Pass along an axis that continues northwest across the river to the highlands north of Island in the Sky. As the road rounds the high point of this initial climb, it descends on the Kayenta past dinosaur tracks which identify this layer with its wet-laid, stream-deposited origins. The dugway takes the road deeper into the southwestward-rising strata, and by the time Kane Springs Canyon widens (mile 8.9), you've descended through five distinct formations in a cumulative elevation GAIN of less than one hundred feet! (Not mentioned were the rather amorphous Moenkopi and Chinle formations, the components of the talus slopes fringing the Wingate cliffs that define this

valley's rim.) After crossing Kane Creek, the climb up the anticline continues on the contact of the brick red Cutler sandstone with the Moenkopi mud- and shalestone. The rock that appears like a cruise ship's smokestack is one of the thickest cross-sections of Moenkopi around. It looks like it would melt in the first stiff rain, and indeed, since it is bereft of harder caprock layers, it is eroding much more rapidly than the Kayenta-protected Wingate walls.

Logistics: No permit or shuttle is necessary.

Trailhead Access: This ride leaves from Main x Center St.'s in Moab.

Mileage Log and Route Description:
0.0 Head west to 1st (100) West, turn right, then left onto Williams Way. From its "T" with 5th West, go left, then right onto Kane Creek Road.
2.8 (L) Trailhead for the Moab Rim Trail
4.7 (L) (Unposted) trailhead for Pritchett Canyon (Hunters Canyon) Trail
5.9 (R) Inconspicuous (unposted) trailhead for the Amasa Back Trail
6.5 (R) At the top of the hill, this spur goes to a sheerly gorgeous (literally) view of Kane Creek, and a scramble up above this point accesses Funnel Arch.
10.3 (R) The Happy Turk is one of the many animated characters found in the Cutler formation. The white and light blue flecks in the rock are probably unoxidized iron.
11.4 (L) Just before the sign, this spur continues up Kane Springs Canyon clear out to Highway 191 on an unridably sandy jeep trail.
14.4 (Hip Hip) Hurrah Pass.

Intricate erosions as viewed from Dead Horse Point

255

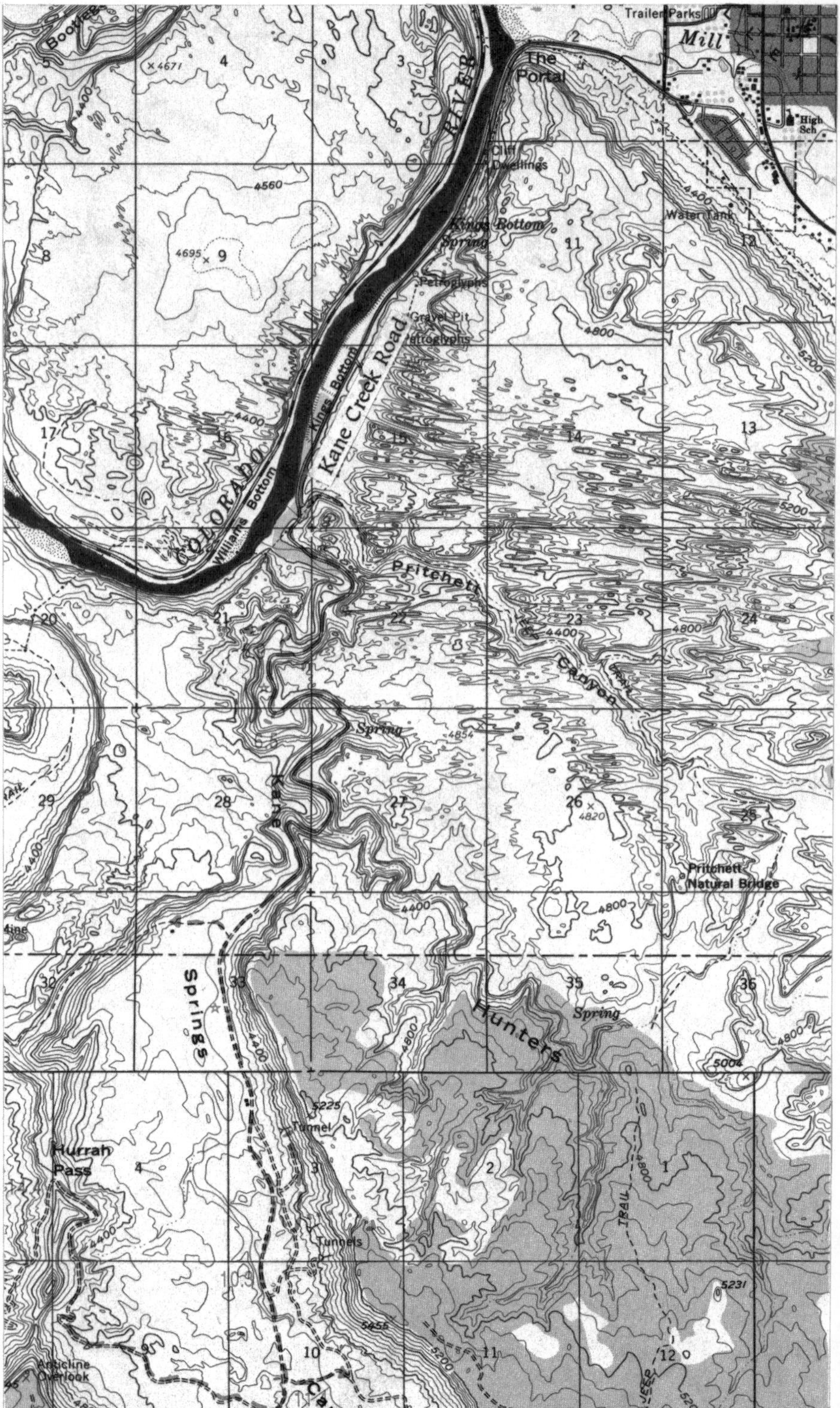

Bootleg
Trailer Parks
Mill
High Sch
The Portal
RIVER
Cliff Dwellings
Water Tank
Kings Bottom
Spring
Petroglyphs
Gravel Pit
Petroglyphs
Kane Creek Road
Kings Bottom
COLORADO
Williams Bottom
Pritchett
Canyon
Spring
Kane
Pritchett Natural Bridge
Mine
Springs
Hunters
Spring
Tunnel
Tunnels
Hurrah Pass
Anticline Overlook
Canyon
TRAIL
JEEP
4671
4560
4695
4400
4800
5200
4854
4820
5004
5225
5455
5231

HURRAH PASS TO AMASA BACK

Type: Loop
Length: 32.9 miles, including 9.6 miles on pavement
Difficulty: Physically gonzo-abusive / Technically difficult
Best Season: Spring and fall
Elevation: Trailhead/-tail/Low—3,965 ft., High—4,740 ft.
Land Agency: BLM
Route Summary: After the easy ride to Hurrah Pass from Moab, a ledgy descent drops nearly to the Colorado River and wiggles down a sandy creekbed, then takes limestone ledges around the southern tip of Amasa Back to Jackson Hole, an abandoned river meander of the Colorado. The trail arcs around a monolith on a fearsomely sandy route to begin the 350 ft. vertical portage up a talus chute through the Wingate sandstone. From the top of Amasa Back, a ledgy descent to Kane Creek and a "grappler" of a hillclimb up to the Kane Creek Road leave you the easy pedal back to Moab.
Options: Amasa Back offers a short out-and-back spur to a view of the Portal, and an old track beneath this viewpoint provides a rollicking, rocksplitting way down to the mouth of Kane Creek.
Attractions: This is one of those routes just made for mountain biking. It accesses perhaps the loneliest piece of redrock desert within ten miles of Moab, in Jackson Hole. Old miners' shacks and decrepit pipelines reinforce this sense of isolation.
Riding Surface: Gravel, bedrock ledges, loose rock, drift sand and pavement on jeep trail and two-laned roads
Geology: Hurrah Pass is on the crest of the elongate upfold called the Cane Creek Anticline. From Moab, the route passes through six formations to reach it (consult the Hurrah Pass "Geology" summary), then descends via a Cutler ledge to encounter one more formation, the Elephant Canyon limestone. It is peculiarly harder than the sand-, mud- and shalestones on the Moab side of the Pass, and provides the caprock for a series of intricate, but shallow canyons near the river. The fact that Jackson Hole (mile 21.2) once contained the river is seen in the hills braced with polished cobble. Amasa Back is destined to be cut off one day too, as the river seeks the shortest route to the sea. (Commenting on this phenomenon, Mark Twain noted that the rate at which the Mississippi was cutting off its meanders, the river would be something like sixty-four miles long by the turn of the (last) century.) When it does, Jackson Hole will probably flow again. The portage up Jacob's Ladder works from the Chinle deposits through the massive Wingate cliff to the Kayenta, the Wingate's caprock. Kayenta provides the ramp for the road down Amasa Back to Kane Creek, its tilt following the shoulder of the anticline until it disappears beneath the surface.
Notes: Carry extra water and wear shoes comfortable for hiking.

Logistics: No permit or shuttle is necessary, but this ride is made pavement-less and nearly ten miles shorter by driving to the mouth of Kane Creek for your start.

Trailhead Access: Main x Center St.'s, Moab

Mileage Log and Route Description:
0.0 (Refer to the Route Description for the Hurrah Pass Trail.)
14.4 Continue down the wilderness side of the pass.
16.9 Turn right on the spur down this rock-walled wash. A barbed wire fence may be strung across the fill ramp.
21.2 Upon climbing the fossil-bearing limestone ledges, this "T" is reached at Jackson Hole. Both ways arc around the monolith to Jacob's Ladder, but the trail right is "less unridable" and a s'koshe shorter.
23.0 Twin junipers mark the threshold to the portage up the Wingate gap.
23.9 Once on board, you may notice a doubletrack across the flats which follows a series of power poles off the east side of Amasa Back. A cow track descends to the mouth of Kane Creek from this road. It is probably only suitable for aspiring trials riders, but will certainly improve with (ab)use. Continue right to descend the Amasa Back the jeep trail.
26.7 Beyond Kane Creek, one of the most challenging pieces of precision gruntwork around looms between you and the road back to Moab. If you're intent on cleaning it or "clearing" it (shifting every rock), by all means jettison your gear, drop your tire pressure and give it the old "canyon-do."
32.9 Moab

A view from Amasa Back

AMASA BACK

Type: Out-and-back
Length: 21.0 miles
Difficulty: Physically difficult / Technically difficult
Best Season: Spring and fall
Elevation: Trailhead/-tail/Low—3,965 ft., High—5,000 ft.
Land Agency: BLM
Route Summary: From Moab, this trail begins on the Kane Creek Road, then follows the Colorado River to the mouth of Kane Springs Canyon, whose drainage it traces before crossing to climb the rocky ledges of Amasa Back. It levels as it crosses the neck of Amasa Back, then resumes climbing to an indefinite turnaround point high on the cliff's edge above the Colorado River.
Options: Several spurs to river gorge viewpoints, both north and south, and freeform exploring of the Back's distant points can color this ride. Also, you can close an Amasa Back/Kane Springs Canyon loop with the portage and hike-a-bike of the hanging valley on Amasa Back's southern tip.
Attractions: Besides the huge views of Poison Spider Mesa and the upper Canyonlands basin, some nice petroglyphs adorn the varnished walls of Amasa Back near Kane Creek. Up on top, a single bighorn sheep petroglyph and several rock-lined storage cysts indicate that native Americans made use of this out-of-the-way area.
Riding Surface: Bedrock ledges, loose rock, gravel and pavement on jeep trail, two-laned roads and freeform routes
Geology: All of Amasa Back is atilt, a consequence of its proximity to the upfolding effects of Cane Creek Anticline. The Kayenta formation, that of freshwater stream deposit, provides the ledgy bedrock for Amasa Back's jeep trail. As a water deposited formation, we know that Kayenta was laid on a level, but amazingly, this thin formation spans a height differential of 1,000 feet in just two miles. Domes of blonde Navajo sandstone above the mouth of Kane Creek thin out towards the anticline (and the Back's southwest rim), but three similiar, prominent outcrops of it remain to make visible landmarks.
Logistics: No permit or shuttle is required, but nearly ten paved miles of the route can be foregone by driving to the beginning of the gravel on Kane Creek Road.
Trailhead Access: This ride leaves from Main x Center St.'s in Moab.

Mileage Log and Route Description:

0.0 Head west to 1st (100) West, turn right, then left onto Williams Way. From its "T" with 5th West, go left, then right onto Kane Creek Road.
2.8 (L) Trailhead for the Moab Rim Trail
4.7 (L) (Unposted) trailhead for Pritchett Canyon (Hunters Canyon) Trail
5.9 Take the inconspicuous spur to Amasa Back which dives off the gravel halfway up the hillclimb.

Quicksand—the great equalizer —slows even Dave Clark down

7.8 The road forks indistinctly on bedrock, going right to continue out Amasa Back. The second of the three looming, sentinel outcrops of Navajo sandstone is ahead, up on the right.

8.3 (R) This sandy spur goes to a must-see view. Soaring raptors such as peregrine falcons and golden eagles are often spotted from here.

10.2 (R) The lone petroglyph of a bighorn sheep is carved onto the wall of the Back's highest outcrop. Although desert bighorn are now greatly outnumbered by deer, it seems that a thousand years ago, the animals were equally abundant, providing a nearly identical resource for ancient hunters. Modern sheep reflect a calcium deficiency in their diet through "split-end" horns that ancient sheep apparently didn't suffer. They were "reintroduced" to the canyonlands area in the 60's and 70's, but their evasive nature makes it difficult to know how far they've spread. Bighorns are proficient swimmers, yet for some reason it is rare to see them on the south side of the Colorado River. It may be because they thrive on the nearly inaccessible talus slopes of the White Rim.

10.7 The route is lost to a sea of ledgy sandstone. Improvisation is required to reach further rims. The return to Moab is on the identical route by which you arrived, unless you choose to investigate one of the listed options.

Bighorn sheep agraze on a river bottom

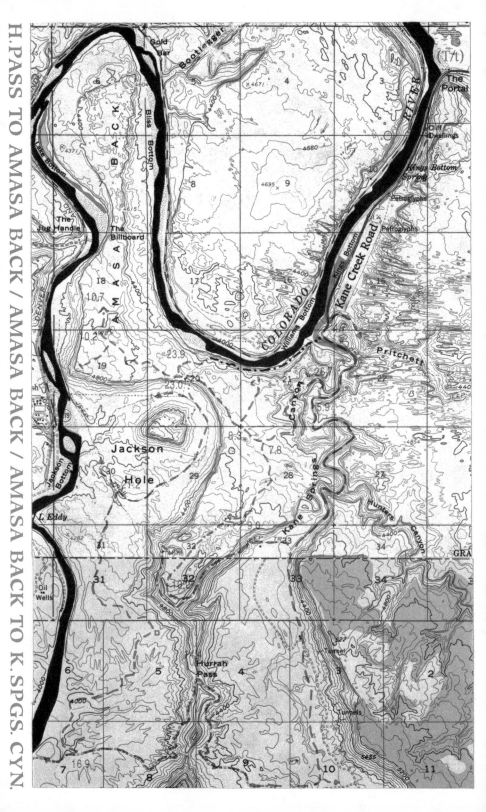

AMASA BACK TO KANE SPRINGS CANYON

Type: Loop
Length: 21.3 miles, including 9.6 miles on pavement
Difficulty: Physically difficult to gonzo-abusive / Technically difficult
Best Season: Spring and fall, but not directly after rain
Elevation: Trailhead/-tail/Low—3,965 ft., High—5,320 ft.
Land Agency: BLM
Route Summary: From a discreet fork on the Amasa Back Trail, this route swings south to enter a slickrock box canyon. Before the road ends, a portage around its head accesses a "hanging valley," whose wash bottom is hike-a-bike-able to the point across from the Anticline Overlook, where an old mining road rounds the southern tip of Amasa Back in its swashbuckling descent to the Kane Creek Road.
Options: From the tip of Amasa Back, the mining road also wraps around towards Jackson Hole on a fun track to end near a mine shaft.
Attractions: Again, this is one of those routes only a mountain biker could execute. Besides the remarkable views (of and) from the hanging valley overlooking the river basin, the mining road descent can provide a delightful, bermed descent on shaly soil if runoff hasn't rutted or slicked it prior to your ride.
Riding Surface: Ledgy rock, wash sand, loose rock and shale, gravel and pavement on jeep trail, washbottoms and two-laned roads
Geology: (Refer to the Hurrah Pass and Amasa Back "Geology" summaries.) The slickrock box canyon is composed of weathered Wingate sandstone, and the hanging valley, which looks as if it might have drained west instead of east, is kin to upper Little Canyon (on the Gemini Bridges, Gold Bar Rim, or Seven Mile/Little Canyon Rim Trails), another Wingate-coamed valley. In each case, the head of the valley has been uplifted by forces from below, anticline or fault offset. The descent to Kane Springs Canyon affords grand views of the brick red Cutler formation below.
Notes: Wear shoes with adequate traction for friction-ing up slickrock.
Logistics: No permit or shuttle is required, but nearly ten paved miles of the route can be foregone by driving to the gravel on Kane Creek Road.
Trailhead Access: This ride leaves from Main x Center St.'s in Moab.

Mileage Log and Route Description:

0.0 Head west to 1st (100) West, turn right, then left onto Williams Way. From its "T" with 5th West, go left, then right onto Kane Creek Road.
5.9 Take the inconspicuous spur to Amasa Back which dives off the gravel halfway up the hillclimb.
7.8 The road forks on bedrock, going right to continue out Amasa Back. Bear left (straight) on this discreet spur.
9.0 At the last bend to the right before the canyon boxes up, you'll find the

most convenient (but steep) portage route. It climbs 100 feet before allowing you a view of the canyon's upper tier, whose drainage you should intersect as directly as possible to continue the hike-a-bike.

10.2 As you come abreast of the Wingate monolith on the rim of Jackson Hole, avoid the lefthand branches of the wash that pinch up, to feel out the old roadbed that climbs left around the three rock knobs, then descends through a rough pass to the Kane Creek Road. This descent becomes rutted after strong rains, but being in Chinle, becomes favorably groomed with frequent riding.

Spu-lash!

The Devil's Golf Ball on the Hurrah Pass Trail

PRITCHETT CANYON (HUNTERS CANYON)

The Colorado River holds promise in an arid land

PRITCHETT CANYON (HUNTERS CANYON)

Type: Out-and-back (or optional loop via Hunters Canyon rim)
Length: 21.7 miles, including 9.6 miles on pavement
Difficulty: Physically difficult / Technically difficult to gonzo-abusive
Best Season: Spring and fall
Land Agency: BLM and private.   At the mouth of Pritchett Canyon, by the Colorado River, the land's owner requires a fee of $1.00 per person to pass through.
Route Summary: From the Kane Creek Road, this route ascends the difficult stream-bed channel and shoreline of beautiful, fin-lined Pritchett Canyon to the pass into Hunters Canyon. The optional continuation stumbles up Yellow Hill to Hunters on a rim-side road out to a point overlooking its confluence with Kane Creek. A 1.5 mile bike-a-hike and portage to Gatherers Canyon drops to the Kane Creek Road. If you decide to ride a loop, consider reversing direction. You can enjoy the descent down Pritchett Canyon and uphill portages are generally safer than downhill.
Attractions: This ride offers many fine hikes through seams in the slickrock fins to petroglyph panels, arches and ruins. Adjacent to Behind the Rocks Wilderness Study Area, Pritchett's intimate and intricate beauty is well accessed by mountain bike, but demands on-foot exploration to be truly understood. It also stands alone as a premiere technical ride along a cottonwood-lined stream, a quick escape into a canyon removed from the common realm, bereft of the *de rigueur* fifty-mile views shared by most other trails.
Riding Surface: Rock-studded sediments, loose cobble, wash and drift sand, bedrock, gravel and pavement on jeep trail, broad ledges and two-laned roads
Geology: Pritchett Canyon is grooved through blonde Navajo sandstone fins, and the trail rides at or below their contact point with the Kayenta, which surfaces most obviously to form the rim of Hunters Canyon.
Logistics: No permit or shuttle is required, but nearly ten paved miles of the route can be foregone by driving to the beginning of the gravel on Kane Creek Road.
Trailhead Access: This ride leaves from Main x Center St.'s in Moab.
Mileage Log and Route Description:
0.0 Head west to 1st (100) West, turn right, then left onto Williams Way. From its "T" with 5th West, go left, then right onto Kane Creek Road.
2.8 (L) Trailhead for the Moab Rim Trail
4.7 This is the (unposted) trailhead for the Pritchett Canyon/(Hunters Canyon) Trail. Just before the pavement ends, take a left up its sandy entrance road.
6.0 (L) This canyon drains out from Teardrop Arch, a mile's hike with never a dull moment. Make your elevation at its mouth.
6.3 (R) A seam through the ledge accesses Bighorn Canyon on the Kane Creek Road via a narrow, glyph-lined corridor.
8.6 (R) The northernmost tip of this spur facilitates access to Hall's Bridge, a massive arch hidden from view.

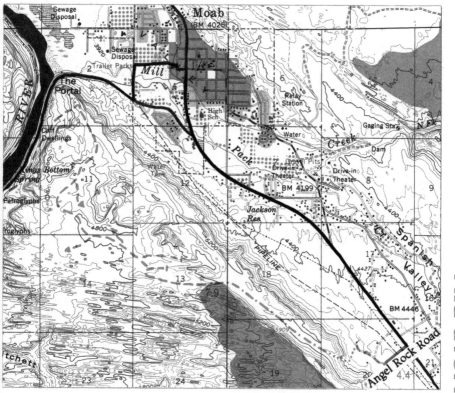

10.2 (R) This spur leads to the trailhead for lovely Pritchett Arch.

10.8 Access down to this lush alcove is had via a talus slope on the far side of the canyon.

12.8 (R) This spur leads to a well preserved, "wet-laid" native American ruin. A pit house or sunken chamber accompanies the turret-shaped granary. The road ends shortly after this spur. The most efficient way to handle the ensuing hike-a-bike (so the author isn't "ensued") is to traverse the slope near the base of the Navajo walls, then after rounding two slight prominences, descend diagonally to the broad bench of Kayenta sandstone. You can ride this bench clear to Gatherers Canyon, with creativity, but have to hike-a-bike along its rim for at least a hundred yards before locating a suitable downclimb to its bottom for the portage out to the Kane Creek Road at Kane Spring.

21.7 Moab

MOAB RIM

Type: Loop
Length: 15.4 miles, including 7.5 miles on pavement
Difficulty: Physically gonzo-abusive/ Technically difficult
Best Season: Spring and fall
Elevation: Trailhead/-tail/Low—3,965 ft., High—5,240 ft.
Land Agency: BLM
Route Summary: A 4.7 mile warmup largely on Highway 191 leads to a severe, mile-long portage up a talus slope to Hidden Valley. A sandy singletrack parallels a valley wall before penetrating the backcountry at a low pass. From this scenic vantage, a jeep road is incurred, and it descends across a valley near walls that are strafed with wonderful petroglyphs. Further towards the river, the trail rises back to the rim of Moab Valley to take a headlong descent of the wrist-wrenching Moab Rim Trail to the Kane Creek Road.

Ultra-strong riders with evolved technical skills may want to grunt up to Moab Rim from theKane Creek Road to end the ride with the loose, stair-stepped descent of the portage route from Angel Rock Road—to take the ride in a counterclockwise direction.

Attractions: Besides the impeccable views, there are several short hiking opportunities to petroglyph panels, ruins, deep potholes, natural caves, and even the token arch.
Riding Surface: Rock-studded sediments, sand, bedrock and pavement on jeep trail, singletrack and two-laned roads and highways.
Geology: From the beginning of the portage, the hiking track ascends through several formations depleted and deformed by their proximity to the fault block that allowed the creation of Moab Valley. These may include remnants of the Paradox, Moenkopi, Chinle and Wingate. The Kayenta sandstone defines the edge of Moab Rim, and the remainder of the route utilizes the dipped ledges of this formation.
Notes: As this trail is in a Wilderness Study Area, it may be closed pending wilderness legislation. In the mean time, keep your bike strictly on roads and trails to preserve wilderness qualities. Wear comfortable hiking shoes, too.
Logistics: No permit or shuttle is necessary.
Trailhead Access: This ride leaves from Main x Center St.'s in Moab.

Mileage Log and Route Description:
0.0 Head south on Highway 191 to turn right onto Angel Rock Road in 4.1 miles.
4.4 At Rimrock Lane, another right leads you to a (posted) trailhead and register box in less than half a mile.
7.9 After summiting the low pass, you intersect the jeep road that will take you all the way back down. The varnished walls to your right include some of the nicest Kokopelli glyphs around. Kokopelli is thought to be symbolic of

one or many intertribal traders who, in his sack of goods, carried also the gift of fertility, which his visit would bestow upon a clan. Anasazi sites have been found to have seashells, tropical bird feathers and beads that could only have been imported along trade routes. Pottery and toolmaking styles amongst different sects show striking similiarities, too, revealing the Pueblo Indian culture as broad spread in its connection to distant cultures.

11.3 At the rim of Moab Valley, a short scramble accesses the "Endless Caves," overlooking the Portal. The steep drop to Kane Creek Road requires good brake control and a discerning eye not to get sidetracked. This was the site of the Fat Tire Festival and Moab Rocks Race' hillclimb in years past, and phenomenal times of just under twelve minutes from road to rim have taken the winner's trophy. (The Festival occurs during the final week in October, culminating in a memorable Halloween party.)

15.3 Moab

Other Roads / Rides in the Moab Area

The sandy ride to Johnson's Up-On-Top can be a short, scenic, enjoyable ride when the sand is firmed up by rain. Other rides which are too sandy for most include the spurs off the Flat Pass Trail towards Lefthand, and the Kane Creek jeep trail from Highway 191 south of Moab to the Kane Creek Road on the Colorado River. There are many roads south of Kane Springs Canyon that cross open country before halting at the rim of Hatch Wash. Across the highway, numerous roads penetrate the Lisbon Industrial Park area.

Please do not ride in Negro Bill Canyon, as it is a Wilderness Study Area and should be afforded all the courtesies of legislated wilderness.

Mountain biking presents a great way to see wildlife. Usually an animal will take off so fast you can't really be sure you saw it. Or maybe it heard you approaching and left before an encounter could even take place. But the speed and stealth given to cycling shifts the element of surprise into our favor.

Raptors will eyeball you from the perch of a scoured cottonwood, until you slow to get your camera out, their cue to depart. The desert bighorn will climb outrageous verticals to escape your scrutiny. But just when they can top a bluff and disappear from view, they hesitate, posture, and return the stare. As soon as a foot is slipped off a pedal onto the ground, however, they bolt. You have become an identifiable threat.

Other animals seem to await your presence. The ever-obstreperous raven will alert its companion that people are nearby, where a neglected bit of lunch becomes a lost lunch. Kangaroo mice might arrive to inspect your campsite come dusk, and they have a knack for making a racket far out of proportion to their size, kicking utensils around, rustling through the garbage, and generally convincing the tentbound human that camp is being ransacked.

While animals such as deer and rabbit are programmed to flee, others can be indifferent to human intrusion. Rarely do you spot a snake that isn't already aware of you, yet the base of the nearest bush is as far away as it feels compelled to go. Lizards approached suddenly may run, scatterbrained, beneath your tires, but when approached tranquilly, may allow you to stroke their chins. Sometimes they challenge you to a pushup contest, climbing higher from the ground after each set in order to establish territorial superiority. Canyon wrens will respond to your whistling with their patented descending arpeggio, and insects from all quarters may gather to counsel with you the moment you stop riding.

Even potholes that are usually dry can teem with life between dormant periods. Animated beads called whirligig beetles weave kaleidoscopic patterns on the water's surface. Tadpole- or fairy shrimp, a horseshoe crab look-alike, perform their pool sweeping duties between trips to the surface for oxygen, when they roll over to attach an air bubble to their ciliated undersides. Bluebottle dragonflies, butterflys on the flutter-by, and ever-active bees flit and bumble amongst the reeds, intent on their rounds.

There is wonder in the desperate lives of "critters"—a wonder that rewards the patient eye.

Navajo sandstone bedding planes—cemented sand dunes

VIII. APPENDICES

Glossary of Terms

acute (spur or doubletrack)—a spur deviating from the main route at an angle of less than 90° from the direction of travel. (An obtuse spur deviates from the direction of travel at between 90° and 180°.)

desert varnish—a dark stain or coating on the surface of rock walls and boulders, sometimes uniform and sometimes occurring as pennons which correspond to water flow across the rock's surface. Moisture leaches iron, manganese, and perhaps even carbon, silicon and aluminum from the rock, leaving a patina on its surface. This process may have a biological component, too, which research has not yet quantified.

doubletrack—parallel tracks made by a jeep or other vehicle, usually with a humped middle and/or vegetation growing between the tracks.

fork—a three-way intersection where two spurs splay in EQUAL angles off of the direction of travel, as distinguished from acute spurs.

formation—the fundamental unit in the local classification of layered rocks, consisting of a bed or beds of similar rock types, and differing from strata above and below. It may be subdivided into "members" and combined with others into "groups."

goathead—a weed that grows small seed pods which function as caltrops. Goatheads are the biggest cause of flat tires in this area, as their spiked horns stick into or catch on wheels and shoes. Their redeeming virtue is that a tea steeped from this plant is an excellent kidney cleanser.

hike-a-bike—usually an unmarked stretch of trail where the bike can only be ridden sporadically, and where some hiking with the bike or portaging it is necessary.

loop—a route which retraces little, if any, common ground in returning to the trailhead/trailtail.

microbiotic crust—the dark mat of microorganisms which is essentially the desert's topsoil, as it stabilizes sand against erosion while fixing nitrogen and other nutrients critical to establishing soil fertility.

obtuse (spur or two track)—[see "acute"]

one-way—a route which starts and ends at different points, thereby requiring a shuttle of some sort.

on-dirt—any road, track, trail, or other ridable surface that is NOT PAVED.

out-and-back—a route which returns on the same trail it went out on.

portage—to shoulder or otherwise carry a bike across terrain where pushing it is too difficult.

pothole—a naturally occurring cistern eroded into slickrock which can hold rainwater.

route—like a trail, it is merely the way, or DIRECTION to go, independent of the type of surface it travels.

sandstone—consolidated rock composed predominantly of quartz sand-sized grains.

singletrack—a type of narrow trail historically used for walking or horseback riding.

slickrock—any rock formation which erodes in a characteristically smooth and rounded way. The name was applied to this region by pioneers who found its surface to be unusually slick beneath the metal horseshoes and wheel rims of their wagons.

split—a trail split is any spur that reconnects with the main route in short order.

spur—any road or track that intersects the through route. (See "acute.")

trail—same as "route."

Weather Statistics for Moab

Ten-year average temperatures, in degrees Fahrenheit:

	Jan	Feb	Mar	Apr	May	Jun	Jul	Aug	Sep	Oct	Nov	Dec
Min.—	17°	26°	33°	42°	51°	54°	64°	63°	56°	41°	29°	21°
Max.—	41°	51°	60°	70°	82°	85°	98°	96°	86°	72°	54°	43°

Ten-year average precipitation, in inches:

Jan	Feb	Mar	Apr	May	Jun	Jul	Aug	Sep	Oct	Nov	Dec
.35	.48	.50	.75	.57	.43	.54	.89	.86	1.15	.52	.67

Index

Acknowledgements

Thanks and hugs to those "everyday heroes" that, for me, inspire excellence by their example:

Janina Schmidt, for revealing the earth's healing ways...
John Groo, for maintaining a sense of "one world"...
Conrad Sorenson, for nurturing higher standards...
Anne Clare Erickson, for a shared love of the canyons...
Kathy Aldous, for unpretentiousness...
Auggie Brooks, for applied "upful-ness"...
Mat Marcus and Lisa Wolfson, for generous and technical "smarts"...
Norm Shrewsbury, for skill and sensitivity...
LE Inskip, for encouragement and non-authoritarian suggestions...
Dave Clark, for being the "control" by not drinking the cow water...
John Graham, for the innocence of Toroweap...
Hugh "Sheriff Roy" Curtis, for making art functional...
Jim Huebner, for a sense of humor beyond the "job description"...
Warren Breslau, for critical goofiness...
Dave Lyle, for demonstrating excellence...
Bill'em and Rob'em Groff, for years of abuse...
Russ Von Koch, Ber Knight, and Peter Haney, for "bridging the gap"...
Rachael Schmidt, for shiny-eyed laughter...
Handsome Anthony Quintile, for Moab's finest bike and trail expertise...
The sometimes awkward, but endearing citizens of Moab...

And, most of all, my beloved family, Ken and Jean, and Mike and Jeff Campbell, who, truth be known, have supported me in unlikelier endeavors, and none so extensive as this book.